What Your Colleagues A

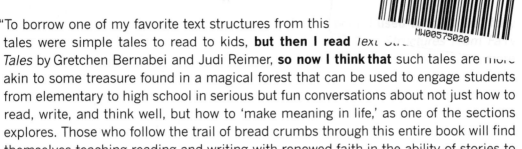

"To borrow one of my favorite text structures from this
tales were simple tales to read to kids, **but then I read** *Text Su...*
Tales by Gretchen Bernabei and Judi Reimer, **so now I think that** such tales are more
akin to some treasure found in a magical forest that can be used to engage students
from elementary to high school in serious but fun conversations about not just how to
read, write, and think well, but how to 'make meaning in life,' as one of the sections
explores. Those who follow the trail of bread crumbs through this entire book will find
themselves teaching reading and writing with renewed faith in the ability of stories to
inspire and instruct. At the end of the trail of bread crumbs you will find not an old
witch trying to stuff you in the oven and cook you, but, instead, two brilliant teachers
who have baked up some of their best ideas yet and are eager to serve them up to you
in this delicious book."

—Jim Burke
Author of *Academic Moves for College and Career Readiness* and
The Common Core Companion Series

"Love fairy tales? Looking for fresh ways to stimulate student thinking and promote
original writing? This book is for you. Gretchen Bernabei and Judi Reimer offer an
inspired approach for using fairy tales as mentor texts and student writing as pre-
reading for analysis of those texts. Their process works in both directions! A wonderful
way to revisit the many uses of enchantment."

—Carol Jago
Long-Time English Teacher,
Past President of the National Council of Teachers of English,
and Associate Director of the California Reading
and Literature Project, UCLA

"*Text Structures From Fairy Tales* by Gretchen Bernabei and Judi Reimer is pure
genius! This book will show teachers the value and importance of students having
a firm foundation in these archetypical stories and use them as springboards
for writing. The authors offer choices for students along with inviting teachers to
'break' suggestions such as using the fairy tales in order and sticking to the authors'
planning structures. Suggested topics for students are broad so they can focus on
what's meaningful to them and their experiences. Each lesson includes examples
from students that teachers can share with their classes. These examples reveal how
students take the theme of a fairy tale and relate it to their relevant experiences.
Fairy tales are magical, and the authors have used them to inspire students to think
and write. A joyful, must-have book!"

—Laura Robb
Author of *Read, Talk, Write*

To Lisa Luedeke
For sharing your magic with so many for so long
and for nurturing enchantment from ordinary beans

Illustration by Dixie Shoopman

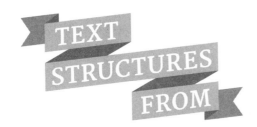

TEXT STRUCTURES FROM

FAIRY TALES

Truisms That Help Students
Write About **Abstract Concepts**…
and Live Happily Ever After

35 LESSONS AND
MENTOR TEXTS

GRADES 4-12

resources.corwin.com/fairytales

GRETCHEN BERNABEI
JUDI REIMER

CORWIN Literacy

For information:

Corwin
A SAGE Company
2455 Teller Road
Thousand Oaks, California 91320
(800) 233-9936
www.corwin.com

SAGE Publications Ltd.
1 Oliver's Yard
55 City Road
London EC1Y 1SP
United Kingdom

SAGE Publications India Pvt. Ltd.
B 1/I 1 Mohan Cooperative Industrial Area
Mathura Road, New Delhi 110 044
India

SAGE Publications Asia-Pacific Pte. Ltd.
18 Cross Street #10–10/11/12
China Square Central
Singapore 048423

Director and Publisher, Corwin Classroom:
    Lisa Luedeke
Editorial Development Manager: Julie Nemer
Senior Editorial Assistant: Sharon Wu
Production Editor: Melanie Birdsall
Copy Editor: Diane DiMura
Typesetter: Integra
Proofreader: Susan Schon
Cover and Interior Designer: Gail Buschman
Marketing Manager: Brian Grimm

Printed in the United States of America

ISBN 978-1-5443-6115-4

This book is printed on acid-free paper.

19 20 21 22 23 10 9 8 7 6 5 4 3 2 1

Contents

online resources

Visit the companion website at **resources.corwin.com/fairytales** for a blank student planning page, the complete collection of text structures, and downloadable versions of the fairy tales.

Acknowledgments

We thank our Corwin Literacy team, whose expertise, professionalism, and sheer goodness leave us shaking our heads in wonder: Lisa Luedeke, Sharon Wu, Julie Nemer, Gail Buschman, Melanie Birdsall, and Diane DiMura.

We are indebted to our colleagues whose enthusiasm and energy resulted in the student writing for this book: Kelly Toepperwein, Alison Vives, Carolyn Karger, Kim Grauer, Morgan Kern, Kathleen Roark, Heather Sargent, Lynda Morgart, Jayne Hover, Susan Diaz, Joseph Clites, Kila Bach, Doris Rico, Jenny Martinez, Victoria Martinez, Andrea Lucas, and Amanda Schmitt.

We also deeply appreciate the warm encouragement from Fran Awbrey, Carol Booth Olsen, Stephanie Cash, Kathy Bieser, Marian Aleta Jones, Christina Clark, Nicole Morales, Nanette Raska, Amy Stengel, Carol Mendenhall, Dottie Hall, and Patricia S. Gray.

Finally, we gratefully acknowledge the love and support from our families, especially Sarah Dawn and Allan Keyes, Lilly and Olivia, Mary Sue King, Bert and Dixie, and Matilde and Julian. And Madeleine and Charlise, the ones who prefer their fairy tales during their tea parties.

Introduction

"If you want your children to be intelligent, read them fairy tales.

If you want them to be very intelligent, read them more fairy tales."

—Commonly attributed to Albert Einstein

I remember sitting behind my mother as she read to us. I'd brush her hair and listen with my brother and sisters as she read fairy tales to us, one after another, night after night. Our family didn't have much money in those days, but we felt rich with magic tables laid out with feasts, dogs with eyes as big as saucers, and pockets crammed full of jewels.

These are the stories of my childhood, stories in their old, archaic forms, cut for length but not for style or content. They are the stories of the Brothers Grimm, of Hans Christian Andersen, of Charles Perrault. They are neither translated into simpler language nor sanitized to remove the gruesome features in the stories. As Judi and I have immersed ourselves in them, we have both been surprised to discover that few characters are purely good or evil. Most embody a perplexing mixture of both, often stimulating conversation about the world.

We do not presume to offer psychological studies of the functions or features of fairy tales; Bruno Bettelheim covered that definitively, we think; but we are convinced that children need stories as much as they need food. They can get by with very little, but both provide nourishment that fortifies a child against witches, against dragons, against starvation. We see what in the world terrifies our children and what worries them, and we remember being comforted by these stories.

"Fairy tales do not tell children that dragons exist.

Children already know that dragons exist.

Fairy tales tell children that dragons can be killed."

—G. K. Chesterton, adapted by Neil Gaiman

How to Use This Book

For any grade level, you can start with reading a story or with writing. Both are fine, as one leads to the other.

Every theme starts with an abstract concept word, like *friendship* or *generosity*. You can help students understand how to develop a theme by expanding concept words into truisms, or life lessons. (See Appendix 11 for a quick lesson.) Truisms are a simple way to ease students into in-depth writing from the heart, without trauma or drudgery.

If You Want to Begin With Reading,

Enjoy the story aloud as a whole group, or quietly. Read it to them. Slowly. Or let student readers read it aloud to the class. Or color-code the story and assign colors to individuals or groups for choral reading. Sometimes we read the story a second time. Highlight parts you like, or annotate using any method you like.

To move to writing, read the prompt on the planning page. Invite students to write truisms, then kernel essays. They may change the words in the structures. You may ask them to use examples from the story to back up their points, or you may want them to draw from other places for examples (their lives, our cultures, history, other literature).

If You Want to Begin With Writing,

Ask students to address the prompt, write a truism, followed by a short kernel essay (demonstrated on the next pages). You might want to introduce the story after they have shared kernels or after they have developed their essays and lead to a discussion about the themes.

If You Want to Begin With Talking,

Use a strategy like the Conversation Strategies from Appendix 5 to get kids thinking about the concept in the prompt. As the conversations progress, their beliefs about the concept crystallize, and they will find it easier to talk on paper if they have talked with actual people first.

Rules You're Welcome to Break

1. Stick to the text structure offered on the planning page.

    You don't have to. In fact, we planted alternatives at the beginning of each section. Choice is essential for good writing. Some situations cry out for freewriting, without a structure at all.

2. Use the fairy tales in order.

    You kidding? You can use them as you like.

3. Don't mess with the words in the text structure boxes.

    Change anything about them you need to (verb tense, point of view, their order, anything).

Thoughts to Embrace

*   Variety is wonderfully refreshing.

*   Writing should be social, and sharing is the main course, not the dessert, in the process.

- Students want to learn and improve, not just repeat the exercises. Give them the gift of great stories and wonderful craft. The Appendix is full of tools to help with this.

- Writers should have as much choice as we can figure out how to give them: to choose their topics, their beliefs, their structures, their devices. If all of the essays seem alike, we need to reexamine what we're asking.

Let's look at the processes of a couple of students.

First, the steps of Alex Calvio, an eleventh grader.

Read the story.

("The Nightingale")

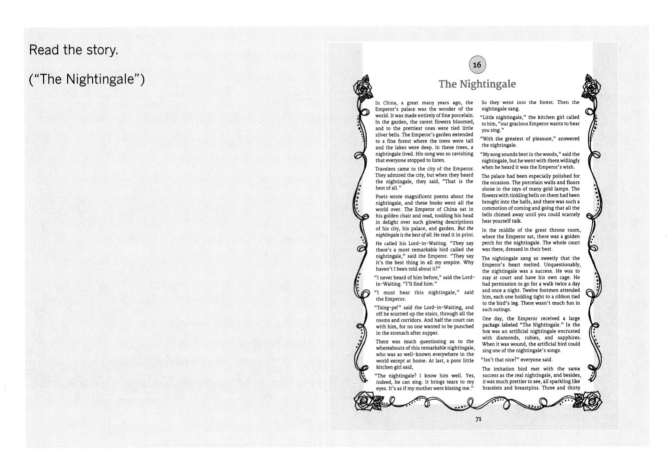

(Continued)

Look at the planning page.

(Identify the topic.)

Read the prompt.

Think about what we love in the world and how we treat it.
Write an essay about pure and simple love.

(Ask yourself, What do I believe about this topic?)

Write your truism.

TRUISM EXAMPLES

1. When a person truly loves, they don't hold grudges.
2. Real love does not expect anything in return.
3. Love should not be one-sided or obsessive.

Choose a structure.

(How will you show your thinking to your reader?)

WRONG ASSUMPTIONS

| I made this wrong assumption | ... happened as a consequence | I learned this truth | So now I believe ... |

And change it if you need to.

WRONG ASSUMPTIONS

| He made this wrong assumption | ... happened as a consequence | He learned this truth | So now I believe ... |

Write a kernel essay.

(Write one sentence for each box in the structure.)

NAME Alex Calvio

Read the story.
Think about what we love in the world and how we treat it.
Write an essay about pure and simple love.

MY TRUISM Unconditional love is the most powerful kind
of love, since it requires forgiveness.

WRONG ASSUMPTIONS

He made this wrong assumption	... happened as a consequence	He learned this truth	So now I believe ...

MY KERNEL ESSAY

1. The Emperor showed unhealthy, selfish love.

2. The nightingale eventually flew away.

3. The Emperor learned that the Nightingale loved him unconditionally.

4. Healthy relationships require selflessness.

TRUISM EXAMPLES

1. When a person truly loves, they don't hold grudges.

2. Real love does not expect anything in return.

3. Love should not be one-sided or obsessive.

Add details from the story

(or from somewhere else).

Alex Calvio

Love can take many shapes and forms, in friendships and relationships. Any interaction involving care could be defined as Love. This means that love should not be one-sided or obsessive.

In the story, "The Nightingale," the Emperor discovers a nightingale that sings beautifully. He orders the bird to be given a cage, attached to a string, and for the bird to sing excessively to the point of exhaustion. This is a representation of an abusive relationship, not necessarily a romantic one, but a relationship between two individuals interacting with one another. This is an abusive relationship because not only does the Emperor ignore the nightingale's wish to stay at home in the forest, he also makes the nightingale feel "loved" and needed in order to lead it back to the palace. Additionally, when the bird finally becomes so worn and tired that it can not sing properly, the Emperor replaces it with a machine, "an artificial nightingale encrusted with diamonds, rubies, and sapphires" and which mechanically reproduces the same song as the nightingale. This action proves that the Emperor does not really love the nightingale, just the song that it sang, and with this the nightingale flies away. [Result: the nightingale flew.]

But the nightingale's love for the Emperor proves to be pure and strong. Even after being abused during their relationship, the nightingale still comes back to save the Emperor from death. This is unconditional love, which is more powerful than any other kind of love since it requires forgiveness. [The Emp. learned about unconditional love.]

In life we can see that successful relationships involve forgiveness along with communication and care. When a relationship is based on negative emotions such as selfishness, it is unhealthy.

"The Nightingale" teaches us how to keep a long lasting and fulfilling type of love. Personally, I may be able to retain healthy relationships by remembering to not use another person's qualities for my own personal benefit. I will give someone space when they require it and love them for their entire selves, not just one part of them. When a relationship is unhealthy, it is best to fly away, like the nightingale. [Healthy relationship require selflessness.]

[showed abuse, not love]

(Continued)

Add craft (rhetorical devices or other devices).

*This essay is visible in regular size in Lesson 16.

Alex Calvio

Love can take many shapes and forms, in friendships and relationships. Any interaction involving care could be defined as Love. This means that love should not be one-sided or obsessive.

In the fairytale, "The Nightingale," the Emperor discovers a nightingale that sings beautifully. He orders the bird to be given a cage, attached to a string, and for the bird to sing excessively to the point of exhaustion. This is a representation of an abusive relationship, not necessarily a romantic one, but a relationship between two individuals interacting with one another. This is an abusive relationship because not only does the Emperor ignore the nightingale's wish to stay at home in the forest, he also makes the Nightingale feel "loved" and needed in order to lead it back to the palace. Additionally, when the bird finally becomes so worn and tired that it can not sing properly, the Emperor replaces it with a machine, "an artificial nightingale encrusted with diamonds, rubies, and sapphires" that could sing the exact same tune that the live Nightingale could. This action proves that the Emperor does not really love the nightingale, just the song that it sang, and with this the nightingale flies away.

But while the Emperor does not love the nightingale, the nightingale does love the Emperor. Even after being abused during their relationship, the nightingale still comes back to save the Emperor from death. This is unconditional love, which is more powerful than any other kind of love since it requires forgiveness.

In life we can see that successful relationships involve forgiveness along with communication and care. When a relationship is based on negative emotions such as selfishness, it can easily become a prison.

"The Nightingale" teaches us how to keep a long lasting and fulfilling type of love. Personally, I may be able to retain healthy relationships by remembering to not use another person's qualities for my own personal benefit. I will give someone space when they require it and love them for their entire selves, not just one part of them. A relationship is a team effort and when someone in a relationship refuses to believe that, it is best to fly away until that relationship can get better, just like the nightingale.

Personification   Anastrophe   Pathos metaphor.   Ethos metaphor

Here's a paper by Ella, a fourth grader:

Read the story.

3
Cinderella

Once there was a gentleman who married, for his second wife, the proudest and most haughty woman that was ever seen. She had two daughters of her own, who were, indeed, exactly like her in all things. He had likewise, a young daughter, but of unparalleled goodness and sweetness of temper.

No sooner were the ceremonies of the wedding over but the stepmother began to show herself in her true colors. She could not bear the good qualities of this pretty girl and employed her in the meanest work of the house. She scoured the dishes and cleaned madam's chamber. She slept on a wretched straw bed, while her sisters slept in fine rooms.

The poor girl bore it all patiently, and she used to go to the chimney corner and sit down there in the cinders and ashes, which caused her to be called Cinderella. However, Cinderella, notwithstanding her coarse apparel, was a hundred times more beautiful than her sisters.

It happened that the king's son gave a ball and invited all persons of fashion to it. Our young misses were mightily delighted at this invitation.

They said to Cinderella, "Would you not like to go to the ball?"

"Alas!" said she, "you only jeer me; it is not for such as I am to go to such a place."

"You are quite right," they replied. "It would make the people laugh to see a Cinderwench at a ball."

They went to court, and Cinderella followed them with her eyes as long as she could. When she lost sight of them, she started to cry.

Her fairy godmother, who saw her all in tears, asked her, "You wish that you could go to the ball; is it not so?"

"Yes," cried Cinderella, with a great sigh.

"Well," said her godmother, "be but a good girl, and I will contrive that you shall go."

Then she took her into her chamber, and said to her, "Run into the garden, and bring me a pumpkin."

Cinderella went immediately and brought it to her godmother. She struck the pumpkin with her wand, and it was instantly turned into a fine coach, gilded all over with gold.

She then went to look into her mousetrap, where she found six mice, all alive. She gave each mouse a little tap with her wand, and made a very fine set of six horses of a beautiful mouse-colored dapple gray.

For a coachman, Cinderella brought a rat, and the fairy touched him with her wand, turning him into a fat, jolly coachman.

After that, she said to her, "Go again into the garden, and you will find six lizards behind the watering pot. Bring them to me."

Her godmother turned them into six footmen, who skipped up immediately behind the coach, with their liveries all bedaubed with gold and silver. The fairy then said to Cinderella, "Well, are you not pleased with it?"

"Oh, yes," she cried; "but must I go in these nasty rags?"

Her godmother then touched her with her wand, and Cinderella's clothes turned into cloth of gold and silver, all beset with jewels. She gave her a pair of glass slippers, the prettiest in the whole world. She got up into her coach; but her godmother, above all things, commanded her not to stay past midnight, telling her that if she stayed one moment longer, the coach would be a pumpkin again, her horses mice, her coachman a rat, her footmen lizards, and that her clothes would become just as they were before.

She promised her godmother to leave the ball before midnight, and then drove away, scarcely able to contain herself for joy. The king's son, who was told that a great

13

Look at the planning page.

(Identify the topic.)

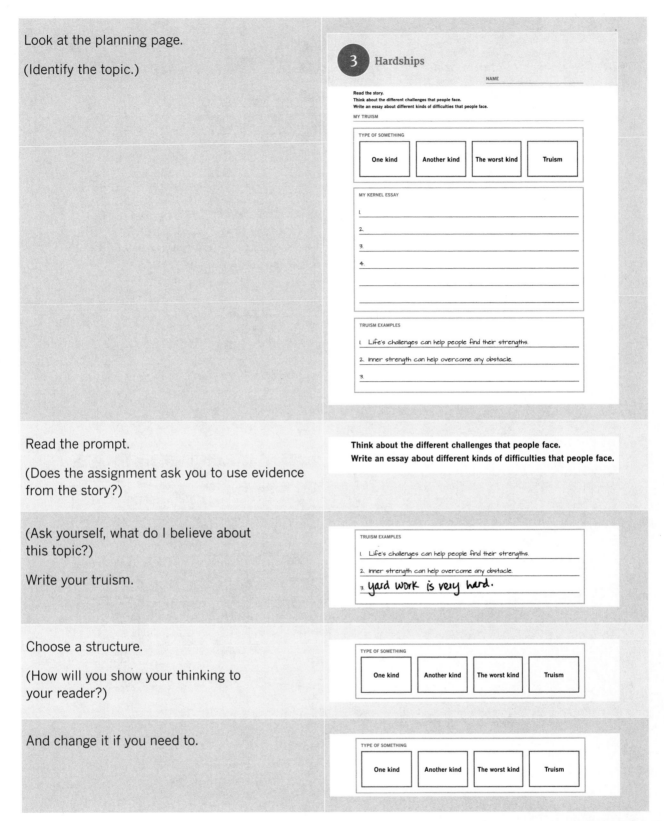

3 Hardships

NAME _____

Read the story.
Think about the different challenges that people face.
Write an essay about different kinds of difficulties that people face.

MY TRUISM

TYPE OF SOMETHING

| One kind | Another kind | The worst kind | Truism |

MY KERNEL ESSAY

1. _____
2. _____
3. _____
4. _____

TRUISM EXAMPLES

1. Life's challenges can help people find their strengths.
2. Inner strength can help overcome any obstacle.
3. _____

Read the prompt.

(Does the assignment ask you to use evidence from the story?)

Think about the different challenges that people face.
Write an essay about different kinds of difficulties that people face.

(Ask yourself, what do I believe about this topic?)

Write your truism.

TRUISM EXAMPLES

1. Life's challenges can help people find their strengths.
2. Inner strength can help overcome any obstacle.
3. yard work is very hard.

Choose a structure.

(How will you show your thinking to your reader?)

TYPE OF SOMETHING

| One kind | Another kind | The worst kind | Truism |

And change it if you need to.

TYPE OF SOMETHING

| One kind | Another kind | The worst kind | Truism |

(Continued)

Write a kernel essay.

(Write one sentence for each box in the structure.)

Add details from the story

(or from somewhere else).

NAME Ella S. Jackson

Read the story.
Think about the different challenges that people face.
Write an essay about different kinds of difficulties that people face.

MY TRUISM   Yard work is hard work

TYPE OF SOMETHING

One kind	Another kind	The worst kind	Truism

MY KERNEL ESSAY

1. Raking leaves and trimming branches is hard.
2. Weeding is tough.
3. Putting down mulch is dirty and hard.
4. Hot and sweaty yard work is rough.

TRUISM EXAMPLES

1. Life's challenges can help people find their strengths.
2. Inner strength can help overcome any obstacle.
3. Yard work is very hard

If you've ever done hours of yard work under a blazing sun, you should have an idea of what yard work at my house is like. The yard work I am used to contains many challenging tasks to be fulfilled!

As a start, I have always done leaves and trimmings first. My Dad hacks away at stray scattered branches, throwing down what seems reasonable, which means there is more to do. The branches that have been chopped off get shoved and squeezed into gargantuan black trash bags that easily weigh a ton each, when they are full. We (my family and I) then work as a team to get the bags to the side of the road. I like this job the least, because I always seem to get numerous scratches and scrapes, but I am always pleased with myself when I finish.

Weeding and raking takes determination if you ever complete it. The grass snarls up the weed pullers and the rake. We sometimes doubtful about their coming out, but by some miracle, somebody gets them out. However, that did not accomplish anything, so we occasionally just do it the old fashioned way: by hand!

Even still, there is more work! An even harder part is putting down mulch. It seems to be the endless chore. The mulch must spread over and over again, so before you could say "I'm as sweaty as a pig!" my arms are limp and feel like lead! Did I mention that mulch gets you so dirty that you look like you slid down the chimney like it was the world's greatest slide"?! Lumbering around with a bag of mulch isn't very fun. So let me tell you YARD WORK IS HARD WORK!

So before you complain, think about how much you'd like hot n' sweaty yard work compared to what you're doing.

-Ella S. Jackson, grade 4

Add craft (rhetorical devices or other devices).

For craft ideas, see the Writer's Toolbox in Appendix 16.

If you've ever done hot sweaty work under a blazing sun, you should have an idea of what yard work at my house is like. The yard work I am used to contains many challenging tasks to be fulfilled!

As a start, I have always done leaves and trimmings first. My Dad hacks away at stray scattered branches that have grown longer than reasonable, which means there is more to do. The branches that have been chopped off get shoved and squeezed into gargantuan black trash bags that seem to weigh a ton each, when they are full. We (my family and I) then work as a team to get the bags to the side of the road. I like this job the least, because I always seem to get numerous scratches and scrapes, but I am always pleased with myself when I finish.

Weeding and raking takes determination if you ever complete it. The grass snarls up the weed pullers and the rake. I'm sometimes doubtful about their coming out, but by some miracle, somebody gets them out. However, that did not accomplish anything, so we occasionally just do it the old fashioned way; by hand!

Even still, there is more work to do an even harder part is putting down mulch. It seems to be the endless sceneiro of "scoop, dump, spread! Over and over again, so before you could say "I'm as sweaty as a pig!" my arms are limp and feel like lead! Did I mention that mulch gets you so dirty, that you look like you slid down the chimney like it was the world's greatest slide"?! Lumbering around with a bag of mulch isn't very fun. So let me tell you YARD WORK IS HARD WORK!

So before you complain, think about how much you'd like hot n' sweaty yard work compared to what you're doing!

-Ella S. Jackson, grade 4

☐ talking   ☐ thinking   ☐ seeing   ☐ doing
☐ simile   ☐ pitchfork

But what about other cultures? Stories from other lands? We invite you to participate in the next collection. If you will send us the stories you remember hearing while in someone's lap, or while brushing someone's hair, we would love to collect and offer them next. (E-mail them to Judi, jreimer2003@hotmail.com.)

Meanwhile, we invite you to share these stories to fortify your children with powerful writing choices while filling their pockets with jewels.

Part I
Structures for Writing About Life Themes

Bank of Text Structure Choices
For Writing About Life Themes

STORY OF MY THINKING

| I used to think (truism) | But this happened | So now I think ... (truism) |

PARTS OF A WHOLE

| The whole | One part | Another part | Truism |

TYPE OF SOMETHING

| One kind | Another kind | The worst kind | Truism |

SHORT- AND LONG-TERM EFFECTS

| What someone said | What surprised me about that | The effect it had at first | The effect it had later | How this will help me later |

WHAT THE CHARACTERS KNOW ABOUT _____

| What it means to most people | One thing she or he knows (and how) | Another thing she or he knows (and how) | What this adds up to for the characters |

1 Appearances

NAME _____

Read the story.
Think about how people are not always as they appear.
Write an essay about first impressions.

MY TRUISM _____

STORY OF MY THINKING

I used to think (truism)	But this happened	So now I think ... (truism)

MY KERNEL ESSAY

1. _____

2. _____

3. _____

_____

_____

_____

_____

TRUISM EXAMPLES

1. First impressions can be so wrong.

2. A glance takes a second; getting to know someone takes a long time.

3. _____

Beauty and the Beast

There was once a very rich merchant, who had six children: three sons and three daughters. His youngest daughter went by the name of Beauty, which made her sisters very jealous. She spent the greatest part of her time in reading good books.

All at once, the merchant lost his whole fortune, excepting a small country house, and told his children with tears in his eyes, they must go there and work for their living. When they came to their country house, Beauty rose at four in the morning and made haste to have the house clean and dinner ready for the family. In less than two months, she grew stronger and healthier than ever. After she had done her work, she read, played on the harpsichord, or else sung whilst she spun.

On the contrary, her two sisters got up at ten and did nothing the whole day. After about a year, the merchant received a letter that a vessel was safely arrived. The two eldest daughters immediately begged of him to buy them new gowns; but Beauty asked for nothing.

"What will you have, Beauty?" said her father. "Since you have the goodness to think of me," answered she, "be so kind to bring me a rose."

The good man went on his journey, and after a great deal of trouble, he came back as poor as before.

He was within thirty miles of his own house, when going through a large forest he lost himself. Night coming on, he began to apprehend being either starved to death with cold and hunger, or else devoured by the wolves, when, on a sudden, he saw a light at some distance; it came from a palace. His horse followed him, and seeing a large stable open, went in, and finding both hay and oats, the poor beast fell to eating very heartily; and entering into a large hall, the man found a good fire, and a table

plentifully set out with but one cover laid. As he was wet quite through with the rain and snow, he drew near the fire to dry himself. "I hope," said he, "the master of the house, or his servants will excuse the liberty I take."

He waited and still nobody came. At last, he was so hungry that he took a chicken and ate it in two mouthfuls, trembling all the while. After this he drank a few glasses of wine, and growing more courageous, he went out of the hall until he came into a chamber, and he concluded it was best to shut the door and go to bed.

It was ten the next morning before the merchant waked, and he was astonished to see a good suit of clothes on a little table. "Thank you, good Madam Fairy," said he aloud.

The good man went to look for his horse, but passing through an arbor of roses, he remembered Beauty's request to him and gathered a branch; immediately, he heard a great noise and saw a frightful Beast coming toward him.

"You are very ungrateful," said the Beast to him, in a terrible voice; "I have saved your life and, in return, you steal my roses, but you shall die for it."

The merchant fell on his knees and said, "I beseech you to forgive me, indeed I had no intention to offend in gathering a rose for one of my daughters."

Replied the monster, "You say you have got daughters. I will forgive you, on condition that one of them come willingly. Go about your business, and swear that if your daughter refuse to die in your stead, you will return within three months."

The merchant had no mind to sacrifice his daughters to the ugly monster, but he thought he should see them once more, so he promised he would return, and the Beast told him he might set out when he pleased.

In a few hours, the good man was at home. When his children came round him, he burst into tears. "Here, Beauty," said he, "take these roses, but how dear they are like to cost your unhappy father;" and then related his fatal adventure.

Answered Beauty, "My father shall not suffer upon my account, since the monster will accept of one of his daughters, I will deliver myself up to all his fury, and I am very happy in thinking that my death will save my father's life."

The horse took the direct road to the palace. The good man and his daughter came into the great hall, where they found a table splendidly served up, and two covers. When they had supped, they heard a great noise. Beauty was sadly terrified at the beast's horrid form, but she took courage as well as she could, and the monster having asked her if she came willingly; "Ye – e – es," said she, trembling.

The beast responded, "You are very good, and I am greatly obliged to you; honest man, go your way tomorrow morning, but never think of coming here again," and immediately the monster withdrew.

"Oh, daughter," said the merchant, embracing Beauty, "I am almost frightened to death, believe me, you had better go back, and let me stay here."

"No, father," said Beauty, in a resolute tone, "you shall set out tomorrow morning and leave me to the care and protection of providence."

As soon as he was gone, Beauty sat down in the great hall, and fell a crying, for she firmly believed Beast would eat her up that night. However, she thought she might as well walk about this fine castle; it was a delightful pleasant place, and she was extremely surprised at seeing a door, over which was written, "Beauty's Apartment." She opened it hastily and was quite dazzled with the magnificence, a large library, a harpsichord, and several music books. "Well," said she to herself, "Were I but to stay here a day, there would not have been all these preparations." This consideration inspired her with fresh courage; and opening the library, she took a book and read these words, in letters of gold:

Welcome Beauty, banish fear,

You are queen and mistress here.

Speak your wishes, speak your will,

Swift obedience meets them still.

"Alas," said she, with a sigh, "there is nothing I desire so much as to see my poor father, and know what he is doing." She had no sooner said this, when casting her eyes on a great looking glass, to her great amazement, she saw her own home, where her father arrived with a very dejected countenance. A moment after, everything disappeared.

At noon she found dinner ready, though without seeing anybody. But at night, as she was going to sit down to supper, she heard the noise Beast made and could not help being sadly terrified. "Beauty," said the monster, "will you give me leave to see you sup?" "That is as you please," answered Beauty trembling.

"No," replied the Beast, "you alone are mistress here; you need only bid me gone. Tell me, do not you think me very ugly?" "That is true," said Beauty, "for I cannot tell a lie, but I believe you are very good natured."

"Yes, yes," said the Beast, "my heart is good, but still I am a monster." "Among mankind," says Beauty, "there are many that deserve that name more than you, and I prefer you, just as you are, to those, who, under a human form, hide a treacherous, corrupt, and ungrateful heart."

Beauty ate a hearty supper and had almost conquered her dread of the monster when he said to her, "Beauty, will you be my wife?"

She said trembling, "No Beast." Beast said, in a mournful voice, "then farewell, Beauty," and only turned back to look at her as he went out.

Beauty spent three months very contentedly in the palace. Every evening Beast paid her a visit, and Beauty daily discovered some valuable qualifications in the monster. Every night, the monster always asked her, if she would be his wife. One day she said to him, "Beast, I am too sincere to make you believe that will ever happen; I shall always esteem you as a friend."

Said the Beast, "I love you with the tenderest affection. Promise me never to leave me." "I could," answered she, "indeed, promise never to leave you entirely, but I have so great a desire to see my father that I shall fret to death." "I will send you to your father, you shall remain with him, and poor Beast will die with grief." "No," said Beauty, weeping, "I love you too well to be the cause of your death. I give you my promise to return in a week."

"You shall be there tomorrow morning," said the Beast, "but remember your promise. You need only lay your ring on a table before you go to bed, when you have a mind to come back. Farewell Beauty." Beast sighed, bidding her good night. When she waked the next morning, she found herself at her father's, who, thought he should have died with joy to see his dear daughter again.

Beauty's sisters sickened with envy, when they saw her dressed like a princess, and more beautiful than ever. When the week was expired, they cried, and she promised to stay a week longer.

On the tenth night she spent at her father's, she dreamed that she saw Beast, dying. Beauty started out of her sleep, and bursting into tears. "Am I not very wicked," said she, "to act so unkindly to Beast?" Beauty having said this, rose, put her ring on the table, and then laid down again and fell asleep. When she waked the next morning, she was overjoyed to find herself in the Beast's palace.

She waited for evening. At last the wished-for hour came, the clock struck nine, yet no Beast appeared. Beauty then feared she had been the cause of his death; she recollected her dream, and flew to the canal in the garden, where she dreamed she saw him. There she found poor Beast stretched out, quite senseless, and, as she imagined, dead. She threw herself upon him without any dread, and found his heart beat still. But

Beast opened his eyes, and said to Beauty, "You forgot your promise, but since I have the happiness of seeing you once more, I die satisfied."

"No, dear Beast," said Beauty, "you must not die. Live to be my husband. The grief I now feel convinces me, that I cannot live without you." Beauty scarce had pronounced these words, when she saw the palace sparkle with light. She turned to her dear Beast, but how great was her surprise! Beast was disappeared, and she saw, at her feet, one of the loveliest princes that eye ever beheld; but she could not forbear asking where Beast was.

"You see him at your feet," said the prince. Beauty, agreeably surprised, gave the charming prince her hand to rise; they went together into the castle, and Beauty was overjoyed to find, in the great hall, her father and his whole family.

The prince married Beauty and lived with her many years; and their happiness—as it was founded on virtue—was complete.

Anissa De La Luz, 11th grade

Growing up, I lived on the Westside, a place that wasn't necessarily crime ridden but it wasn't rainbows and sunshine either. So it wasn't hard to believe that I started making generalizations about people based on their appearances. In addition to my observations of people in my neighborhood, media sources like the news also supported my generalizations when they would show mugshots of criminals covered in tattoos and various piercings. In my mind, tattoos and piercings were the basic staples of a sketchy person who was up to no good.

So one day when I went to Walmart, I couldn't find the item that I needed and realized that I needed help from an employee. After looking around, one of the only employees that I saw was a guy covered in skull-themed tattoos and facial piercings. I immediately deemed him as rude and sketchy, dismissing any idea of asking him for help because of his intimidating look.

I continued around the store looking for what I needed but I still required some help; so I continued my search for an employee for help. I finally stumbled upon a girl employee who had a smile as bright as the sun on her face and a perfectly placed ponytail. I decided that she looked harmless enough and walked up to her to ask her for her help. As soon as I did, I was flabbergasted because she turned to me, rolled her eyes and sighed loudly.

She was undoubtedly annoyed with the question I asked her and "tried her best to help me." She gave up within a minute of helping me and said that she would get someone else to help me. I was astonished to find out that she got the guy I had seen earlier to help me out. When he walked up to me he was well-mannered. He told me hello, asked how I was doing, and what he could do to help me out. I told him what I needed and he immediately asked me to follow him. I did and he quickly helped me find the item that I had been looking for.

I had completely misjudged who he was just because I only took his appearance into consideration. I couldn't believe that the person I expected to be amazingly kind was amazingly awful instead. After this experience, I realized that I shouldn't judge people solely based off of their appearances because people aren't always what you think people are going to be.

Amber Smith, 9th grade

What you see when meeting someone doesn't tell you the full story, or the quality of the person. When you first meet someone, it's easy to characterize their personality by what you see on the outside, like their clothes, hair, or even facial expressions. There is more to a person than what you see when you first meet them, like in "Beauty and the Beast."

Fairy tales are one of the first teachers and inspiration for children. "Beauty and the Beast" taught me, like many children, there is always more to a person's story. When Beauty first met the Beast, she saw a rough and mean exterior. She saw a killer, not the kind man that he was. Later in the story, Beauty opens up her mind and heart and welcomes the Beast into her life. When she did this, she found a beautiful person with a kind heart, a person who just wanted to be accepted.

True character is what people show you with their actions, not with the clothes they wear. "Beauty and the Beast" teaches the most important aspect of life is to be accepting of everyone, no matter what you think when you first meet them.

Notes

2 Family

NAME

Read the story.
Think about how everyone needs family.
Write an essay about what a family provides to an individual.

MY TRUISM

PARTS OF A WHOLE

The whole	One part	Another part	Truism

MY KERNEL ESSAY

1.

2.

3.

4.

TRUISM EXAMPLES

1. All families have some things in common.
2. Some families seem unusual.
3.

The Bremen Town Musicians

A certain man had a donkey, which had carried the corn sacks to the mill indefatigably for many a long year; but his strength was going, and he was growing more and more unfit for work. Seeing that no good wind was blowing, the donkey ran away and set out on the road to Bremen. "There," he thought, "I can surely be town musician." When he had walked some distance, he found a hound lying on the road, gasping like one who had run till he was tired. "What are you gasping so for, you big fellow?" asked the donkey.

"Ah," replied the hound, "as I am old, and daily grow weaker, and no longer can hunt, my master wanted to kill me, so I took to flight; but now how am I to earn my bread?"

"I tell you what," said the donkey, "I am going to Bremen, and shall be town musician there; go with me. I will play the lute, and you shall beat the kettledrum."

The hound agreed, and on they went.

Before long, they came to a cat, sitting on the path, with a face like three rainy days! "Now then, old shaver, what has gone askew with you?" asked the donkey.

"Who can be merry when his neck is in danger?" answered the cat. "Because I am now getting old, and I prefer to sit by the fire rather than hunt about after mice, my mistress wanted to drown me, so I ran away. Where am I to go?"

"Go with us to Bremen. You can be a town musician." The cat thought well of it and went with them.

After this, the three fugitives came to a farmyard, where the cock was sitting upon the gate, crowing with all his might. Said the donkey, "What is the matter?"

Said the cock, "Guests are coming for Sunday, so the housewife has no pity, and has told the cook that she intends to eat me in the soup tomorrow, and this evening I am to have my head cut off. Now I am crowing at full pitch while I can."

"Ah, but red-comb," said the donkey, "you had better come away with us. We are going to Bremen; you can find something better than death everywhere. You have a good voice, and if we make music together, it must have some quality!"

The cock agreed to this plan, and all four went on together. They could not, however, reach the city of Bremen in one day, and in the evening, they came to a forest. The donkey and the hound laid themselves down under a large tree. The cat and the cock settled themselves in the branches; but the cock flew right to the top, where he was most safe. Before he went to sleep, he looked round on all the four sides and thought he saw in the distance a little spark burning; so he called out to his companions that there must be a house not far off, for he saw a light. The donkey said, "If so, we had better get up and go on, for the shelter here is bad." The hound thought that a few bones with some meat on would do him good too!

So they made their way to the place where the light was a well-lighted robber's house. The donkey, as the biggest, went to the window and looked in.

"What do you see, my grey-horse?" asked the cock. "What do I see?" answered the donkey. "A table covered with good things to eat and drink, and robbers sitting at it enjoying themselves." "That would be the sort of thing for us," said the cock. "Yes, yes; ah, how I wish we were there!" said the donkey.

Then the animals thought of a plan to drive away the robbers. The donkey was to place himself with his forefeet upon the window ledge, the hound was to jump on the donkey's back, the cat was to climb upon the dog, and lastly the cock was to fly up and perch upon the head of the cat.

When this was done, they began to perform their music together: the donkey brayed, the hound barked, the cat mewed, and the cock crowed; then they burst through the window into the room, so that the glass clattered! At this horrible din, the robbers sprang up, thinking that a ghost had come in, and fled in a great fright out into the forest. The four companions now sat down at the table and ate as if they were going to fast for a month.

As soon as the four minstrels had done, they put out the light, and each sought for himself a sleeping place according to his nature and to what suited him. The donkey laid himself down upon some straw in the yard, the hound behind the door, the cat upon the hearth near the warm ashes, and the cock perched himself upon a beam of the roof; and being tired with their long walk, they soon went to sleep.

When it was past midnight, and the robbers saw from afar that the light was no longer burning in their house, and all appeared quiet, the captain said, "We ought not to have let ourselves be frightened out of our wits," and ordered one of them to go and examine the house.

The messenger finding all still, went into the kitchen to light a candle, and, taking the glistening fiery eyes of the cat for live coals, he held a lucifer-match to them to light it. But the cat flew in his face, spitting and scratching. He was dreadfully frightened, and ran to the back door, but the dog, who lay there, sprang up and bit his leg; and as he ran across the yard by the straw heap, the donkey gave him a smart kick with its hind foot. The cock, too, who had been awakened by the noise, and had become lively, cried down from the beam, "Cock-a-doodle-doo!"

Then, the robber ran back as fast as he could to his captain, and said, "Ah, there is a horrible witch sitting in the house, who spat on me and scratched my face with her long claws; and by the door stands a man with a knife, who stabbed me in the leg; and in the yard, there lies a black monster, who beat me with a wooden club; and above, upon the roof, sits the judge, who called out, 'Bring the rogue here to me!' so I got away as well as I could."

After this the robbers did not trust themselves in the house again; but the four musicians of Bremen did not care to leave it any more. And the mouth of him who last told this story is still warm.

Dallas Smith, 9th grade

1. Although family can cause problems, family can help cope with problems too by being supportive.

2. Family can cause problems by overreacting to small situations.

3. Family can be supportive of you, like when you do something wrong like not washing the dishes.

4. Families are like roller coasters; they have their ups and downs, they sometimes make you sick to your stomach, but overall it's totally worth it.

Annie Booth, 8th grade

1. Families are not always related by blood. The girls in my Girl Scout troop are just like my family because it's like living together when we go camping. Once we got to sleep overnight inside NASA and once in the Houston Aquarium.

2. In the "Bremen Town Musicians," the animals feel like family when they work together. They save each other from being killed, they huddle under a tree at night to keep warm, and they scare off the robbers.

3. My friends in Girl Scouts also act like a family when we help other people by making blankets for homeless shelters and pet shelters. We love to sell Girl Scout cookies together.

4. You don't always have to be related to be a family.

Appie Aguirre, 10th grade

1. What makes a perfect family? The money they have? The clothes they wear? Don't you ever get curious? The truth of it is, I don't think there is a perfect family. Maybe the family's problems are what hold them together.

2. Problems happen in every family, all kinds of problems. Some have children, nephews, cousins, or parents in jail. Some have problems with abuse, drugs, and alcohol. I think we all know of a person in our family who struggles with some of these.

3. Other families have more domestic household-type problems. Maybe the Smith family is always clogging their toilet, thus resulting in tons of money out the window. Other families have different types of financial problems.

4. All families have problems, but that is just what makes a family.

NAME _____

Read the story.
Think about the different challenges that people face.
Write an essay about different kinds of difficulties that people face.

MY TRUISM _____

TYPE OF SOMETHING

One kind	Another kind	The worst kind	Truism

MY KERNEL ESSAY

1. _____

2. _____

3. _____

4. _____

_____

_____

TRUISM EXAMPLES

1. Life's challenges can help people find their strengths.

2. Inner strength can help overcome any obstacle.

3. _____

Cinderella

Once there was a gentleman who married, for his second wife, the proudest and most haughty woman that was ever seen. She had two daughters of her own, who were, indeed, exactly like her in all things. He had likewise, a young daughter, but of unparalleled goodness and sweetness of temper.

No sooner were the ceremonies of the wedding over but the stepmother began to show herself in her true colors. She could not bear the good qualities of this pretty girl and employed her in the meanest work of the house. She scoured the dishes and cleaned madam's chamber. She slept on a wretched straw bed, while her sisters slept in fine rooms.

The poor girl bore it all patiently, and she used to go to the chimney corner and sit down there in the cinders and ashes, which caused her to be called Cinderella. However, Cinderella, notwithstanding her coarse apparel, was a hundred times more beautiful than her sisters.

It happened that the king's son gave a ball and invited all persons of fashion to it. Our young misses were mightily delighted at this invitation.

They said to Cinderella, "Would you not like to go to the ball?"

"Alas!" said she, "you only jeer me; it is not for such as I am to go to such a place."

"You are quite right," they replied. "It would make the people laugh to see a Cinderwench at a ball."

They went to court, and Cinderella followed them with her eyes as long as she could. When she lost sight of them, she started to cry.

Her fairy godmother, who saw her all in tears, asked her, "You wish that you could go to the ball; is it not so?"

"Yes," cried Cinderella, with a great sigh.

"Well," said her godmother, "be but a good girl, and I will contrive that you shall go."

Then she took her into her chamber, and said to her, "Run into the garden, and bring me a pumpkin."

Cinderella went immediately and brought it to her godmother. She struck the pumpkin with her wand, and it was instantly turned into a fine coach, gilded all over with gold.

She then went to look into her mousetrap, where she found six mice, all alive. She gave each mouse a little tap with her wand, and made a very fine set of six horses of a beautiful mouse-colored dapple gray.

For a coachman, Cinderella brought a rat, and the fairy touched him with her wand, turning him into a fat, jolly coachman.

After that, she said to her, "Go again into the garden, and you will find six lizards behind the watering pot. Bring them to me."

Her godmother turned them into six footmen, who skipped up immediately behind the coach, with their liveries all bedaubed with gold and silver. The fairy then said to Cinderella, "Well, are you not pleased with it?"

"Oh, yes," she cried; "but must I go in these nasty rags?"

Her godmother then touched her with her wand, and Cinderella's clothes turned into cloth of gold and silver, all beset with jewels. She gave her a pair of glass slippers, the prettiest in the whole world. She got up into her coach; but her godmother, above all things, commanded her not to stay past midnight, telling her that if she stayed one moment longer, the coach would be a pumpkin again, her horses mice, her coachman a rat, her footmen lizards, and that her clothes would become just as they were before.

She promised her godmother to leave the ball before midnight, and then drove away, scarcely able to contain herself for joy. The king's son, who was told that a great princess had arrived, ran out to receive her. He gave her his hand and led her into the hall. There was immediately a profound silence. Nothing was then heard but a confused noise of, "How beautiful she is! How beautiful she is!"

The king's son led her to the most honorable seat, and afterward took her out to dance with him. She danced so very gracefully that they all more and more admired her.

She thought that it was no later than eleven when she counted the clock striking twelve. She jumped up and fled, as nimble as a deer. The prince followed but could not overtake her. She left behind one of her glass slippers, which the prince picked up most carefully. She reached home, but quite out of breath, and in her nasty old clothes, having nothing left of all her finery but one of the little slippers.

As she was eagerly telling her godmother everything that had happened at the ball, her two sisters knocked at the door, which Cinderella ran and opened.

"You stayed such a long time!" she cried, gaping, rubbing her eyes and stretching herself as if she had been sleeping.

"If you had been at the ball," said one of her sisters, "you would not have been tired with it. The finest princess was there, the most beautiful that mortal eyes have ever seen."

They told her that this princess hurried away with so much haste that she dropped one of her little glass slippers, which the king's son had picked up, and that most certainly he was very much in love with the beautiful person who owned the glass slipper.

What they said was very true; for a few days later, the king's son had it proclaimed that he would marry her whose foot this slipper would just fit. They began to try it on all the court, but in vain; it was brought to the two sisters, who did all they possibly could to force their foot into the slipper, but they did not succeed.

Cinderella knew that it was her slipper and said, "Let me see if it will not fit me."

Her sisters burst out laughing, but the gentleman who was sent to try the slipper looked earnestly at Cinderella, and said that he had orders to let everyone try.

He had Cinderella sit down, and he found that it went on very easily, fitting her as if it had been made of wax. Her two sisters were greatly astonished, but then even more so, when Cinderella pulled out of her pocket the other slipper. Then in came her godmother and touched her wand to Cinderella's clothes, making them richer and more magnificent than any of those she had worn before.

And now her two sisters threw themselves at her feet to beg pardon. Cinderella embraced them and said that she forgave them with all her heart, and wanted them always to love her.

She was taken to the young prince. He thought she was more charming than before, and, a few days after, married her. Cinderella gave her two sisters lodgings in the palace, and that very same day matched them with two great lords of the court.

Moral: Beauty in a woman is a rare treasure that will always be admired. Graciousness, however, is priceless and of even greater value.

Ella Jackson, 4th grade

If you've ever done hot sweaty work under a blazing sun, you should have an idea of what yard work at my house is like. The yard work I am used to contains many challenging tasks to be fulfilled!

As a start, I have always done leaves and trimmings first. My Dad hacks away at stray scattered branches that have grown longer than reasonable, which means there is more to do. The branches that have been chopped off get shoved and squeezed into gargantuan black trash bags that seem to weigh a ton each, when they are full. We (my family and I) then work as a team to get the bags to the side of the road. I like this job the least because I always seem to get numerous scratches and scrapes, but I am always pleased with myself when I finish.

Weeding and raking take determination if you ever complete it. The grass snarls up the weed pullers and the rake. I'm sometimes doubtful about their coming out, but by some miracle, somebody gets them out. However, that does not accomplish anything, so we occasionally just do it the old fashioned way; by hand!

Even still, there is more work to do; an even harder part is putting down mulch. It seems to be the endless scenario of "scoop, dump, spread!" over and over again, so before you could say "I'm as sweaty as a pig!" my arms are limp and feel like lead! Did I mention that mulch gets you so dirty that you look like you slid down the chimney like it was the world's greatest slide? Lumbering around with a bag of mulch isn't very fun. So let me tell you YARD WORK IS HARD WORK!

So before you complain, think about how much you'd like hot n' sweaty yard work compared to what you're doing!

Read the story.

Think about how clearly we remember kind or mean things other people have said to us.

Write an essay about the impact that words can have on other people.

MY TRUISM

SHORT- AND LONG-TERM EFFECTS

What someone said	What surprised me about that	The effect it had at first	The effect it had later	How this will help me later

---

MY KERNEL ESSAY

1. _____

2. _____

3. _____

4. _____

5. _____

_____

TRUISM EXAMPLES

1. Mean words can make a person miserable. _____

2. Words can be an accidental weapon. _____

3. _____

Diamonds and Toads

Once upon a time there was a widow who had two daughters. The elder was so disagreeable and so proud. The younger, who was the very picture of sweetness of temper and virtue, was withal one of the most beautiful girls ever seen. This mother doted on her elder daughter, and at the same time had a great aversion for the younger. She made her eat in the kitchen and work continually.

Among other things, this unfortunate child had to go twice a day to draw water more than a mile and a half from the house, and bring home a pitcherful of it. One day, as she was at this fountain, there came to her a poor woman, who begged of her to let her drink.

"Oh, yes, with all my heart, Goody," said this pretty little girl. Rinsing the pitcher at once, she took some of the clearest water from the fountain and gave it to her, holding up the pitcher all the while that she might drink the easier.

The good woman having drunk, said to her:

"You are so pretty, so good and courteous, that I cannot help giving you a gift." For this was a fairy, who had taken the form of a poor country woman, to see how far the civility and good manners of this pretty girl would go. "I will give you for a gift," continued the Fairy, "that, at every word you speak, there shall come out of your mouth either a flower or a jewel."

When this pretty girl returned, her mother scolded her for staying so long at the fountain.

"I beg your pardon, mamma," said the poor girl, "for not making more haste."

And in speaking these words there came out of her mouth two roses, two pearls, and two large diamonds.

"What is it I see there?" said her mother, quite astonished. "I think pearls and diamonds come out of the girl's mouth! How happens this, my child?"

This was the first time she had ever called her "my child."

The girl told her frankly all the matter, not without dropping out great numbers of diamonds.

"Truly," cried the mother, "I must send my own dear child thither. Fanny, look at what comes out of your sister's mouth when she speaks. Would you not be glad, my dear, to have the same gift? Go and draw water out of the fountain, and when a poor woman asks you to let her drink, give it to her very civilly."

"I should like to see myself going to the fountain to draw water," said this ill-bred minx.

"I insist you shall go," said the mother, "and that instantly."

She went, but grumbled all the way, taking with her the best silver tankard in the house.

She no sooner reached the fountain than she saw coming out of the wood, a magnificently dressed lady, who came up to her, and asked to drink. This was the same fairy who had appeared to her sister, but she had now taken the air and dress of a princess, to see how far this girl's rudeness would go.

"Am I come hither," said the proud, ill-bred girl, "to serve you with water, pray? I suppose this silver tankard was brought purely for your ladyship, was it? However, you may drink out of it, if you have a fancy."

"You are scarcely polite," answered the fairy, without anger. "Well, then, since you are so disobliging, I give you for gift that at every word you speak there shall come out of your mouth a snake or a toad."

So soon as her mother saw her coming, she cried out:

"Well, daughter?"

"Well, mother?" answered the unhappy girl, throwing out of her mouth a viper and a toad.

4 "Oh, mercy!" cried the mother, "what is it I see? It is her sister who has caused all this, but she shall pay for it," and immediately she ran to beat her. The poor child fled away from her, and went to hide herself in the forest nearby.

The King's son, who was returning from the chase, met her, and seeing her so beautiful, asked her what she did there alone and why she cried.

"Alas! sir, my mother has turned me out of doors."

The King's son, who saw five or six pearls and as many diamonds come out of her mouth, desired her to tell him how that happened. She told him the whole story. The King's son fell in love with her, and, considering that such a gift was worth more than any marriage portion another bride could bring, conducted her to the palace of the King, his father, and there married her.

As for her sister, she made herself so much hated that her own mother turned her out of doors. The miserable girl, after wandering about and finding no one to take her in, went to a corner of the wood, and there died.

Student Work Samples: Power of Words

Clarissa Gutierrez, 9th grade

1. One night when I was 7, my aunt told me, "Don't cry or be sad, but I love your brother more."

2. I was too little to really shake it off and to not let it bother me.

3. In my head I always went back to that day and it would just tear me down.

4. It's made me stronger as a person and that's why if someone says anything about me, it doesn't get to me.

5. This has already begun to help me because I'm being me and if you don't like it, that's not my problem.

Anna Riggs, 11th grade

During my sophomore year, I took a class on how to write a novel. When we were studying novelists' writing processes, my teacher gave me a book called *The Writer's Life*, a compilation of essays from *The Washington Post* written by several eminent novelists. Joanna Trollope, an English novelist who has written several bestsellers, writes, "I sometimes wish people wouldn't try to write fiction before they are 35—or at least, to realize that they will write infinitely better fiction after they are 35."

This sparked a period of indignance toward this writer. It surprised me that an author would say that one should wait to write in the first place: I have only heard from successful authors telling young writers to write as much as possible, and when you're not writing, recommend to have your nose stuffed in a book. To me, Trollope's philosophy was bitter and dismissive of all the students majoring in creative writing or the young English teachers who are determined to finish a novel in the time they spend not grading papers and writing lesson plans and teaching, and even the young novelists who are bestsellers and get paid to continue crafting their fantasies. Her ideology entails that noteworthy writing is a goal unobtainable by young people, as if *Frankenstein* wasn't written by Mary Shelley when she was nineteen, or Steinbeck didn't publish his first novel when he was twenty-seven.

For me to remember reading this sentence over a year after finishing my writing class meant I must have felt considerably discouraged by Trollope's essay. Just as in any situation, if something is put eloquently, it is more persuasive. For as insignificant as a single essay is, this one carried weight.

But in the long term, I learned that Trollope had a point. While I was indignant about it at the time, she was right. I, a teenager, was unable to finish writing a novel. Writing demands unfaltering attention, which I realistically won't have time for until I am, perhaps, thirty-five. Now, a year after reading *A Writer's Life*, I realize I couldn't have made a commitment to finish a novel anyway. I look at Joanna's "rule" differently and actually understand it better because of this current phase of my life. In a setting ridden with deadlines and commitments, I spread myself and my time thinly. This year alone, I have worked harder than I ever have in school all while juggling time-consuming extracurriculars like theatre, or finding more personal values and goals after the March For Our Lives movement began. Furthermore, chances of success for finishing a novel (and publishing), are arguably higher for older individuals who have more control over their lives and time.

This realization doesn't change the fact that at the beginning of that semester, I thought I would spend practically the rest of my time in high school writing a novel, but by the end of the year, I had forgotten about that aspiration. Over time, I grew to be more practical and realistic. With the help of that op-ed essay by Joanna Trollope, I can see her quote in a more positive light. As writers, we can spend our younger years spending days alone wandering around art museums in Chicago, going to gun violence protests in Boston, or going to quinceñeras and local bands' concerts every weekend when I'm home in San Antonio. Without this irreplaceable time of youth, I'd have no inspiration later on. Overall, while it was difficult to admit at the time, Trollope's words are powerful and true.

NAME

Read the story.

Think about how people act when they receive gifts.

Write an essay about how people react when they feel grateful.

MY TRUISM

WHAT THE CHARACTERS KNOW ABOUT _____

| What it means to most people | One thing she or he knows (and how) | Another thing she or he knows (and how) | What this adds up to for the characters |

MY KERNEL ESSAY

1. _____

2. _____

3. _____

4. _____

_____

_____

TRUISM EXAMPLES

1. People have the power to repay kindness.

2. Sometimes help arrives when nobody has asked for it.

3. _____

The Elves and the Shoemaker

There was once a shoemaker, who worked very hard and was very honest; but still he could not earn enough to live upon; and at last all he had in the world was gone, save just leather enough to make one pair of shoes.

Then he cut his leather out, all ready to make up the next day, meaning to rise early in the morning to his work. His conscience was clear and his heart light amidst all his troubles; so he went peaceably to bed, left all his cares to Heaven, and soon fell asleep. In the morning after he had said his prayers, he sat himself down to his work; when, to his great wonder, there stood the shoes already made upon the table. The good man knew not what to say or think at such an odd thing happening. He looked at the workmanship; there was not one false stitch in the whole job; all was so neat and true that it was quite a masterpiece.

The same day a customer came in, and the shoes suited him so well that he willingly paid a price higher than usual for them; and the poor shoemaker, with the money, bought leather enough to make two pairs more. In the evening, he cut out the work and went to bed early, that he might get up and begin betimes next day; but he was saved all the trouble, for when he got up in the morning, the work was done ready to his hand. Soon in came buyers, who paid him handsomely for his goods, so that he bought leather enough for four pair more. He cut out the work again overnight and found it done in the morning, as before; and so it went on for some time: What was got ready in the evening was always done by daybreak, and the good man soon became thriving and well off again.

One evening, about Christmas-time, as he and his wife were sitting over the fire chatting together, he said to her, "I should like to sit up and watch tonight, that we may see who it is that comes and does my work for me." The wife liked the thought; so they left a light burning and hid themselves in a corner of the room, behind a curtain that was hung up there, and watched what would happen.

As soon as it was midnight, there came in two little naked dwarfs; and they sat themselves upon the shoemaker's bench, took up all the work that was cut out, and began to ply with their little fingers, stitching and rapping and tapping away at such a rate, that the shoemaker was all wonder and could not take his eyes off them. And on they went, till the job was quite done, and the shoes stood ready for use upon the table. This was long before daybreak; and then they bustled away as quick as lightning.

The next day the wife said to the shoemaker. "These little wights have made us rich, and we ought to be thankful to them, and do them a good turn if we can. I am quite sorry to see them run about as they do; and indeed it is not very decent, for they have nothing upon their backs to keep off the cold. I'll tell you what, I will make each of them a shirt, and a coat and waistcoat, and a pair of pantaloons into the bargain; and do you make each of them a little pair of shoes."

The thought pleased the good cobbler very much; and one evening, when all the things were ready, they laid them on the table, instead of the work that they used to cut out, and then went and hid themselves to watch what the little elves would do.

About midnight in they came, dancing and skipping, hopped round the room, and then went to sit down to their work as usual; but when they saw the clothes lying for them, they laughed and chuckled, and seemed mightily delighted.

Then, they dressed themselves in the twinkling of an eye and danced and capered and sprang about, as merry as could be, till at last they danced out at the door, and away over the green.

The good couple saw them no more; but everything went well with them from that time forward, as long as they lived.

Student Work Samples: Gratitude

Thomas Mora, 8th grade

1. A gift is a powerful thing. No matter the size of the gift, whoever you give the gift to, they feel happy.

2. A gift tells people many things. It tells them that you appreciate them.

3. It also tells them that they are worth you taking time and money out of your day to get them a gift.

4. All this joy and happiness makes the other person want to do something for you or someone else, therefore carrying on the cycle.

Kelly Dinkle, 10th grade

1. Who doesn't just love and appreciate a random act of kindness?

2. Typically, you're grateful for something someone has done for you that was not expected or necessary. The shoemaker and his wife did not expect help. They stayed up late out of amazement just to see who would do this kind thing for them.

3. You find that the fact that the person even thought about you enough to do something worth feeling grateful for, often outweighs what they even did for you. You just think about the fact that they did it!

4. Sometimes help comes your way when you don't even ask for it, but you'll look back and greatly appreciate it and possibly repay the favor out of gratefulness.

Julian Ponce, 7th grade

1. Gratitude means being thankful to other people.

2. One thing I know is that it can have to do with food. I felt grateful to my friend Sofia when she brought me a bag of Takis.

3. Another thing I know about gratitude is that it's even better to make other people happy by doing things for them. I brought Takis to everyone at my lunch table last year, and they were happy. I could see they felt gratitude when they said "thanks!" and opened the Takis up and started eating them instantly.

4. All together, this means that when you make someone happy, they can do the same for you. People are thankful for what they get, whether it's food or friendship or help.

Notes

Part II
Structures for Explaining a Concept

Bank of Text Structure Choices

For Explaining a Concept

CASE STUDY

Question	My (or someone else's) experience	What that shows	Truism

COMPARING NOTES

Some people think …	Other people think …	But I think …	So I will …

THE ONION

Truism	How do I know this? (one way)	If that had not happened, how else would I know this?	If that had not happened, how else would I know this?	Truism

RECONSIDERING A BELIEF

Most people think …	… because (one way it's good)	But … (one way it's bad)	So … (truism)

LIFE LESSON

Truism	How it's true in the story	How it's true in life	How this will help me

NAME

Read the story.
Think about how people go along with the crowd, even when they disagree deep down.
Write an essay about how hard it is to disagree with a group.

MY TRUISM

CASE STUDY

Question	My (or someone else's) experience	What that shows	Truism

MY KERNEL ESSAY

1. _____

2. _____

3. _____

4. _____

_____

_____

TRUISM EXAMPLES

1. It's easy to state your opinion when you know everyone else agrees with it.

2. It's easy to keep quiet when you disagree with a group.

3. _____

The Emperor's New Clothes

Many years ago, there was an Emperor, who was so excessively fond of new clothes that he spent all his money in dress. He had a different suit for each hour of the day.

One day, two rogues, calling themselves weavers, made their appearance at the court. They gave out that they knew how to weave the most beautiful colors and elaborate patterns, the clothes manufactured from which should have the wonderful property of remaining invisible to everyone who was unfit for the office he held, or who was extraordinarily simple in character.

"These must, indeed, be splendid clothes!" thought the Emperor. "Had I such a suit, I might at once find out what men in my realms are unfit for their office and also be able to distinguish the wise from the foolish! This stuff must be woven for me immediately." And he caused large sums of money to be given to both the weavers in order that they might begin their work directly.

So the two pretended weavers set up two looms and affected to work very busily, though in reality they did nothing at all. They asked for the most delicate silk and the purest gold thread, put both into their own knapsacks, and then continued their pretended work at the empty looms until late at night.

"I should like to know how the weavers are getting on with my cloth," said the Emperor to himself, after some little time had elapsed; he was, however, rather embarrassed, when he remembered that a simpleton, or one unfit for his office, would be unable to see. All the people throughout the city had heard of the wonderful property the cloth was to possess; and all were anxious to learn how wise, or how ignorant, their neighbors might prove to be.

The Emperor now sent an officer of his court to see how the men were getting on, and to ascertain whether the cloth would soon be ready. He surveyed the looms on all sides, but could see nothing at all but the empty frames.

The impostors requested him very courteously to be so good as to come nearer their looms and then asked him whether the design pleased him, and whether the colors were not very beautiful, at the same time pointing to the empty frames. The poor old minister looked and looked: There was nothing there. "What!" thought he. "Is it possible that I am a simpleton? I have never thought so myself; and no one must know it now if I am so. Can it be that I am unfit for my office? No, that must not be said either. I will never confess that I could not see the stuff."

"Well, Sir Minister!" said one of the knaves, still pretending to work. "You do not say whether the stuff pleases you."

"Oh, it is excellent!" replied the old minister, looking at the loom through his spectacles. "This pattern, and the colors, yes. I will tell the Emperor without delay how very beautiful I think them."

"We shall be much obliged to you," said the impostors.

The whole city was talking of the splendid cloth, and now the Emperor himself wished to see the costly manufacture. He went to the crafty impostors, who, as soon as they were aware of the Emperor's approach, went on working more diligently than ever, although they still did not pass a single thread through the looms.

"Is not the work absolutely magnificent?" said two officers of the crown. "If your Majesty will only be pleased to look at it! What a splendid design! What glorious colors!" and at the same time, they pointed to the empty frames; for they imagined that everyone else could see this exquisite piece of workmanship.

"How is this?" said the Emperor to himself. "I can see nothing! This is indeed a terrible affair!" "Oh! The cloth is charming," said he aloud. And he smiled most graciously, and looked closely at the empty looms. All his retinue now strained their eyes, but they could see no more than the others; nevertheless, they all exclaimed, "Oh, how beautiful!" and advised his majesty to have some new clothes made from this splendid material, for the approaching procession. "Magnificent! Charming! Excellent!" resounded on all sides.

The rogues sat up the whole of the night before the day on which the procession was to take place, and had sixteen lights burning, so that everyone might see how anxious they were to finish the Emperor's new suit. They pretended to roll the cloth off the looms, cut the air with their scissors, and sewed with needles without any thread in them. "See!" cried they, at last. "The Emperor's new clothes are ready!"

And now the Emperor came to the weavers; and the rogues raised their arms, saying, "Here are your Majesty's trousers! Here is the scarf! Here is the mantle! The whole suit is as light as a cobweb; that, however, is the great virtue of this delicate cloth."

"Yes indeed!" said all the courtiers, although not one of them could see anything of this exquisite manufacture.

"If your Imperial Majesty will be graciously pleased to take off your clothes, we will fit on the new suit, in front of the looking glass."

The Emperor was accordingly undressed, and the rogues pretended to array him in his new suit, the Emperor turning round, from side to side, before the looking glass.

"How splendid his Majesty looks in his new clothes, and how well they fit!" everyone cried out. "What a design! What colors! These are indeed royal robes!"

"I am quite ready," answered the Emperor. "Do my new clothes fit well?" asked he, turning himself round again before the looking glass, in order that he might appear to be examining his handsome suit.

The lords of the bedchamber, who were to carry his Majesty's train, pretended to be carrying something, for they would by no means betray anything like simplicity or unfitness for their office.

So now the Emperor walked under his high canopy in the midst of the procession, through the streets of his capital; and all the people standing by, and those at the windows, cried out, "Oh! How beautiful are our Emperor's new clothes!" In short, no one would allow that he could not see these much-admired clothes; because, in doing so, he would have declared himself either a simpleton or unfit for his office.

"But the Emperor has nothing at all on!" said a little child.

"Listen to the voice of innocence!" exclaimed his father; and what the child had said was whispered from one to another.

"But he has nothing at all on!" at last cried out all the people. The Emperor was vexed, for he knew that the people were right; but he thought the procession must go on now! And the lords of the bedchamber took greater pains than ever, to appear holding up a train, although, in reality, there was no train to hold.

Student Work Sample: Peer Pressure

Emily Rivera, 9th grade

My Truism: It is easy to keep quiet when you disagree with a group.

1. Why is it so easy to keep quiet when you disagree with a group?

2. The Emperor and his people were fooled.

3. To maintain or avoid an image, people will go against their own opinions.

4. Peer pressure can manipulate and silence people's inner personalities.

Why is it so easy to keep quiet when you disagree with a group? Peer pressure plays on your desire to fit in. The fear of possibly being the odd one out causes you to change your views to stay in the group.

An emperor who loved fashion was told by two con artists that they knew "how to weave the most beautiful colors and elaborate patterns." They promised that these clothes would be invisible to those who are simpletons or were unsuited for their title. Eager, the emperor employed them with two large payments. The con men never began production. They only pretended, and the result was nothing. Everyone who laid eyes on the "clothing" described its beauty but in reality they viewed nothing at all.

These people had a fear of being called a simpleton or unsuited for their office, so they lied, and created phony descriptions of the "clothing" in order to save face. This proves that people will go against their own opinions to maintain or avoid a certain image.

Peer pressure can manipulate and silence individuals' inner positions. It takes bravery and confidence to resist it.

7 Greed

Read the story.

Think about how people always wish they had more.

Write an essay about whether it's better to try to achieve more or to be happy with what you have.

MY TRUISM

COMPARING NOTES

| Some people think ... | Other people think ... | But I think ... | So I will ... |

MY KERNEL ESSAY

1. _____

2. _____

3. _____

4. _____

_____

_____

TRUISM EXAMPLES

1. There is no such thing as "enough."

2. Greed makes a person unhappy.

3. _____

The Fisherman and His Wife

There was once a fisherman who lived with his wife in a pigsty, close by the seaside. One day, as he sat on the shore, looking at the sparkling waves and watching his line, all on a sudden he pulled out a great fish. But the fish said, "Pray let me live! I am not a real fish; I am an enchanted prince. Put me in the water again and let me go!" "Oh, ho!" said the man, "I will have nothing to do with a fish that can talk; so swim away, sir!" Then he put him back into the water, and the fish darted straight down to the bottom.

When the fisherman went home to his wife in the pigsty, he told her. "Did not you ask it for anything?" said the wife. "We live very wretchedly here, in this nasty dirty pigsty; do go back and tell the fish we want a snug little cottage."

The fisherman did not much like the business. However, he went to the seashore; and the water looked all yellow and green. And he stood at the water's edge and said:

"O man of the sea! Hearken to me! My wife Ilsabill will have her own will and hath sent me to beg a boon of thee!"

Then the fish came swimming to him and said, "Well, what does your wife want?" "Ah!" said the fisherman, "She says that when I had caught you, I ought to have asked you for something before I let you go; she does not like living any longer in the pigsty and wants a snug little cottage." "Go home, then," said the fish; "she is in the cottage already!" So the man went home and saw his wife standing at the door of a nice trim little cottage. There was a parlor, a bedchamber, a kitchen, and a little garden, planted with all sorts of flowers and fruits. "Ah!" said the fisherman, "How happily we shall live now!" "We will try to do so, at least," said his wife.

Everything went right for a week or two, and then Dame Ilsabill said, "Husband, there is not near room enough for us in this cottage; the courtyard and the garden are a great deal too small. I should like to have a large stone castle to live in. Go to the fish again and tell him to give us a castle." "Wife," said the fisherman, "I don't like to go to him again." "Nonsense!" said the wife. "He will do it very willingly, I know; go along and try!"

The fisherman went, but his heart was very heavy. And when he came to the sea, it looked blue and gloomy, though it was very calm; and he went close to the edge of the waves, and said:

"O man of the sea! Hearken to me! My wife Ilsabill will have her own will, and hath sent me to beg a boon of thee!"

"Well, what does she want now?" said the fish. "Ah!" said the man, dolefully, "My wife wants to live in a stone castle." "Go home, then," said the fish. "She is standing at the gate of it already." So away went the fisherman and found his wife standing before the gate of a great castle. "See," said she, "is not this grand?" With that, they went into the castle together and found a great many servants there, and the rooms all richly furnished, and full of golden chairs and tables; and in the courtyard were stables and cow-houses. "Well," said the man, "now we will live cheerful and happy in this beautiful castle for the rest of our lives." "Perhaps we may," said the wife.

The next morning when Dame Ilsabill said, "Husband, bestir yourself, for we must be king of all the land." "Wife, wife," said the man, "why should we wish to be the king? I will not be king." "Then I will," said she. "But, wife," said the fisherman, "how can you be king?" "Husband," said she, "go and try! I will be king." So the man went away quite sorrowful. This time, the sea looked a dark grey color, as he cried out:

"O man of the sea! Hearken to me! My wife Ilsabill will have her own will, and hath sent me to beg a boon of thee!"

"Well, what would she have now?"' said the fish. "Alas!" said the poor man. "My wife wants to be king." "Go home," said the fish; "She is king already."

7

Then the fisherman went home; and as he came close to the palace, he saw a troop of soldiers and heard the sound of drums and trumpets. And when he went in, he saw his wife sitting on a throne of gold and diamonds, with a golden crown upon her head. "Well, wife," said the fisherman, "are you king?" "Yes," said she, "I am king." And when he had looked at her for a long time, he said, "Ah, wife! What a fine thing it is to be king! Now we shall never have anything more to wish for as long as we live." "I don't know how that may be," said she. "Never is a long time. I think I should like to be emperor." "Alas, wife! Why should you wish to be emperor?" said the fisherman. "Husband," said she, "go to the fish! I say I will be emperor." "Ah, wife!" replied the fisherman, "The fish cannot make an emperor, I am sure, and I should not like to ask him for such a thing." "I am king," said Ilsabill, "so go at once!"

So the fisherman muttered as he went along, "This will come to no good, it is too much to ask; the fish will be tired at last, and then we shall be sorry for what we have done." He soon came to the seashore; and the water was quite black and muddy, and a mighty whirlwind blew over the waves, but he went to the water's brink, and said:

"O man of the sea! Hearken to me! My wife Ilsabill will have her own will, and hath sent me to beg a boon of thee!"

"What would she have now?" said the fish. "Ah!" said the fisherman, "She wants to be emperor." "Go home," said the fish, "she is emperor already."

So he went home again; and as he came near, he saw his wife Ilsabill sitting on a very lofty throne made of solid gold, with a great crown on her head a full two-yards high; and on each side of her stood her guards and attendants in a row. The fisherman went up to her and said, "Wife, are you emperor?" "Yes," said she, "I am emperor." "Ah!" said the man, as he gazed upon her. "What a fine thing it is to be emperor!" "Husband," said she, "why should we stop at being emperor? I will be pope next." "O wife, wife!" said he. "How can you be pope?" "Husband," said she, "I will be pope this very day. Go and try him."

So the fisherman went. But when he came to the shore, the wind was raging and the sea was tossed up and down in boiling waves. At this sight, the fisherman was dreadfully frightened, and he trembled so that his knees knocked together: but still he went down near to the shore and said:

"O man of the sea! Hearken to me! My wife Ilsabill will have her own will, and hath sent me to beg a boon of thee!"

"What does she want now?" said the fish. "Ah!" said the fisherman. "My wife wants to be pope." "Go home," said the fish; "she is pope already."

Then the fisherman went home and found Ilsabill sitting on a throne two-miles high. And she had three great crowns on her head, and around her stood all the pomp and power of the Church. "Wife," said the fisherman, as he looked at all this greatness, "are you pope?" "Yes," said she, "I am pope." "Well, wife," replied he, "it is a grand thing to be pope." Then they went to bed; but Dame Ilsabill could not sleep all night for thinking what she should be next. At last, as she was dropping asleep, morning broke, and the sun rose. At this, she was very angry, and wakened her husband, and said, "Husband, go to the fish and tell him I must be lord of the sun and moon." The fisherman was half asleep, but he fell out of bed. "Alas, wife!" said he. "Cannot you be easy with being pope?" "No," said she, "I am very uneasy as long as the sun and moon rise without my leave. Go to the fish at once!"

Then the man went shivering with fear; and as he was going down to the shore, a dreadful storm arose, the sea with great black waves, swelling up like mountains with crowns of white foam upon their heads. And the fisherman crept towards the sea and cried out, as well as he could:

"O man of the sea! Hearken to me! My wife Ilsabill will have her own will, and hath sent me to beg a boon of thee!"

"What does she want now?" said the fish. "Ah!" said he. "She wants to be lord of the sun and moon." "Go home," said the fish, "to your pigsty again."

And there they live to this very day.

Emmanuel Mendez, 11th grade

My truism: He who is not content with what he has, would not be content with what he would like to have.

1. Some people think that material things in their life will make them happier.

2. Other people think that one can be satisfied with what they have, however minimalist and modest, by seeking happiness through methods such as human connection.

3. But I think that if someone wants something they hope will make them happy, they should make their choices wisely and put in sufficient work and effort to get it.

4. So I will make sure to put in effort to earn things that I want while making my choices wisely and remember to also seek happiness beyond material goods.

Kayla Cosme, 10th grade

Some people think we should be grateful for what we have. There are millions of people out there in the world that don't have a fraction of the things we do, so we should cherish the everyday things that seem little to us but are huge to others. If we are constantly trying to get the luxury things of life that everyone is supposed to love, it will be like an agonizing task that will turn that stuff into a chore. These luxuries may also appear worthwhile because we are continuously working to get the next "best" thing. Being happy with what you're given gives us the chance to look around and see everything we are blessed with—like family, friends, or just being alive because some people don't even get that chance.

Other people think that the sky is the limit. Some people just want more. Not more of things and money, but more of life. As human beings, we do not like to settle. We are always working toward something; whether it is getting accepted into your dream school or that promotion at work, we all have a goal in our lives. What's the point of living if we aren't trying to live toward someone or something. There is a reason everyone is alive. We aren't here to take up space. We are here to make our mark on the world and achieving more will do that.

But I think we should be determined for something better while remembering what we are blessed with. There is nothing wrong with wanting more in life. If we didn't want more, there would be no improvement in the world. We would still be living in caves and traveling by foot. However, as we improve, we need to remember the things we couldn't live without and make us truly happy because at the end of the day, with all the advances in the world, that is the only thing that matters.

So I will live life reaching for the stars while remembering to keep my feet on the ground. I will drive to my goal of a better life and purpose. However, while doing so, I will remember to see what I am given and to appreciate all that I have.

8 Selfishness

Read the story.

Think about how some people are generous while others are selfish.

Write an essay about how people can benefit from everyone near by us, even from selfish people.

MY TRUISM

THE ONION

Truism	How do I know this? (one way)	If that had not happened, how else would I know this?	If that had not happened, how else would I know this?	Truism

MY KERNEL ESSAY

1. _____

2. _____

3. _____

4. _____

5. _____

TRUISM EXAMPLES

1. Sometimes bad motives produce good results. _____

2. Nobody actually tries to be selfish, so we should treat everyone with care. _____

3. _____

The Frog Prince

One fine evening, a young princess put on her bonnet and clogs and went out to take a walk by herself in a wood; and when she came to a cool spring of water, she sat herself down to rest a while. Now she had a golden ball in her hand; and she was tossing it up into the air and catching it again as it fell. After a time, the ball bounded away and fell down into the spring. The princess looked into the spring after her ball, but it was very deep, so deep that she could not see the bottom of it. Then she began to bewail her loss, and said, "Alas! if I could only get my ball again, I would give all my fine clothes and jewels, and everything that I have in the world."

Whilst she was speaking, a frog put its head out of the water, and said, "Princess, why do you weep so bitterly?" "Alas!" said she. "What can you do for me, you nasty frog? My golden ball has fallen into the spring." The frog said, "I want not your pearls and jewels and fine clothes; but if you will love me, and let me live with you and eat from off your golden plate, and sleep upon your bed, I will bring you your ball again." "What nonsense!" thought the princess. "He can never even get out of the spring to visit me, and therefore, I will tell him he shall have what he asks." So she said to the frog, "Well, if you will bring me my ball, I will do all you ask." Then the frog put his head down and dived deep under the water; and after a little while, he came up again, with the ball in his mouth. As soon as the young princess saw her ball, she ran to pick it up; and she was so overjoyed that she never thought of the frog but ran home with it as fast as she could.

The next day, just as the princess had sat down to dinner, she heard a strange noise—tap, tap—plash, plash—as if something was coming up the marble staircase: and soon afterward, there was a gentle knock at the door, and a little voice cried out and said:

"Open the door, my princess dear, Open the door to thy true love here! And mind the words that thou and I said

By the fountain cool, in the greenwood shade."

Then the princess ran to the door and opened it, and there she saw the frog, whom she had quite forgotten. At this sight, she was sadly frightened, and, shutting the door as fast as she could, came back to her seat. The king, her father, seeing that something had frightened her, asked her what was the matter. "There is a nasty frog," said she, "at the door, that lifted my ball for me out of the spring this morning: I told him that he should live with me here, thinking that he could never get out of the spring; but there he is at the door, and he wants to come in."

Then the king said to the young princess, "As you have given your word you must keep it; so go and let him in." She did so, and the frog hopped into the room, and then straight on—tap, tap—plash, plash—from the bottom of the room to the top, till he came up close to the table where the princess sat. "Pray lift me upon your chair," said he to the princess, "and let me sit next to you." As soon as she had done this, the frog said, "Put your plate nearer to me, that I may eat out of it." This she did, and when he had eaten as much as he could, he said, "Now I am tired; carry me upstairs and put me into your bed." And the princess did and put him upon the pillow of her own bed, where he slept all night long. As soon as it was light, he jumped up, hopped downstairs, and went out of the house. "Now, then," thought the princess, "at last he is gone, and I shall be troubled with him no more."

But she was mistaken; for when night came again, she heard the same tapping at the door.

And when the princess opened the door, the frog came in and slept upon her pillow

8 as before, till the morning broke. And the third night, he did the same. But when the princess awoke on the following morning, she was astonished to see, instead of the frog, a handsome prince, gazing on her with the most beautiful eyes she had ever seen, and standing at the head of her bed.

He told her that he had been enchanted by a spiteful fairy, who had changed him into a frog; and that he had been fated so to abide till some princess should take him out of the spring, let him eat from her plate, and sleep upon her bed for three nights. "You," said the prince, "have broken his cruel charm, and now I have nothing to wish for but that you should go with me into my father's kingdom, where I will marry you, and love you as long as you live."

The young princess, you may be sure, was not long in saying "Yes" to all this. They then took leave of the king, got into the coach with eight horses, and all set out, full of joy and merriment, for the prince's kingdom, which they reached safely; and there they lived happily a great many years.

Maya Garcia, 4th grade

1. Everyone is selfish at times. I know this because on Halloween, my cousins take all the candy instead of taking only one piece.

2. And once I was being selfish, too, because when my little cousin Hunter comes over he always changes the channel; so when I was told he was coming, I hid the remote.

3. I have another example. My cousin Hannah hid all her lip glosses from her sister Haley because she didn't want her to use any of them.

4. So as you can see, everyone is selfish at times, and even generous people can be selfish.

5. Sometimes selfishness takes over.

Alex Calvio, 11th grade

1. Most people think that being selfish is a bad quality.

2. However, being selfish can actually benefit an individual. When someone is selfish, they are meeting their needs.

3. This doesn't mean that being selfish is entirely good. When someone is selfish, they can harm others.

4. So, even if being selfish has benefits, it is important to realize that there are many bad results that could happen as well.

Alejandro Varelo, 4th grade

1. Everyone at times can be selfish, especially my family.

2. Sometimes I play video games in the morning so no one can go on my PS4 except me.

3. One day my brother was super selfish! He ate all my chips and then lied and said that my mom ate them.

4. My dog Lisa hates her brother Lucky, so one time Lisa ate all of the dog food so Lucky got nothing to eat. She did that because he didn't share his toy; so both of them were selfish.

5. So what I'm saying is that everyone can be selfish at times. So make someone's day and don't be selfish.

9 Confidence

Read the story.

Think about how confidence can lead to a win or a loss.

Write an essay about how a person's attitude can cause success or failure.

MY TRUISM

RECONSIDERING A BELIEF

| Most people think ... | ... because (one way it's good) | But ... (one way it's bad) | So ... (truism) |

MY KERNEL ESSAY

1. _____

2. _____

3. _____

4. _____

_____

_____

TRUISM EXAMPLES

1. Nobody can win forever.

2. Being a sore winner is worse than being a sore loser.

3. _____

The Gingerbread Boy

Now you shall hear a story that somebody's great-great-grandmother told a little girl ever so many years ago:

There was once a little old man and a little old woman, who lived in a little old house in the edge of a wood. They would have been a very happy old couple but for one thing—they had no little child, and they wished for one very much. One day, when the little old woman was baking gingerbread, she cut a cake in the shape of a little boy and put it into the oven.

Presently she went to the oven to see if it was baked. As soon as the oven door was opened, the little gingerbread boy jumped out, and he began to run away as fast as he could go.

The little old woman called her husband, and they both ran after him. But they could not catch him. And soon the gingerbread boy came to a barn full of threshers. He called out to them as he went by, saying:

> *"I've run away from a little old woman,*
>
> *A little old man,*
>
> *And I can run away from you, I can!"*

Then the barn full of threshers set out to run after him. But, though they ran fast, they could not catch him. And he ran on till he came to a field full of mowers. He called out to them:

> *"I've run away from a little old woman,*
>
> *A little old man,*
>
> *A barn full of threshers,*
>
> *And I can run away from you, I can!"*

Then the mowers began to run after him, but they couldn't catch him. And he ran on till he came to a cow. He called out to her:

> *"I've run away from a little old woman,*
>
> *A little old man,*
>
> *A barn full of threshers,*
>
> *A field full of mowers,*
>
> *And I can run away from you, I can!"*

But, though the cow started at once, she couldn't catch him. And soon he came to a pig. He called out to the pig:

> *"I've run away from a little old woman,*
>
> *A little old man,*
>
> *A barn full of threshers,*
>
> *A field full of mowers,*
>
> *A cow,*
>
> *And I can run away from you, I can!"*

But the pig ran and couldn't catch him. And he ran till he came across a fox, and to him he called out:

> *"I've run away from a little old woman,*
>
> *A little old man,*
>
> *A barn full of threshers,*
>
> *A field full of mowers,*
>
> *A cow and a pig,*
>
> *And I can run away from you, I can!"*

Then the fox set out to run. Now foxes can run very fast, and so the fox soon caught the gingerbread boy and began to eat him up.

Presently the gingerbread boy said:

> *"Oh dear! I'm quarter gone!"*
>
> *And then, "Oh, I'm half gone!"*
>
> *And soon, "I'm three-quarters gone!"*
>
> *And at last, "I'm all gone!"*

and never spoke again.

Yadira Campay, 9th grade

The Gingerbread Boy believed he was faster than everyone on the farm. Because he could outrun a couple of things, he was confident about himself. When he outran one group, he would brag about it to the next group and would keep running.

The Gingerbread Boy at first ran faster than the old lady and old man when they were chasing him. He would then go to a different group (near him) and brag to anyone around. They got mad that he was bragging and thought the fox could outrun him.

Once again, the Gingerbread Boy thought because he had outrun everyone else that he could also outrun the fast fox. The Gingerbread Boy soon found out he was too confident in himself, and his running skills were not enough. The fox caught up with him (because foxes are fast animals), and the fox ended up eating the Gingerbread Boy.

The Gingerbread Boy was overconfident, and that led up to him being eaten. Being confident in yourself is good but being overconfident about things can end up badly.

Julian Herrerra, 9th grade

Your words fuel your actions. This is a mentality that defines the line between success or failure. Whether it's talking about all the ways something could go wrong, a negative attitude, or hyping yourself up, a positive attitude, you perform in relation to what you say and think, the nature of your attitude.

The thinking behind the idea is to help ensure success through the use of positive attitude. A simple scenario would be a huddle before a sports game where the players bask in positive words to mold their attitude into the performance of the team during the game.

Having brought the bright side of the subject up, it's important to understand the negative. As an individual, negative words and attitudes lead to failure. This can be seen when a student is preparing for a future test If the student repeatedly sees themselves having a negative performance, they will only underperform because of their negative attitude.

All in all, the attitude of an individual decides whether or not the individual will succeed or fail. It's the words you say that shape the attitude. So the more positive the speaker is, the more favorable the attitude will be. The direction at which you point your words is the direction your actions will take you.

Notes

10 Laughter

Read the story.
Think about how you feel better after you laugh really hard.
Write an essay about the importance of laughter in our lives.

MY TRUISM

LIFE LESSON

| Truism | How it's true in the story | How it's true in life | How this will help me |

MY KERNEL ESSAY

1. _____

2. _____

3. _____

4. _____

_____

_____

TRUISM EXAMPLES

1. Laughter is better than medicine.

2. Everyone needs a good laugh now and then.

3. _____

The Golden Goose

There was a man who had three sons, the youngest of whom was called Dummling, who was despised, mocked, and sneered at on every occasion.

It happened that the eldest wanted to go into the forest to hew wood, and before he went, his mother gave him a beautiful sweet cake and a bottle of wine in order that he might not suffer from hunger or thirst.

When he entered the forest, he met a little grey-haired old man who bade him good day, and said: "Do give me a piece of cake out of your pocket, and let me have a draught of your wine; I am so hungry and thirsty." But the clever son answered, "If I give you my cake and wine, I shall have none for myself; be off with you," and he left the little man standing and went on.

But when he began to hew down a tree, it was not long before he made a false stroke, and the axe cut him in the arm so that he had to go home and have it bound up. And this was the little grey man's doing.

After this, the second son went into the forest, and his mother gave him, like the eldest, a cake and a bottle of wine. The little old grey man met him likewise and asked him for a piece of cake and a drink of wine. But the second son, too, said sensibly enough, "What I give you will be taken away from myself; be off!" and he left the little man standing and went on. His punishment, however, was not delayed; when he had made a few blows at the tree, he struck himself in the leg, so that he had to be carried home.

Then Dummling said, "Father, do let me go and cut wood." The father answered, "Your brothers have hurt themselves with it; leave it alone; you do not understand anything about it." But Dummling begged so long that at last he said, "Just go then; you will get wiser by hurting yourself." His mother gave him a cake made with water and baked in the cinders, and with it a bottle of sour beer.

When he came to the forest, the little old grey man met him likewise, and greeting him, said, "Give me a piece of your cake and a drink out of your bottle; I am so hungry and thirsty." Dummling answered, "I have only cinder cake and sour beer; if that pleases you, we will sit down and eat." So they sat down, and when Dummling pulled out his cinder cake, it was a fine sweet cake, and the sour beer had become good wine. So they ate and drank, and after that, the little man said, "Since you have a good heart and are willing to divide what you have, I will give you good luck. There stands an old tree; cut it down, and you will find something at the roots. I do this because you were kind to me." Then the little man took leave of him.

Dummling went and cut down the tree, and when it fell, there was a goose sitting in the roots with feathers of pure gold. He lifted her up, and taking her with him, went to an inn where he thought he would stay the night. Now the host had three daughters, who saw the goose and were curious to know what such a wonderful bird might be and would have liked to have one of its golden feathers.

The eldest thought, "I shall soon find an opportunity of pulling out a feather," and as soon as Dummling had gone out, she seized the goose by the wing, but her finger and hand remained sticking fast to it.

The second came soon afterward, thinking only of how she might get a feather for herself, but she had scarcely touched her sister than she was held fast.

At last, the third also came with the like intent, and the others screamed out, "Keep away; for goodness' sake keep away!" But she did not understand why she was to keep away. "The others are there," she thought. "I may as well be there too," and ran to them; but as soon as she had touched her sister, she remained sticking fast to her. So they had to spend the night with the goose.

The next morning Dummling took the goose under his arm and set out, without troubling himself about the three girls who were hanging on to it. They were obliged to run after him continually, now left, now right, wherever his legs took him.

In the middle of the fields, the parson met them, and when he saw the procession he said, "For shame, you good-for-nothing girls; why are you running across the fields after this young man? Is that seemly?" At the same time, he seized the youngest by the hand in order to pull her away, but as soon as he touched her, he likewise stuck fast and was himself obliged to run behind.

Before long, the sexton came by and saw his master, the parson, running behind three girls. He was astonished at this and called out, "Hi! your reverence. Whither away so quickly? Do not forget that we have a christening today!" and running after him, he took him by the sleeve but was also held fast to it.

Whilst the five were trotting thus one behind the other, two laborers came with their hoes from the fields; the parson called out to them and begged that they would set him and the sexton free. But they had scarcely touched the sexton when they were held fast, and now there were seven of them running behind Dummling and the goose.

Soon afterward, he came to a city, where a king ruled who had a daughter who was so serious that no one could make her laugh. So he had put forth a decree that whosoever should be able to make her laugh should marry her. When Dummling heard this, he went with his goose and all her train before the king's daughter, and as soon as she saw the seven people running on and on, one behind the other, she began to laugh quite loudly, and as if she would never stop. Thereupon, Dummling asked to have her for his wife; but the king did not like the son-in-law and made all manner of excuses and said he must first produce a man who could drink a cellarful of wine. Dummling thought of the little grey man, who could certainly help him; so he went into the forest, and in the same place where he had felled the tree, he saw a man sitting, who had a very sorrowful face. Dummling asked him what he was taking to heart so sorely, and he answered, "I have such a great thirst and cannot quench it; cold water I cannot stand, a barrel of wine I have just emptied, but that to me is like a drop on a hot stone!"

"There, I can help you," said Dummling. "Just come with me and you shall be satisfied."

He led him into the king's cellar, and the man bent over the huge barrels and drank and drank till his loins hurt, and before the day was out, he had emptied all the barrels. Then Dummling asked once more for his bride, but the king was vexed that such an ugly fellow, whom everyone called Dummling, should take away his daughter, and he made a new condition: He must first find a man who could eat a whole mountain of bread. Dummling did not think long, but went straight into the forest, where in the same place there sat a man who was tying up his body with a strap, and making an awful face, and saying, "I have eaten a whole ovenful of rolls, but what good is that when one has such a hunger as I? My stomach remains empty, and I must tie myself up if I am not to die of hunger."

At this, Dummling was glad and said, "Get up and come with me; you shall eat yourself full." He led him to the king's palace where all the flour in the whole Kingdom was collected, and from it, the king caused a huge mountain of bread to be baked. The man from the forest stood before it, began to eat, and by the end of one day, the whole mountain had vanished. Then Dummling for the third time asked for his bride; but the king again sought a way out and ordered a ship which could sail on land and on water. "As soon as you come sailing back in it," said he, "you shall have my daughter for wife."

Dummling went straight into the forest, and there sat the little grey man to whom he had given his cake. When he heard what Dummling wanted, he said, "Since you have given me to eat and to drink, I will give you the ship; and I do all this because you once were kind to me."

Then he gave him the ship which could sail on land and water, and when the king saw that, he could no longer prevent him from having his daughter. The wedding was celebrated, and after the king's death, Dummling inherited his kingdom and lived for a long time contentedly with his wife.

Faith Kinney, 10th grade

1. To laugh is to be happy and happiness is what we crave above all else.

2. The happiness that the princess felt at laughing carried through her marriage.

3. We spend money and time trying to be happy.

4. Laughter is the job of life and if we can't have that then what's the point?

Everyone's heard the saying that laughter is the best medicine. It's not quite that simple. To laugh is to be happy and happiness is what we crave above everything else.

The happiness that the princess felt at laughing at the people brought her a husband. The love that a married couple feel for each other is no more than the highest degree of happiness. She undoubtedly laughed a great deal during the rest of her life because of this wonderful marriage.

As Americans, we spend a great deal of time and money trying to be happy. Everything from tourist attractions to amusement parks to places like Las Vegas were and still are being built to make people happy. It is the lack of happiness that drives people to do things like commit or attempt suicide, shootings, and terrorism.

If we can make each other laugh and keep the joy of life alive, then we would be much better off, both on small and large scales. Kindness and happiness go hand in hand and the more we show, the better our lives will be.

Part III
Structures for Character Analysis

Bank of Text Structure Choices

For Character Analysis

EVOLUTION OF A TERM

What the word meant to me when I was little	What it meant when I was a little older	What it means to me now	What it will mean to me later in my life	What all this says to me

CHAIN REACTION

One thing that happened	What that caused	What else that caused	How it turned out	Truism

DOUBLE TAKE

What happened	A negative way to view this	A positive way to view this	Which way I think is stronger	Truism

NEWS/GOSSIP: TELL ME, TELL ME

At the time ...	All of a sudden ...	This was surprising because ...	People said ...	It just goes to show you:

CHANGE OF PLANS

Where I was going (and why)	Something unexpected that happened	How my plans changed	What I think (truism)

NAME _____

Read the story.

Think about how many important things have happened because someone did or did not listen.

Write an essay about the importance of listening.

MY TRUISM

EVOLUTION OF A TERM

| What the word meant to me when I was little | What it meant when I was a little older | What it means to me now | What it will mean to me later in my life | What all this says to me |

MY KERNEL ESSAY

1. _____

2. _____

3. _____

4. _____

5. _____

TRUISM EXAMPLES

1. Listening to others can save a person's life. _____

2. It's important to know who to listen to and who to ignore. ____

3. _____

Hansel and Gretel

Hard by a great forest dwelt a poor wood-cutter with his wife and his two children. The boy was called Hansel and the girl Gretel. He had little to bite and to break, and he could no longer procure daily bread. Now when he thought over this by night in his bed, and tossed about in his anxiety, he said to his wife, "What is to become of us?"

"I'll tell you what, husband," answered the woman. "Early tomorrow morning we will take the children out into the forest and leave them alone. They will not find the way home again, and we shall be rid of them."

"No, wife," said the man.

"O, thou fool!" said she, "Then we must all four die of hunger."

The two children had also not been able to sleep for hunger and had heard what their stepmother had said. Gretel wept bitter tears.

"Be quiet, Gretel," said Hansel. "I will find a way to help us." And when the old folks had fallen asleep, he got up and crept outside. The moon shone brightly, and the white pebbles which lay in front of the house glittered like real silver pennies. Hansel put as many of them in the little pocket of his coat as he could possibly get in. Then he lay down again in his bed.

When day dawned, the woman awoke the two children, saying, "Get up, you sluggards! We are going into the forest to fetch wood." She gave each a little piece of bread. When they had walked a short time, Hansel stood still and peeped back at the house, and did so again and again, constantly throwing one of the white pebble stones on the road.

When they had reached the middle of the forest, the father said, "Now, children, pile up some wood, and I will light a fire."

The woman said, "Now, children, lay yourselves down by the fire and rest; we will go cut some wood. When we have done, we will come back and fetch you."

Hansel and Gretel sat by the fire, and they fell fast asleep. When at last they awoke, it was dark night. Gretel began to cry, but Hansel comforted her and said, "Just wait a little, and we will find the way." And when the full moon had risen, Hansel took his little sister by the hand, and followed the pebbles which shone like newly coined silver pieces.

They walked the whole night long, and by break of day came to their father's house. When the woman saw them, she said, "You naughty children." The father, however, rejoiced, for it had cut him to the heart to leave them behind alone.

Not long afterward, the children heard their stepmother saying to their father, "Everything is eaten again; we have one half loaf left. The children must go; we will take them farther into the wood."

The children were, however, still awake and had heard the conversation. When the old folks were asleep, Hansel again got up, and wanted to go out and pick up pebbles, but the woman had locked the door.

Early in the morning the woman took the children out of their beds. Their bit of bread was given to them, and Hansel crumbled his in his pocket, and often threw a morsel on the ground.

The woman led the children still deeper into the forest. Then a great fire was again made, and the stepmother said, "Just sit there, you children; we are going to cut wood, and we will come and fetch you." When it was noon, Gretel shared her piece of bread with Hansel, and then they fell asleep. They did not awake until it was dark night. Hansel said, "Just wait, Gretel, until the moon rises, and then we shall see our way home again."

When the moon came, they set out, but they found no crumbs for the birds had picked them all up. They got deeper into the forest. At last, they reached a little house and they saw that it was built of bread and covered with cakes, but that the windows were of clear sugar. Hansel broke off a little of the roof to try, and Gretel leant against the window and nibbled at the panes. Then a soft voice cried from the room,

"Nibble, nibble, gnaw,

Who is nibbling at my little house?"

The children answered,

"The wind, the wind,

The heaven-born wind,"

and went on eating. Suddenly the door opened, and a very, very old woman came creeping out. Hansel and Gretel were so terribly frightened that they let fall what they had in their hands. The old woman, however, nodded her head, and said, "Oh, you dear children, do come in, and stay with me." She took them both by the hand, and led them into her little house. Then good food was set before them, milk and pancakes, with sugar, apples, and nuts. Afterward two pretty little beds were covered with clean white linen, and Hansel and Gretel lay down in them and thought they were in heaven.

The old woman had only pretended to be so kind; she was in reality a wicked witch, who lay in wait for children, and had only built the little bread house in order to entice them there. When a child fell into her power, she killed it, cooked and ate it, and that was a feast day with her.

Early in the morning, she seized Hansel with her shriveled hand, carried him into a little stable, and shut him in with a grated door. Then she went to Gretel, shook her till she awoke and cried, "Get up, lazy thing, fetch some water, and cook something good for thy brother; he is in the stable outside. When he is fat, I will eat him." Gretel began to weep bitterly, but she was forced to do what the wicked witch ordered her.

And now the best food was cooked for poor Hansel, but Gretel got nothing but crab shells. Every morning the woman cried, "Hansel, stretch out thy finger that I may feel if thou wilt soon be fat." Hansel, however, stretched out a little bone to her, and the old woman, who had dim eyes, thought it was

Hansel's finger. When four weeks had gone by, she would not wait any longer. "Gretel," she cried, "fat or lean, to-morrow I will kill him and cook him." Ah, how the poor little sister did lament.

Early in the morning, Gretel had to go out and hang up the cauldron with the water and light the fire. "Creep in," said the witch, "and see if the oven is properly heated."

But Gretel said, "How do you get in?" "Silly goose," said the old woman. "The door is big enough; just look, I can get in myself!" And she crept up and thrust her head into the oven. Then Gretel gave her a push and shut the iron door, and fastened the bolt. Oh! then the witch began to howl quite horribly, and she was miserably burnt to death.

Gretel ran like lightning to Hansel, opened his little stable, and cried, "Hansel, we are saved! The old witch is dead!" How they did rejoice and embrace each other and dance about and kiss each other! And they went into the witch's house, and in every corner there stood chests full of pearls and jewels. "These are far better than pebbles!" said Hansel, and thrust into his pockets whatever could be got in, and Gretel said, "I, too, will take something home with me," and filled her pinafore full.

When they had walked for hours, they came to their father's house. Then they threw themselves into their father's arms. The man had not known one happy hour since he had left the children in the forest; the woman, however, was dead. Gretel emptied her pinafore until pearls and precious stones ran about the room, and Hansel threw one handful after another out of his pocket to add to them. Then all anxiety was at an end, and they lived together in perfect happiness.

Kennedy Hagan, 9th grade

1. Putting a seatbelt on was annoying when I was little.

2. It's important because of the accident.

3. When I have kids, I want them safe.

4. Things are told to us for a reason.

5. Not listening can be catastrophic!

Rules are everywhere, at home, at school, in stores, and most of them get ignored quite often. Well, rules are set in place for a reason. Listening to others can save a person's life.

As children, we're all told to put a seatbelt on. Well, if you're like me, you hated that rule. I never understood why I had to wear one. My grandparents told me they never wore seatbelts, and my mom was a good driver so I started to ignore that rule. It didn't seem fair to me.

When I was in 8th grade, one of my teachers was in a car accident and her son didn't have a seatbelt on, so he ended up with a broken collarbone and a broken arm. She told us that at a stop sign, a car behind her didn't stop and rammed into them. After hearing this, I realized I was forced to wear a seatbelt because another car could do damage and it was not just my mom's driving that mattered.

As I start driving, I'll always keep this in mind because if I don't have a seatbelt, I could get seriously injured or even killed. And when I have my own kids one day, I'll want them to be safe too!

Rules are told to us for a reason. And even if we don't understand, we will one day. So listening to them is a good idea because if you don't the results can be catastrophic!

12 Fear

Read the story.
Think about how scary news can go viral.
Write an essay about public fear.

MY TRUISM

CHAIN REACTION

One thing that happened	What that caused	What else that caused	How it turned out	Truism

MY KERNEL ESSAY

1. _____

2. _____

3. _____

4. _____

5. _____

_____

TRUISM EXAMPLES

1. It's easy to whip up public fear over nothing.

2. Fear can make people act stupid.

3. _____

Henny Penny

One day Henny-penny was picking up corn in the brickyard when—whack!—an acorn hit her upon the head. "Goodness gracious me," said Henny-penny, "the sky's a-going to fall; I must go and tell the King."

So she went along, and she went along, and she went along, till she met Cocky-locky. "Where are you going, Henny-penny?" says Cocky-locky. "Oh! I'm going to tell the King the sky's a-falling," says Henny-penny. "May I come with you?" says Cocky-locky. "Certainly," says Henny-penny. So Henny-penny and Cocky-locky went to tell the King the sky was falling.

They went along, and they went along, and they went along, till they met Ducky-daddles. "Where are you going to, Henny-penny and Cocky-locky?" says Ducky-daddles. "Oh! we're going to tell the King the sky's a-falling," said Henny-penny and Cocky-locky. "May I come with you?" says Ducky-daddles. "Certainly," said Henny-penny and Cocky-locky. So Henny-penny, Cocky-locky, and Ducky-daddles went to tell the King the sky was a-falling.

So they went along, and they went along, and they went along, till they met Goosey-poosey. "Where are you going to, Henny-penny, Cocky-locky, and Ducky-daddles?" said Goosey-poosey. "Oh! we're going to tell the King the sky's a-falling," said Henny-penny and Cocky-locky and Ducky-daddles. "May I come with you?" said Goosey-poosey. "Certainly," said Henny-penny, Cocky-locky, and Ducky-daddles. So Henny-penny, Cocky-locky, Ducky-daddles, and Goosey-poosey went to tell the King the sky was a-falling.

So they went along, and they went along, and they went along, till they met Turkey-lurkey. "Where are you going, Henny-penny, Cocky-locky, Ducky-daddles, and Goosey-poosey?" says Turkey-lurkey. "Oh! we're going to tell the King the sky's a-falling," said Henny-penny, Cocky-locky, Ducky-daddles, and Goosey-poosey. "May I come with you, Henny-penny, Cocky-locky, Ducky-daddles, and Goosey-poosey?" said Turkey-lurkey. "Oh, certainly, Turkey-lurkey," said Henny-penny, Cocky-locky, Ducky-daddles, and Goosey-poosey. So Henny-penny, Cocky-locky, Ducky-daddles, Goosey-poosey, and Turkey-lurkey all went to tell the King the sky was a-falling.

So they went along, and they went along, and they went along, till they met Foxy-woxy, and Foxy-woxy said to Henny-penny, Cocky-locky, Ducky-daddles, Goosey-poosey, and Turkey-lurkey, "Where are you going, Henny-penny, Cocky-locky, Ducky-daddles, Goosey-poosey, and Turkey-lurkey?" And Henny-penny, Cocky-locky, Ducky-daddles, Goosey-poosey, and Turkey-lurkey said to Foxy-woxy, "We're going to tell the King the sky's a-falling." "Oh! but this is not the way to the King, Henny-penny, Cocky-locky, Ducky-daddles, Goosey-poosey, and Turkey-lurkey," says Foxy-woxy; "I know the proper way; shall I show it you?" "Oh, certainly, Foxy-woxy," said Henny-penny, Cocky-locky, Ducky-daddles, Goosey-poosey, and Turkey-lurkey. So Henny-penny, Cocky-locky, Ducky-daddles, Goosey-poosey, Turkey-lurkey, and Foxy-woxy all went to tell the King the sky was a-falling.

So they went along, and they went along, and they went along, till they came to a narrow and dark hole. Now this was the door of Foxy-woxy's burrow. But Foxy-woxy said to Henny-penny, Cocky-locky, Ducky-daddles, Goosey-poosey, and Turkey-lurkey, "This is the shortcut to the King's palace; you'll soon get there if you follow me. I will go first and you come after, Henny-penny, Cocky-locky, Ducky-daddles, Goosey-poosey, and Turkey-lurkey." "Why, of course, certainly, without doubt, why not?" said Henny-penny, Cocky-locky, Ducky-daddles, Goosey-poosey, and Turkey-lurkey.

So Foxy-woxy went into his burrow, and he didn't go very far but turned round to wait for Henny-penny, Cocky-locky, Ducky-daddles,

Goosey-poosey, and Turkey-lurkey. Now Turkey-lurkey was the first to go through the dark hole into the burrow. He hadn't got far when—

"Hrumph!"

Foxy-woxy snapped off Turkey-lurkey's head and threw his body over his left shoulder. Then Goosey-poosey went in, and—

"Hrumph!"

Off went her head and Goosey-poosey was thrown beside Turkey-lurkey. Then Ducky-daddles waddled down, and—

"Hrumph!"

Foxy-woxy had snapped off Ducky-daddles' head and Ducky-daddles was thrown alongside Turkey-lurkey and Goosey-poosey. Then Cocky-locky strutted down into the burrow, and he hadn't gone far when—

"Hrumph!"

But Cocky-locky will always crow whether you want him to do so or not, and so he had just time for one "Cock-a-doo-dle d—" before he went to join Turkey-lurkey, Goosey-poosey, and Ducky-daddles over Foxy-woxy's shoulders.

Now when Henny-penny, who had just got into the dark burrow, heard Cocky-locky crow, she said to herself:

"My goodness! it must be dawn. Time for me to lay my egg."

So she turned round and bustled off to her nest; so she escaped, but she never told the King the sky was falling!

Jimi Perez, 11th grade

Because of my irrational fear of heights, it took several minutes before my dad could finally convince me to help him strip the roof down to the beams. He wanted to replace the old rotten boards with new wood to fix the leaks that were getting worse. The old wood was rotting from the moisture of the rain seeping in.

Even though I had already agreed to help my dad work on the roof, there was my fear of heights to deal with once I was up there. We started off cleaning the entire roof of any debris and leftover materials such as sticks and a lot of nails. After the roof was clean, we proceeded to tear up the old rotted boards to expose the beam structure below.

The way we ripped the boards off the beams left all the nails in the beams which would be a big problem when we wanted to put the new wood down as the nails would protrude and create gaps between boards, allowing water to leak in again.

To avoid the problem of the nails protruding, my dad had me go around on the beams and take the nails out of them as they were already slightly ripped up from tearing the boards off previously. As a result, I could see just how high from the ground I was. Although I wasn't terribly high, only one story up, I could not stop the feeling that I would fall. Despite this, I still needed to get the nails out so that we could continue to fix the roof.

After a couple hours of stripping the roof and removing nails, we decided to take a break. However, the ladder was originally set up in the area that we first started removing wood, so near the ladder was no board at all, only beam. I was too terrified to get anywhere near the ladder because I could not bring myself to walk on the beams even though they were just as wide as the curb which I always walk on.

Even though I could not get down, my dad still wanted to go on a break, so he moved the ladder closer to where I was to help me get down from the roof. After several minutes of trying to convince me to get down the ladder, I really couldn't do it so he threw me up a Powerade and went on his way.

One hour later, my dad came back and was stunned to see me still on the roof. He helped me come down the ladder and I was able to feel stable ground once more.

I try to pride myself on being a logical thinker. Now I realize that I probably could've jumped off and been fine, but I was so scared that I was unable to think critically. Sometimes fear can paralyze a person.

NAME

Read the story.

Think about how the same act can be seen as an act of resourcefulness or as thievery.

Write an essay about whether stealing is ever justifiable.

MY TRUISM

DOUBLE TAKE

| What happened | A negative way to view this | A positive way to view this | Which way I think is stronger | Truism |

MY KERNEL ESSAY

1. _____

2. _____

3. _____

4. _____

5. _____

_____

TRUISM EXAMPLES

1. People might do anything to help their families survive.

2. Desperation can change a person's values.

3. _____

Jack and the Beanstalk

A long, long time ago, there lived a boy called Jack. One morning the good hard-working mother sobbed, "We must sell our cow and live on the money."

So, Jack set off to sell the cow. He saw a little old man on the road who called out, "Good morning! And where may you be going?"

"I am going to market to sell our cow—and I mean to make a good bargain."

"So you will!" chuckled a little old man. And he drew out of his pocket five beans.

"What!" Jack said. "My Milky-White for five common beans!"

"But they aren't common beans," put in the little old man. "If you plant these beans over-night, by morning they will have grown up right into the very sky." Jack was too flabbergasted even to open his mouth. "It's a good bargain, Jack," said the old man.

"Right as a trivet," cried Jack, without stopping to think, and the next moment he found himself standing on an empty road.

So whistling, he trudged home cheerfully. His mother was watching anxiously for him at the gate. "Tell me quick how much you got for her."

Jack held out the beans triumphantly.

His mother said, "What! Them beans?"

"Yes," replied Jack, beginning to doubt his own wisdom; "but they're *magic* beans. Oh! Please don't hit so hard!"

And she flung the miserable beans out of window and sent him, supperless, to bed.

When he woke, everything in the room showed greenish. He was out of bed in a trice, and the next moment was climbing up the biggest beanstalk you ever saw.

So he climbed until he saw a tall, shining white house. And on the doorstep stood a great big woman with a black porridge pot in her hand. Now Jack, having had no supper, was hungry as a hunter, and he said politely,

"Good-morning, ma'am. I wonder if you could give me some breakfast?"

Whereat the ogre's wife laughed and bade Jack come in. But he had hardly finished the porridge when the house began to tremble. It was the ogre coming home!

Thump! THUMP!! THUMP!!!

"Into the oven with you, sharp!" cried the ogre's wife; and the iron oven door was just closed when the ogre strode in. Jack could see him through the little peephole slide at the top.

The ogre began sniffing about the room. Then he frowned horribly and began the real ogre's rhyme:

"Fee-fi-fo-fum,

I smell the blood of an Englishman.

Be he alive, or be he dead,

I'll grind his bones to make my bread."

"Don't be silly," said his wife. "It's the bones of the little boy you had for supper that I'm boiling down for soup! Come, eat your breakfast. There's a good ogre!"

So the ogre ate his three sheep, and when he had done, he went to a big oaken chest and took out three big bags of golden pieces. And by and by his head began to nod, and at last he began to snore so loud that the whole house shook.

Then Jack nipped out of the oven and, seizing one of the bags of gold, he ran till he came to the beanstalk. He flung his burden down, and climbed after it.

And when he came to the bottom, there was his mother picking up gold pieces out of the garden as fast as she could.

Then he turned to look for the beanstalk; but, lo and behold, it wasn't there at all! So he knew, then, it was all real magic.

After that they lived happily on the gold pieces for a long time, but at last, a day came when there was not one more. That night Jack slept like a top, and when he woke ... another bean had grown in the night. In a trice, Jack found himself before the tall white house, where the ogre's wife was standing with the black porridge pot in her hand.

He heard the ogre coming—

Thump! THUMP! THUMP!

The ogre began sniffing and calling out,

"Fee-fi-fo-fum,

I smell the blood of an Englishman.

Be he alive, or be he dead,

I'll grind his bones to make my bread."

"Twaddle!" said the ogre's wife. "It's only the bones of the boy you had last week that I've put into the pig bucket!"

"Umph!" said the ogre harshly; but he ate, and then he said to his wife, "Bring me my hen that lays the magic eggs. I want to see gold." So the ogre's wife brought him a great big black hen with a shiny red comb.

Then the ogre said, "Lay!" and it promptly laid—what do you think?—a beautiful, shiny, yellow, golden egg!

Jack could hardly believe his eyes, and made up his mind that he would have that hen. So, when the ogre began to doze, he just out like a flash from the oven seized the hen, and ran for his life!

How Jack got down the beanstalk he never knew, but get down he did. And the very moment Jack touched ground, he called out, "Lay!" and the black hen ceased cackling and laid a great, big, shiny, yellow, golden egg. So everyone was satisfied.

But one fine moonlight midsummer night before he went to bed, Jack stole out to the garden with a big watering can and watered the ground under his window. Then he slept like a top. When he woke, there he was in an instant on the beanstalk, climbing, climbing, climbing for all he was worth. But this time, he just hid in some bushes, and then he slipped out and hid himself in the copper pot.

And by and by he heard—

Thump! THUMP! THUMP!

"Fee-fi-fo-fum,

I smell the blood of an Englishman.

Be he alive, or be he dead,

I'll grind his bones to make my bread."

"Well, I declare, so do I!" exclaimed the ogre's wife. "It will be that horrid boy who stole the bag of gold and the hen. If so, he's hid in the oven!"

But when she opened the door, lo and behold, Jack wasn't there! And when the ogre had finished his breakfast, he called out to his wife, "Bring me my magic harp!"

So she brought out a little harp and put it on the table. And the ogre leant back in his chair and said lazily,

"Sing!" And, lo and behold, the harp began to sing, and the ogre fell asleep. Then Jack stole out of the copper pot like a mouse, crept to the table, and laid hold of the magic harp.

But it cried out quite loud, "Master! Master!" So the ogre woke, saw Jack, and rushed after him.

Jack just flung himself on to the stalk and began to go down as fast as he could, while the harp kept calling, "Master! Master!" Then Jack climbed down faster and shouted, "Mother! Mother! Bring an axe!"

Now his mother ran out. At that moment Jack touched ground, and he flung down the harp and he seized the axe and gave a great chop at the beanstalk.

And the ogre and all came toppling down, and, of course, the ogre broke his crown, so that he died on the spot.

After that everyone was quite happy. For they had gold to spare. Jack became quite a useful person. And the last bean is still in the garden.

Olivia Blackman, 8th grade

1. When Jack climbed the magic beanstalk, he found an ogre who had lots of treasures. Jack decided to steal his magic bag of gold because he and his mother were very poor.

2. A negative way to view this situation is that Jack just kept stealing things from the ogre, and stealing is wrong even from someone who has more than you.

3. A positive thing about this is that Jack needed to find a way to get money fast because his mother was desperate and mad at him for selling their cow.

4. I think the positive outlook is stronger because even though Jack stole, he still had good intentions.

5. Stealing is a bad act that can come from good intentions.

Sherri Fisher, 9th grade

1. Back in October, my friend stole a lip gloss from Urban Outfitters and got away with it.

2. A negative way to look at this is that Urban Outfitters lost money. Sure, it was only $3.00 but money is money and if everyone does it it's all gonna add up and then Urban Outfitters will lose more money.

3. A positive way to view this would be that Urban Outfitters deserves to be ripped off because they sell t-shirts that deeply offend so many social and ethnic groups with their politics.

4. Overall, despite Urban Outfitters being sucky, it's not right to steal. Lots of smaller companies sometimes sell their stuff there and it's not fair to steal from them.

5. No matter what, stealing is just wrong.

John Stapleton, 10th grade

1. Is there a situation where stealing is okay? Is it always wrong or can there be a good enough reason to do it? Is something like stealing tacos from your school lunch line, as my friend did, ever justified?

2. I guess the negatives of stealing from the lunch line just by walking past the cashier would be that you're cheating other students that are waiting to pay. Maybe you're cheating the funds that the money would go to. You might just be a jerk for not paying when there are actually families who cannot afford to pay.

3. The positive to stealing those tacos would be that you just simply didn't spend any money. My friend got some good laughs out of those tacos, so I'd say that's a positive.

4. Overall, I think stealing is not justifiable. Maybe just learn some patience instead of stealing food. Just think how your parents would react. Think about the people you could be disappointing.

5. Desperation can change a person's values and enable them to do things they normally wouldn't do, like steal tacos. However, unless it's a desperate situation, it's important to always think so that simple desperation for food doesn't get to you.

NAME _____

Read the story.

Think about how some people are generous and often help others.

Write an essay about what happens to people who are generous to others.

MY TRUISM _____

NEWS/GOSSIP: TELL ME, TELL ME				
At the time ...	**All of a sudden ...**	**This was surprising because ...**	**People said ...**	**It just goes to show you:**

MY KERNEL ESSAY

1. _____

2. _____

3. _____

4. _____

5. _____

_____

TRUISM EXAMPLES

1. If you're too generous, people will mistreat you.

2. It's good to give and take, with balance.

3. _____

The Little Red Hen

A Little Red Hen lived in a barnyard. She spent almost all of her time walking about the barnyard in her picketty-pecketty fashion, scratching everywhere for worms.

She dearly loved fat, delicious worms and felt they were absolutely necessary to the health of her children. As often as she found a worm, she would call "Chuck-chuck-chuck!" to her chickies.

When they were gathered about her, she would distribute choice morsels of her tidbit. A busy little body was she!

A cat usually napped lazily in the barn door, not even bothering herself to scare the rat who ran here and there as he pleased. And as for the pig who lived in the sty—he did not care what happened so long as he could eat and grow fat.

One day the Little Red Hen found a seed. It was a wheat seed, but the Little Red Hen was so accustomed to bugs and worms that she supposed this to be some new and perhaps very delicious kind of meat. She bit it gently and found that it resembled a worm in no way whatsoever as to taste, although because it was long and slender, a Little Red Hen might easily be fooled by its appearance.

Carrying it about, she made many inquiries as to what it might be. She found it was a wheat seed and that, if planted, it would grow up and when ripe, it could be made into flour and then into bread.

When she discovered that, she knew it ought to be planted. She was so busy hunting food for herself and her family that, naturally, she thought she ought not to take time to plant it.

So she thought of Pig—upon whom time must hang heavily—and of Cat who had nothing to do, and of the great fat Rat with his idle hours, and she called loudly, "Who will plant the seed?"

But Pig said, "Not I," and Cat said, "Not I," and Rat said, "Not I."

"Well, then," said the Little Red Hen, "I will."

And she did.

Then she went on with her daily duties through the long summer days, scratching for worms and feeding her chicks, while Pig grew fat, and Cat grew fat, and Rat grew fat, and the wheat grew tall and ready for harvest.

So one day, the Little Red Hen chanced to notice how large the wheat was and that the grain was ripe, so she ran about calling briskly, "Who will cut the wheat?"

Pig said, "Not I," Cat said, "Not I," and Rat said, "Not I."

"Well, then," said the Little Red Hen, "I will."

And she did.

She got the sickle from among the farmer's tools in the barn and proceeded to cut off all of the big plant of wheat.

On the ground lay the nicely cut wheat, ready to be gathered and threshed, but the newest and yellowest and downiest of Mrs. Hen's chicks set up a "peep-peep-peeping" in their most vigorous fashion, proclaiming to the world at large, but most particularly to their mother, that she was neglecting them.

Poor Little Red Hen! She felt quite bewildered and hardly knew where to turn. Her attention was sorely divided between her duty to her children and her duty to the wheat, for which she felt responsible.

So, again, in a very hopeful tone, she called out, "Who will thresh the wheat?"

But Pig, with a grunt, said, "Not I," and Cat, with a meow, said, "Not I," and Rat, with a squeak, said, "Not I."

So the Little Red Hen, looking, it must be admitted, rather discouraged, said, "Well, I will, then."

And she did.

Of course, she had to feed her babies first, though, and when she had gotten them all to sleep for their afternoon nap, she went out and threshed the wheat. Then she called out, "Who will carry the wheat to the mill to be ground?"

Turning their backs with snippy glee, Pig said, "Not I," and Cat said, "Not I," and Rat said, "Not I."

So the good Little Red Hen could do nothing but say, "I will then."

And she did.

Carrying the sack of wheat, she trudged off to the distant mill. There she ordered the wheat ground into beautiful white flour. When the miller brought her the flour, she walked slowly back all the way to her own barnyard in her own picketty-pecketty fashion.

She even managed, despite her load, to catch a nice juicy worm now and then and had one left for the babies when she reached them. Those cunning little fluff-balls were so glad to see their mother. For the first time, they really appreciated her.

After this really strenuous day, Mrs. Hen retired to her slumbers earlier than usual—indeed, before the colors came into the sky to herald the setting of the sun, her usual bedtime hour.

She would have liked to sleep late in the morning, but her chicks, joining in the morning chorus of the hen yard, drove away all hopes of such a luxury.

Even as she sleepily half opened one eye, the thought came to her that today that wheat must, somehow, be made into bread.

She was not in the habit of making bread, although, of course, anyone can make it if he or she follows the recipe with care, and she knew perfectly well that she could do it if necessary.

So after her children were fed and made sweet and fresh for the day, she hunted up Pig, Cat and Rat.

Still confident that they would surely help her some day she sang out, "Who will make the bread?"

Alas for the Little Red Hen! Once more her hopes were dashed! For Pig said, "Not I," Cat said, "Not I," and Rat said, "Not I."

So the Little Red Hen said once more, "I will then," and she did.

Feeling that she might have known all the time that she would have to do it all herself, she went and put on a fresh apron and spotless cook's cap. First of all she set the dough, as was proper. When it was time, she brought out the molding board and the baking tins, molded the bread, divided it into loaves, and put them into the oven to bake.

All the while, Cat sat lazily by, giggling and chuckling. And close at hand, the vain Rat powdered his nose and admired himself in a mirror. In the distance could be heard the long-drawn snores of the dozing Pig.

At last the great moment arrived. A delicious odor was wafted upon the autumn breeze. Everywhere the barnyard citizens sniffed the air with delight.

The Red Hen ambled in her picketty-pecketty way toward the source of all this excitement.

Although she appeared to be perfectly calm, in reality, she could only with difficulty restrain an impulse to dance and sing, for had she not done all the work on this wonderful bread? Small wonder that she was the most excited person in the barnyard!

She did not know whether the bread would be fit to eat, but—joy of joys!—when the lovely brown loaves came out of the oven, they were done to perfection. Then, probably because she had acquired the habit, the Red Hen called,

"Who will eat the bread?"

All the animals in the barnyard were watching hungrily and smacking their lips in anticipation, and Pig said, "I will," Cat said, "I will," Rat said, "I will."

But the Little Red Hen said,

"No, you won't. I will."

And she did.

Student Work Sample: Generosity

Rose Taylor, 12th grade

It was a hot afternoon in July and my friends and I went to Walmart to shop. As we tumbled out of the car, we noticed a family standing under a tree in a green space near the parking lot. They looked hot and tired. The father held a sign saying, "Family hungry and homeless—Please Help!" One of my friends said, "Aw, that's terrible." The other two girls didn't say anything but seemed annoyed by the family. I walked over and handed them the $20 bill that I had planned on spending in the store. The father took the money, smiled, and said, "Bless you! This really helps! Thank you!" As I returned to my friends, they said that I had done a good thing. I felt good inside and went in the store feeling like I had made a difference for that family.

As we were leaving and walking to the car, I saw that same family load up into what looked like a brand new pickup that probably cost $40,000. I was so shocked but relieved that my friends had not seen them. I felt like such a fool! I told myself that I never would give a stranger money who begged for it. In fact, I was furious with that family, but it was too late to do anything about it.

All the way home and throughout the day, I couldn't stop thinking about it. I felt so stupid and I was afraid to tell anyone what happened. My mom came in my room as I lay on the bed staring at the ceiling. She asked me what was wrong and I started telling her the story and crying that I was so gullible to believe that I helped someone. Mom took my hand and said that no matter what, I had done a good thing. That sometimes the right thing to do is more powerful than not doing anything at all. Although I felt stupid, I wasn't. I did what I thought was right and that's the important thing. She then took me downstairs and we baked cookies together.

I have thought about that day often. Although someone fooled me, there are many other people who need help. I can't walk by someone who asks for a handout. I know that sometimes they may do bad things with the dollar or two I give them, but it makes me feel good, and maybe just maybe, I made a difference to someone.

15 Distractions

Read the story.
Think about how easy it is to get distracted from a task or goal.
Write an essay about how distractions in your path can help you or hurt you.

MY TRUISM

CHANGE OF PLANS

| Where I was going (and why) | Something unexpected that happened | How my plans changed | What I think (truism) |

MY KERNEL ESSAY

1. _____

2. _____

3. _____

4. _____

_____

_____

TRUISM EXAMPLES

1. Distractions can help you see that you're not serious about a goal.

2. Occasional breaks can help a person arrive at a destination.

3. _____

Little Red Riding Hood

Once upon a time, there was a dear little girl who was loved by everyone who looked at her, but most of all by her grandmother, and there was nothing that she would not have given to the child. Once she gave her a little cape of red velvet, which suited her so well that she would never wear anything else; so she was always called "Little Red Riding Hood."

One day, her mother said to her, "Come, Little Red Riding Hood; here is a piece of cake and a bottle of wine; take them to your grandmother as she is ill and weak, and they will do her good. Set out before it gets hot, and when you are going, walk nicely and quietly and do not run off the path or you may fall and break the bottle; and when you go into her room, don't forget to say, 'Good morning.'"

"I will take great care," said Little Red Riding Hood to her mother.

The grandmother lived out in the wood, half a league from the village, and just as Little Red Riding Hood entered the wood, a wolf met her. Red Riding Hood did not know what a wicked creature he was and was not at all afraid of him.

"Good day, Little Red Riding Hood," said he.

"Thank you kindly, wolf."

"Whither away so early, Little Red Riding Hood?"

"To my grandmother's."

"What have you got in your apron?"

"Cake and wine; my poor sick grandmother is to have something good, to make her stronger."

"Where does your grandmother live, Little Red Riding Hood?"

"A good quarter of a league farther on in the wood. Her house stands under the three large oak trees; you surely must know it," replied Little Red Riding Hood.

So the wolf walked for a short time by the side of Little Red Riding Hood, and then he said, "See, Little Red Riding Hood, how pretty the flowers are about here—why do you not look round? You do not hear how sweetly the little birds are singing; you walk gravely along as if you were going to school, while everything else out here in the wood is merry."

Little Red Riding Hood raised her eyes, and when she saw the sunbeams dancing here and there through the trees, and pretty flowers growing everywhere, she thought, "Suppose I take grandmother a fresh nosegay; that would please her too. It is so early in the day that I shall still get there in good time." And so she ran from the path into the wood to look for flowers.

Meanwhile, the wolf ran straight to the grandmother's house and knocked at the door.

"Who is there?"

"Little Red Riding Hood," replied the wolf. "She is bringing cake and wine; open the door."

"Lift the latch," called out the grandmother. "I am too weak, and cannot get up."

The wolf lifted the latch, the door sprang open, and without saying a word, he went straight to the grandmother's bed and devoured her. Then he put on her clothes, dressed himself in her cap, laid himself in bed, and drew the curtains.

Little Red Riding Hood, however, had been running about picking flowers, and when she had gathered so many that she could carry no more, she remembered her grandmother and set out on the way to her.

She was surprised to find the cottage-door standing open, and when she went into the room, she called out, "Good morning," but received no answer; so she went to the bed and drew back the curtains. There lay her grandmother with her cap pulled far over her face, and looking very strange.

"Oh! grandmother," she said, "what big ears you have!"

"The better to hear you with, my child," was the reply.

"But, grandmother, what big eyes you have!" she said.

"The better to see you with, my dear."

"But, grandmother, what large hands you have!"

"The better to hug you with."

"Oh! but, grandmother, what a terrible big mouth you have!"

"The better to eat you with!"

And scarcely had the wolf said this, than with one bound, he was out of bed and swallowed up Red Riding Hood.

When the wolf had appeased his appetite, he lay down again in the bed, fell asleep, and began to snore very loud. The huntsman was just passing the house, and thought to himself, "How the old woman is snoring! I must just see if she wants anything." So he went into the room, and when he came to the bed, he saw that the wolf was lying in it. "Do I find you here, you old sinner!" said he. "I have long sought you!" Then just as he was going to fire at him, it occurred to him that the wolf might have devoured the grandmother, and that she might still be saved; so he did not fire, but took a pair of scissors, and began to cut open the stomach of the sleeping wolf. When he had made two snips, he saw the little Red Riding Hood shining, and then he made two snips more, and the little girl sprang out, crying, "Ah, how frightened I have been! How dark it was inside the wolf"; and after that, the aged grandmother came out alive also, but scarcely able to breathe. Red Riding Hood, however, quickly fetched great stones with which they filled the wolf's belly, and when he awoke, he wanted to run away, but the stones were so heavy that he collapsed at once, and fell dead.

Then all three were delighted. The huntsman drew off the wolf's skin and went home with it; the grandmother ate the cake and drank the wine which Red Riding Hood had brought, and revived. But Red Riding Hood thought to herself, "As long as I live, I will never by myself leave the path to run into the wood, when my mother has forbidden me to do so."

Student Work Samples: Distractions

Brandon Dross, 4th grade

1. We were going to buy a new house.

2. We went to eat.

3. Someone else bought the house.

4. I think you should never be distracted.

Aiyana Arriaga, 4th grade

1. I was cutting a piece of cake and was about to put it on the plate when my cousins asked me to get them a water.

2. I looked at the cake in my hand and it was on the floor.

3. I didn't get to eat the cake.

4. Distractions get you off course.

Melissa Casarrubias, 4th grade

1. I was putting milk in a cup for my brother and I was not paying attention.

2. I spilled milk all over.

3. I had to clean up instead of play.

4. Distractions can make you make bad decisions.

Part IV
Structures for Analyzing a Theme in Literature

Bank of Text Structure Choices

For Analyzing a Theme in Literature

WRONG ASSUMPTIONS

I made this wrong assumption	... happened as a consequence	I learned this truth	So now I believe ...

FINDING OUT FOR SURE

I've never been sure if ...	But I've always suspected that ...	Because once I experienced ...	Which made me think that ...	And finally I realized that ...

DEFINITION

Definition of something	How to tell if something fits this definition	One example that fits	Truism

---

THE 11-MINUTE ESSAY

Truism	How it's true in a story	How it's true in a movie	How it's true in my life	I wonder ...

TEVYE'S DEBATE

On one hand ...	On the other hand ...	But on the other hand ...	But on the other hand ...	So ...

NAME _____

Read the story.

Think about what we love in the world and how we treat it.

Write an essay about pure and simple love.

MY TRUISM _____

WRONG ASSUMPTIONS

| I made this wrong assumption | ... happened as a consequence | I learned this truth | So now I believe ... |

MY KERNEL ESSAY

1. _____

2. _____

3. _____

4. _____

_____

_____

TRUISM EXAMPLES

1. When a person truly loves, they don't hold grudges. _____

2. Real love does not expect anything in return. _____

3. _____

The Nightingale

In China, a great many years ago, the Emperor's palace was the wonder of the world. It was made entirely of fine porcelain. In the garden, the rarest flowers bloomed, and to the prettiest ones were tied little silver bells. The Emperor's garden extended to a fine forest where the trees were tall and the lakes were deep. In these trees, a nightingale lived. His song was so ravishing that everyone stopped to listen.

Travelers came to the city of the Emperor. They admired the city, but when they heard the nightingale, they said, "That is the best of all."

Poets wrote magnificent poems about the nightingale, and these books went all the world over. The Emperor of China sat in his golden chair and read, nodding his head in delight over such glowing descriptions of his city, his palace, and garden. *But the nightingale is the best of all.* He read it in print.

He called his Lord-in-Waiting. "They say there's a most remarkable bird called the nightingale," said the Emperor. "They say it's the best thing in all my empire. Why haven't I been told about it?"

"I never heard of him before," said the Lord-in-Waiting. "I'll find him."

"I must hear this nightingale," said the Emperor.

"Tsing-pe!" said the Lord-in-Waiting, and off he scurried up the stairs, through all the rooms and corridors. And half the court ran with him, for no one wanted to be punched in the stomach after supper.

There was much questioning as to the whereabouts of this remarkable nightingale, who was so well-known everywhere in the world except at home. At last, a poor little kitchen girl said,

"The nightingale? I know him well. Yes, indeed, he can sing. It brings tears to my eyes. It's as if my mother were kissing me."

So they went into the forest. Then the nightingale sang.

"Little nightingale," the kitchen girl called to him, "our gracious Emperor wants to hear you sing."

"With the greatest of pleasure," answered the nightingale.

"My song sounds best in the woods," said the nightingale, but he went with them willingly when he heard it was the Emperor's wish.

The palace had been especially polished for the occasion. The porcelain walls and floors shone in the rays of many gold lamps. The flowers with tinkling bells on them had been brought into the halls, and there was such a commotion of coming and going that all the bells chimed away until you could scarcely hear yourself talk.

In the middle of the great throne room, where the Emperor sat, there was a golden perch for the nightingale. The whole court was there, dressed in their best.

The nightingale sang so sweetly that the Emperor's heart melted. Unquestionably, the nightingale was a success. He was to stay at court and have his own cage. He had permission to go for a walk twice a day and once a night. Twelve footmen attended him, each one holding tight to a ribbon tied to the bird's leg. There wasn't much fun in such outings.

One day, the Emperor received a large package labeled "The Nightingale." In the box was an artificial nightingale encrusted with diamonds, rubies, and sapphires. When it was wound, the artificial bird could sing one of the nightingale's songs.

"Isn't that nice?" everyone said.

The imitation bird met with the same success as the real nightingale, and besides, it was much prettier to see, all sparkling like bracelets and breastpins. Three and thirty times it sang the selfsame song without tiring. No one noticed the real nightingale flying out the open window, back to his home in the green forest.

All the courtiers slandered the nightingale, whom they called a most ungrateful wretch and praised the artificial bird beyond measure.

Five years passed by, and a real sorrow befell the whole country. Their Emperor fell ill, ill unto death. A new Emperor was chosen in readiness.

Cold and pale lay the Emperor. All the courtiers thought he was dead and went to do homage to the new Emperor. The poor Emperor could hardly breathe. It was as if something were sitting on his chest. Opening his eyes he saw it was Death who sat there, wearing the Emperor's crown, handling the Emperor's gold sword, and carrying the Emperor's silk banner.

"Music, music!" the Emperor called. "Sing, my precious little golden bird, sing! I have given you gold and precious presents. Sing, I pray you, sing!"

But the bird stood silent. There was no one to wind it. Death kept staring through his great hollow eyes, and it was quiet, deadly quiet.

Suddenly, through the window came a burst of song. It was the little live nightingale. Death listened, and said, "Go on, little nightingale, go on!"

"But," said the little nightingale, "will you give back that sword, that banner, that Emperor's crown?"

And Death gave back these treasures for a song. The nightingale sang on. It sang of the quiet churchyard where white roses grow. Death longed for his garden and departed.

"Thank you, thank you!" the Emperor said. "Little bird from Heaven, I know you of old. I banished you once from my land, and yet you have sung away Death from my heart. How can I repay you?"

"You have already rewarded me," said the nightingale. "I brought tears to your eyes when first I sang for you. To the heart of a singer those are more precious than any precious stone."

"You must stay with me always," said the Emperor. "Sing to me only when you please."

But the nightingale said, "Let me come as I will. Then, I shall sit on the spray by your window and sing things that will make you happy and thoughtful too, if you will promise me one thing."

"All that I have is yours," cried the Emperor.

"One thing only," the nightingale asked. "You must not let anyone know that you have a little bird who tells you everything." And away he flew.

The servants came in to look after their dead Emperor—and there they stood. And the Emperor said, "Good morning."

Alex Calvio, 11th grade

Love can take many shapes and forms, in friendships and relationships. Any interaction involving care could be defined as love. This means that love should not be one-sided or obsessive.

In the fairytale, "The Nightingale," the Emperor discovers a nightingale that sings beautifully. He orders the bird to be given a cage, attached to a string, and for the bird to sing excessively to the point of exhaustion. This is a representation of an abusive relationship, not necessarily a romantic one, but a relationship between two individuals interacting with one another. This is an abusive relationship because not only does the Emperor ignore the nightingale's wish to stay at home in the forest, he also makes the Nightingale feel "loved" and needed in order to lead it back to the palace. Additionally, when the bird finally becomes so worn and tired that it cannot sing properly, the Emperor replaces it with a machine, "an artificial nightingale encrusted with diamonds, rubies, and sapphires" that could sing the exact same tune that the live Nightingale could. This action proves that the Emperor does not really love the nightingale, just the song that it sang, and with this, the nightingale flies away.

But while the Emperor does not love the nightingale, the nightingale does love the Emperor. Even after being abused during their relationship, the nightingale still comes back to save the Emperor from death. This is unconditional love, which is more powerful than any other kind of love since it requires forgiveness.

In life, we can see that successful relationships involve forgiveness along with communication and care. When a relationship is based on negative emotions such as selfishness, it can easily become a prison.

"The Nightingale" teaches us how to keep a long-lasting and fulfilling type of love. Personally, I may be able to retain healthy relationships by remembering to not use another person's qualities for my own personal benefit. I will give someone space when they require it and love them for their entire selves, not just one part of them. A relationship is a team effort and when someone in a relationship refuses to believe that, it is best to fly away until that relationship can get better, just like the nightingale.

17 Humiliation

Read the story.

Think about how people treat someone who is different.

Write an essay about the effects of humiliation.

MY TRUISM

FINDING OUT FOR SURE

| I've never been sure if ... | But I've always suspected that ... | Because once I experienced ... | Which made me think that ... | And finally I realized that ... |

MY KERNEL ESSAY

1.

2.

3.

4.

5.

TRUISM EXAMPLES

1. People humiliate each other over ridiculous stuff.

2. It's easy to feel shame when others point out your flaws.

3.

One-Eye, Two-Eyes, and Three-Eyes

There was once a woman who had three daughters, the eldest of whom was called One-eye, because she had only one eye in the middle of her forehead; and the second, Two-eyes, because she had two eyes like other folks; and the youngest, Three-eyes, because she had three eyes. However, as Two-eyes saw just as other human beings did, her sisters and her mother could not endure her. They said to her, "Thou, with thy two eyes, art no better than the common people; thou dost not belong to us!" They pushed her about, and did everything that they could to make her unhappy. It came to pass that Two-eyes had to go out into the fields and tend the goat, but she was still quite hungry because her sisters had given her so little to eat. So she sat down on a ridge and began to weep. And when she looked up in her grief, a woman was standing beside her, who said, "Wipe away thy tears, Two-eyes; just say to thy goat,

> 'Bleat, my little goat, bleat,
>
> Cover the table with something to eat,'

and then a clean, well-spread little table will stand before thee, with the most delicious food upon it, and when thou hast had enough, just say,

> 'Bleat, bleat, my little goat, I pray,
>
> And take the table quite away,'

and then it will vanish again from thy sight." Hereupon the wise woman departed. Two-eyes said,

> "Bleat, my little goat, bleat,
>
> Cover the table with something to eat,"

and a little table, covered with a white cloth, was standing there, and on it was the most delicious food. Then Two-eyes helped herself to some food. And when she was satisfied, she said,

> "Bleat, bleat, my little goat, I pray,
>
> And take the table quite away,"

and immediately the little table and everything on it was gone again. Two-eyes was quite glad and happy.

In the evening, when she went home, she found a small dish with some food, which her sisters had set ready for her, but she did not touch it. As it happened every time, they said, "Two-eyes always leaves her food untasted, and she used to eat up everything." They resolved to send One-eye with Two-eyes when she went to the pasture, to observe. So when Two-eyes set out the next time, One-eye went to her and said, "I will go with you to the pasture." But Two-eyes knew what was in One-eye's mind, and said, "Come, One-eye, we will sit down, and I will sing something to you." One-eye sat down and was tired with the unaccustomed walk, and Two-eyes sang constantly,

> "One-eye, wakest thou?
>
> One-eye, sleepest thou?"

until One-eye shut her one eye and fell asleep, and Two-eyes said,

> "Bleat, my little goat, bleat,
>
> Cover the table with something to eat,"

and seated herself at her table and ate and drank until she was satisfied, and then she again cried,

> "Bleat, bleat, my little goat, I pray,
>
> And take the table quite away,"

and in an instant all was gone. Two-eyes now awakened One-eye, and said, "Come, let us go home again." One-eye could not tell her mother why Two-eyes would not eat, and said, "I fell asleep when I was out."

Next day the mother said to Three-eyes, "This time thou shalt go and observe, for she must eat and drink in secret." So Three-eyes went to Two-eyes, and said, "I will go with you." But Two-eyes knew what was in Three-eyes' mind, and said, "We will sit down, and I will sing something to you, Three-eyes."

Three-eyes sat down, and Two-eyes began the same song as before, and sang,

"Three-eyes, are you waking?"

but then, instead of singing,

"Three-eyes, are you sleeping?"

as she ought to have done, she thoughtlessly sang,

"Two-eyes, are you sleeping?"

Then two of the eyes which Three-eyes had, shut and fell asleep, but the third did not sleep. And when Two-eyes thought that Three-eyes was fast asleep, she used her little charm,

"Bleat, my little goat, bleat,

Cover the table with something to eat,"

and ate and drank as much as her heart desired, and then ordered the table to go away again, saying

"Bleat, bleat, my little goat, I pray,

And take the table quite away."

Three-eyes had seen everything. When they got home, Three-eyes told the mother, "When she is out, she calls to the little goat and a table appears before her covered with the best of food and she eats all she wants. I watched everything closely." Then the envious mother fetched a knife and killed the goat.

When Two-eyes saw that, she went out and wept bitter tears. Suddenly, the wise woman once more stood by her side, and said, "Two-eyes, why art thou weeping?" She answered. "The goat has been killed by my mother." The wise woman said, "Two-eyes, ask thy sisters to give thee the heart of the slaughtered goat, and bury it in the ground in front of the house." Two-eyes went home and said to her sisters, "Dear sisters, do give me the heart of my goat." Then they told her she could have it. So Two-eyes buried the heart quietly in the evening.

Next morning, when they all awoke, there stood a strangely magnificent tree with leaves of silver, and fruit of gold, standing on the exact spot where she had buried the heart. Then the mother said to One-eye, "Climb up, my child, and gather some of the fruit for us." One-eye climbed up, but the branch escaped from her hands, and she could not pluck a single apple. Then said the mother, "Three-eyes, do you climb up." Three-eyes was not more skillful, and the golden apples always escaped her. At length, the mother climbed up herself but could not get hold of the fruit. Then Two-eyes climbed up, and the golden apples came into her hand of their own accord, so that she brought a whole apronful down with her. The mother took them away from her, and treated her still more cruelly.

It so befell that once when they were all standing together by the tree, a young knight came up. He was a handsome lord, who stopped and admired the magnificent gold and silver tree, and said to the sisters, "To whom does this fine tree belong? Anyone who would bestow one branch of it on me might in return for it ask whatsoever he desired." Then Two-eyes came forth, and the knight was surprised at her great beauty. Two-eyes said, "That I certainly shall be able to do, for the tree belongs to me." And she climbed up, and broke off a branch with beautiful silver leaves and golden fruit, and gave it to the knight. Then said the knight, "What shall I give thee for it?" "Alas!" answered Two-eyes, "I suffer from hunger; if you would take me with you, I should be happy." So the knight lifted Two-eyes on to his horse, and took her home with him to his father's castle, and there he married her, and the wedding was solemnized with great rejoicing.

Her two sisters grudged her good fortune. "The wonderful tree, however, still remains with us," thought they, "and everyone will come and admire it." But next morning, the tree had vanished. When Two-eyes looked out of the window of her own little room, to her great delight the tree was standing in front of it, and so it had followed her.

Two-eyes lived a long time in happiness. Once, two poor women came to her in her castle and begged for alms. She looked in their faces and recognized her sisters, One-eye, and Three-eyes, who had fallen into such poverty that they had to beg. Two-eyes made them welcome and was kind to them so that they both with all their hearts repented the evil that they had done their sister in their youth.

Student Work Sample: Humiliation

Tristan Bayless, 11th grade

1. I've never been sure if humiliation was a good thing.

2. But I've always suspected that humiliation was a semi-good thing.

3. Because I once experienced humiliation.

4. Which made me think that humiliation was a bad feeling.

5. And I finally realized that humiliation was a way to make us feel better.

I've never been sure if humiliation was a good thing. When one is humiliated, he or she feels distrust and anger at the person who humiliated them.

But I've always suspected that humiliation could be a semi-good thing because it tells us how others see and feel about us.

Because I once felt humiliation. It happened on a Sunday when I was eating lunch with my extended family. My brother told my uncle's girlfriend not to sit next to me because I stank, and I somewhat did.

At that moment, I felt like humiliation was a bad feeling. I got angry and lashed out at my brother in a passive aggressive way. I turned my humiliation into anger, which was what he wanted.

But after that experience, I always cleaned up and dressed nicely before a family gathering. And I finally realized that humiliation was a way to make us feel better, because it helps us to see our flaws. But it can work in your favor based on your mindset if you use the humiliation to improve yourself.

18 Tests

Read the story.
Think about all the kinds of tests people face in life.
Write an essay about how to tell if a test is fair.

MY TRUISM

DEFINITION

| Definition of something | How to tell if something fits this definition | One example that fits | Truism |

MY KERNEL ESSAY

1. _____

2. _____

3. _____

4. _____

_____

_____

TRUISM EXAMPLES

1. If the challenge is made by a bully, you can be sure the test will not be fair.

2. Some tests are scams.

3. _____

The Princess and the Pea

There was once a prince who wanted to marry a princess. But she must be a real princess, mind you. So he traveled all round the world, seeking such a one, but everywhere something was in the way. Not that there was any lack of princesses, but he could not seem to make out whether they were real princesses; there was always something not quite satisfactory.

Therefore, home he came again, quite out of spirits, for he wished so much to marry a real princess.

One evening a terrible storm came on. It thundered and lightninged, and the rain poured down; indeed, it was quite fearful. In the midst of it there came a knock at the town gate, and the old king went out to open it.

It was a princess who stood outside. But O dear, what a state she was in from the rain and bad weather! The water dropped from her hair and clothes, it ran in at the tips of her shoes and out at the heels; yet she insisted she was a real princess.

"Very well," thought the old queen; "that we shall presently see." She said nothing, but went into the bedchamber and took off all the bedding, then laid a pea on the sacking of the bedstead. Having done this, she took twenty mattresses and laid them upon the pea and placed twenty eider-down beds on top of the mattresses.

The princess lay upon this bed all the night. In the morning, she was asked how she had slept.

"Oh, most miserably!" she said. "I scarcely closed my eyes the whole night through. I cannot think what there could have been in the bed. I lay upon something so hard that I am quite black and blue all over. It is dreadful!"

It was now quite evident that she was a real princess, since through twenty mattresses and twenty eider-down beds she had felt the pea. None but a real princess could have such delicate feeling.

So the prince took her for his wife, for he knew that in her he had found a true princess. And the pea was preserved in the cabinet of curiosities, where it is still to be seen unless someone has stolen it.

And this, mind you, is a real story.

Student Work Samples: Tests

Reijahl Torrevillas, 5th grade

1. *IMPOSSIBLE* definition: something that isn't possible.

2. People think something isn't possible if it is hard.

3. An example is trying to sneeze with your eyes open. It is both hard and impossible.

4. Some tests are impossible to pass.

John Edwards, 8th grade

1. "An accordance with the rules or standards"—that's the definition of *fair*. So when someone tells you rules, it's fair if you follow it, and there's a good outcome that's a fair test.

2. How to tell if a test is fair: Does it follow the rules of the test?

3. If you get all the questions right on the test but you don't explain your answers, and it says answers must be explained in the test instructions, and your score is a zero, then it's fair in my eyes because you're the one that didn't follow the directions.

4. If they explain the directions and you don't follow them, then it's on you. If it's the other way around, then it's not fair.

Jayne Hover, educator

1. *Fear*: something that has the ability to squelch dreams.

2. If you cannot move toward your dream, then you are in fear.

3. I wasn't sure I could fly, but I needed to get somewhere quickly which meant I had to get on a plane.

4. Sometimes life gives us a test to prove to ourselves that we can overcome anything.

Notes

19 Reputation

Read the story.

Think about how a person's reputation can become reality.

Write an essay about people's power to shape our own reputations.

MY TRUISM

THE 11-MINUTE ESSAY

| Truism | How it's true in a story | How it's true in a movie | How it's true in my life | I wonder ... |

MY KERNEL ESSAY

1. _____

2. _____

3. _____

4. _____

5. _____

_____

TRUISM EXAMPLES

1. People believe what they see.

2. People believe they see more than they do.

3. _____

Puss in Boots

Once upon a time, there was a miller who left no more riches to the three sons he had than his mill, his ass, and his cat. The division was soon made. Neither the lawyer nor the attorney was sent for. They would soon have eaten up all the poor property. The eldest had the mill, the second the ass, and the youngest nothing but the cat.

The youngest, as we can understand, was quite unhappy.

The Cat said to him with a grave and serious air,

"Do not thus afflict yourself, my master; you have nothing else to do but to give me a bag, and get a pair of boots made for me, that I may scamper through the brambles, and you shall see that you have not so poor a portion in me as you think."

Though the Cat's master did not think much of what he said, he had seen him play such cunning tricks. When the Cat had what he asked for, he booted himself very gallantly, and putting his bag about his neck, he held the strings of it in his two forepaws, and went into a warren.

Scarcely was he settled but he had what he wanted. A rash and foolish young rabbit jumped into his bag. Proud of his prey, he went with it to the palace and asked to speak with the King. He said,

"I have brought you, sire, a rabbit which my noble Lord, the Master of Carabas" (for that was the title which Puss was pleased to give his master) "has commanded me to present to your Majesty from him."

"Tell thy master," said the King, "that I thank him, and that I am pleased with his gift."

The Cat continued for two or three months thus to carry his Majesty, from time to time, some of his master's game. One day when he knew that the King was to take the air along the riverside, with his daughter, the most beautiful princess in the world, he said to his master,

"If you will follow my advice, your fortune is made. You have nothing else to do but go and bathe in the river, just at the spot I shall show you, and leave the rest to me."

The Marquis of Carabas did what the Cat advised him to. While he was bathing, the King passed by, and the Cat cried out with all his might,

"Help! Help! My Lord the Marquis of Carabas is drowning!"

At this noise, the King put his head out of the coach window, and seeing the Cat who had so often brought him game, he commanded his guards to run immediately to the assistance of his Lordship, the Marquis of Carabas.

While they were drawing the poor Marquis out of the river, the Cat came up to the coach and told the King that, while his master was bathing, there came by some rogues, who ran off with his clothes. The cunning Cat had hidden the clothes under a great stone. The King immediately commanded the officers of his wardrobe to run and fetch one of his best suits for the Lord Marquis of Carabas.

The King's daughter found him very much to her liking, and she fell in love with him. The King would have him come into the coach and take part in the airing. The Cat, overjoyed to see his plan succeed, marched on before, and, meeting with some countrymen, who were mowing a meadow, he said to them,

"Good people, you who are mowing, if you do not tell the King that the meadow you mow belongs to my Lord Marquis of Carabas, you shall be chopped as small as herbs for the pot."

The King did not fail to ask the mowers to whom the meadow they were mowing belonged.

"To my Lord Marquis of Carabas," answered they all together, for the Cat's threat had made them afraid.

"You have a good property there," said the King to the Marquis of Carabas.

"You see, sire," said the Marquis, "this is a meadow which never fails to yield a plentiful harvest every year."

The Master's Cat, who went always before, said the same thing to all he met, and the King was astonished at the vast estates of my Lord Marquis of Carabas.

Monsieur Puss came at last to a stately castle, the master of which was an Ogre, the richest ever known; for all the lands which the King had then passed through belonged to this castle. The Cat, who had taken care to inform himself who this Ogre was and what he could do, asked to speak with him, saying he could not pass so near his castle without paying his respects to him.

The Ogre received him as civilly as an Ogre could do, and made him sit down.

"I have been assured," said the Cat, "that you have the gift of being able to change yourself into all sorts of creatures you have a mind to; that you can, for example, transform yourself into a lion, or elephant, and the like."

"That is true," answered the Ogre, roughly; "and to convince you, you shall see me now become a lion."

Puss was so terrified at the sight of a lion so near him that he immediately climbed into the gutter, not without much trouble and danger, because of his boots, which were of no use at all to him for walking upon the tiles. A little while after, when Puss saw that the Ogre had resumed his natural form, he came down and owned he had been very much frightened.

"I have, moreover, been informed," said the Cat, "but I know not how to believe it, that; you have also the power to take on you the shape of the smallest animals; for example, a rat or a mouse, but I must own to you I take this to be impossible."

"Impossible!" cried the Ogre; "you shall see." And at the same time he changed himself into a mouse and began to run about the floor. Puss no sooner perceived this than he fell upon him and ate him up.

Meanwhile, the King, who saw, as he passed, this fine castle of the Ogre's, had a mind to go into it. Puss ran out, and said to the King, "Your Majesty is welcome to this castle of my Lord Marquis of Carabas."

"What! my Lord Marquis," cried the King, "and does this castle also belong to you? There can be nothing finer than this courtyard."

The Marquis gave his hand to the young Princess, and followed the King, who went first. They passed into the great hall. His Majesty, charmed with the good qualities of my Lord of Carabas, as was also his daughter, who had fallen violently in love with him, and seeing the vast estate he possessed, said to him,

"It will be owing to yourself only, my Lord Marquis, if you are not my son-in-law."

The Marquis, with low bows, accepted the honor which his Majesty conferred upon him, and forthwith that very same day married the Princess.

Student Work Sample: Reputation

Sebastian Herrera, 11th grade

I believe that a reputation can completely change a person. A reputation is like a chip on your shoulder. A reputation can not only change the way a person is but it can completely change who they are, and affect people around them in a positive or a negative way, but most likely negatively. If you think you are the best at what you do, then that's how you will feel about yourself.

In *The Great Gatsby,* Gatsby likes Daisy but he lets his reputation get in the way of it and he lets Daisy go and get married to another guy he knows is cheating on her. But he never tells her because that would go against his reputation as a party animal and a player. Gatsby lets his reputation change his whole future.

In the film *Zookeeper*, the zookeeper liked his job, but at the same time, he was in love with one of his co-workers. When he was offered a job as a car salesman, he started to work with higher class people. He began to forget who he really was and where he came from. He wanted to escape his lowly reputation.

Then the woman he liked decided to take a job out of the state so he finally realized that he couldn't let her leave without telling her how he felt about her. His inner character became more important than his reputation.

In my life, when I started working at Chick-fil-A, I had to be very polite and have great manners to the customers. This training caused me to continue to use those manners even while off work and living my regular everyday life. My own behavior was shaped because of the company's reputation.

I wonder if people can ever go back to the way they used to be before they changed who they originally were. Maybe some part of that reputation becomes part of our internal selves.

20 Companionship

Read the story.

Think about how some people are comfortable by themselves and other people prefer being around people.

Write an essay about how much companionship is too much.

MY TRUISM

TEVYE'S DEBATE

On one hand ...	On the other hand ...	But on the other hand ...	But on the other hand ...	So ...

MY KERNEL ESSAY

1. _____

2. _____

3. _____

4. _____

5. _____

_____

TRUISM EXAMPLES

1. People need the companionship of others.

2. Spending time alone can have its advantages.

3. _____

Rapunzel

There were once a man and a woman who had long in vain wished for a child. At length, the woman hoped that God was about to grant her desire. These people had a little window at the back of their house from which a splendid garden could be seen, which was full of the most beautiful flowers and herbs. It was, however, surrounded by a high wall, and no one dared to go into it because it belonged to an enchantress, who had great power and was dreaded by all the world.

One day, the woman was standing by this window and looking down into the garden, when she saw a bed which was planted with the most beautiful rampion (rapunzel), and it looked so fresh and green that she longed for it and had the greatest desire to eat some.

This desire increased every day, and as she knew that she could not get any of it, she quite pined away and looked pale and miserable. Then her husband was alarmed, and asked, "What aileth thee, dear wife?" "Ah," she replied, "if I can't get some of the rampion, which is in the garden behind our house, to eat, I shall die." The man, who loved her, thought, "Sooner than let thy wife die, bring her some of the rampion thyself, let it cost thee what it will." In the twilight of evening, he clambered down over the wall into the garden of the enchantress, hastily clutched a handful of rampion, and took it to his wife. She at once made herself a salad of it, and ate it with much relish. She, however, liked it so much, so very much, that the next day, she longed for it three times as much as before.

In the gloom of evening, therefore, he let himself down again; but when he had clambered down the wall, he saw the enchantress standing before him. "How canst thou dare," said she with angry look, "to descend into my garden and steal my rampion like a thief? Thou shalt suffer for it!" "Ah," answered he, "let mercy take the place of justice. I only made up my mind to do it out of necessity. My wife saw your rampion from the window, and felt such a longing for it that she would have died if she had not got some to eat." Then the enchantress allowed her anger to be softened, and said to him,

"I will allow thee to take away with thee as much rampion as thou wilt, only I make one condition, thou must give me the child which thy wife will bring into the world; it shall be well treated, and I will care for it like a mother."

The man in his terror consented to everything, and when the woman was brought to bed, the enchantress appeared at once, gave the child the name of Rapunzel, and took it away with her.

Rapunzel grew into the most beautiful child beneath the sun. When she was twelve years old, the enchantress shut her into a tower, which lay in a forest, and had neither stairs nor door, but quite at the top was a little window. When the enchantress wanted to go in, she placed herself beneath this, and cried,

> *"Rapunzel, Rapunzel,*
>
> *Let down thy hair to me."*

Rapunzel had magnificent long hair, fine as spun gold, and when she heard the voice of the enchantress she unfastened her braided tresses, wound them round one of the hooks of the window above, and then the hair fell twenty ells down, and the enchantress climbed up by it.

After a year or two, it came to pass that the King's son rode through the forest and went by the tower. Then he heard a song, which was so charming that he stood still and listened. This was Rapunzel, who in her solitude passed her time in letting her sweet voice resound. The King's son wanted to climb up to her, and looked for the door of the tower, but none was to be found. He rode home, but the singing had so deeply touched his heart, that every day he went out into the forest and listened to it. Once when he was thus standing behind a tree, he saw that an enchantress came there, and he heard how she cried,

"Rapunzel, Rapunzel,

Let down thy hair."

Then Rapunzel let down the braids of her hair, and the enchantress climbed up to her. The next day when it began to grow dark, he went to the tower and cried,

"Rapunzel, Rapunzel,

Let down thy hair."

Immediately, the hair fell down and the King's son climbed up.

At first, Rapunzel was terribly frightened when a man such as her eyes had never yet beheld, came to her; but the King's son told her that his heart had been so stirred that he had to see her. Then Rapunzel lost her fear, and when he asked her if she would take him for her husband, and she saw that he was young and handsome, she thought, "He will love me more than old Dame Gothel does;" and she said yes, and laid her hand in his. She said, "I will willingly go away with thee, but I do not know how to get down. Bring with thee a skein of silk every time that thou comest, and I will weave a ladder with it, and when that is ready, I will descend, and thou wilt take me on thy horse." They agreed that he should come to her every evening, for the old woman came by day.

The enchantress remarked nothing of this, until once Rapunzel said to her, "Tell me, Dame Gothel, how it happens that you are so much heavier for me to draw up than the young King's son? He is with me in a moment." "Ah! thou wicked child," cried the enchantress. "What do I hear thee say! I thought I had separated thee from all the world, and yet thou hast deceived me!" In her anger, she clutched Rapunzel's beautiful tresses, wrapped them twice round her left hand, seized a pair of scissors with the right, and snip, snap, they were cut off, and the lovely braids lay on the ground. And she was

so pitiless that she took poor Rapunzel into a desert where she had to live in great grief and misery.

On the same day, however, that she cast out Rapunzel, the enchantress in the evening fastened the braids of hair which she had cut off to the hook of the window, and when the King's son came and cried,

"Rapunzel, Rapunzel,

Let down thy hair,"

she let the hair down.

The King's son ascended, but he did not find his dearest Rapunzel above, but the enchantress, who gazed at him with wicked and venomous looks. "Aha!" she cried mockingly, "Thou wouldst fetch thy dearest, but the beautiful bird sits no longer singing in the nest; the cat has got it, and will scratch out thy eyes as well. Rapunzel is lost to thee; thou wilt never see her more."

The King's son was beside himself with pain, and in his despair he leapt down from the tower. He escaped with his life, but the thorns into which he fell, pierced his eyes. Then he wandered quite blind about the forest, ate nothing but roots and berries, and did nothing but lament and weep over the loss of his dearest wife.

Thus he roamed about in misery for some years, and at length came to the desert where Rapunzel, with the twins to which she had given birth, a boy and a girl, lived in wretchedness. He heard a voice, and it seemed so familiar to him that he went toward it, and when he approached, Rapunzel knew him and fell on his neck and wept. Two of her tears wetted his eyes and they grew clear again, and he could see with them as before. He led her to his kingdom where he was joyfully received, and they lived for a long time afterwards, happy and contented.

Lydia Saldana, 11th grade

Can companionship lead to harm? Most people would say yes because spending time with the wrong type of people can lead kids down a wayward path filled with troublesome behavior, leading them to do things that they don't want to do. One time, my friends were forcing me to jump into a lake. The lake was all murky and we could not see what was at the bottom. We were not even sure if there were snakes around too. I ended up giving in to what they wanted me to do and jumped in. I took this action because I did not want to feel left out and I also wanted to experience something new. After I jumped in it was all fun and games until I got all cut up on my legs from rocks that we could not see. When this happened and I looked down at my legs and saw all of the cuts and scrapes, it looked as if I had just gone through a blender. When I felt the pain, it took me back to when I was a little kid and fell off my bike and scraped my hands and knees. I was also very upset because it was the day right before my big party and my legs were covered in all of these cuts and scrapes.

On the other hand, the same pressure from other friends can be beneficial. For example, one time, I went out with one of my friends to Six Flags. While we were there, she was pressuring me to ride the roller coasters but I didn't want to. She kept pressuring me over and over until I gave in. Again, I didn't want to feel left out and I wanted to try something new, so I decided to get on with her. The outcome of this incident was beneficial because I had so much fun and I overcame my fear of riding roller coasters.

When you need a little encouragement, look for companionship from friends who will help you to overcome your fears, not those who will put you in a situation that can be dangerous or harmful. They can help you spend your time wisely.

Part V
Structures for Commentary About Plot

Bank of Text Structure Choices

For Commentary About Plot

| I used to think (truism) | But this happened | So now I think ... (truism) |

| This bad situation happened | How I should have reacted | How I did react | Now I know ... |

| A big mistake someone made | What this caused | How it turned out | If the mistake had not happened | Truism |

| Truism | A bad way (and why) | A better way (and why) | The best way |

| What it is | Kinds of it | Where you can find it | Parts of it | Truism about it |

NAME

Read the story.
Think about promises you've made or promises other people have made to you.
Write an essay about how hard it can be to keep a promise.

MY TRUISM

STORY OF MY THINKING

| I used to think (truism) | But this happened | So now I think ... (truism) |

MY KERNEL ESSAY

1. _____

2. _____

3. _____

_____

_____

_____

TRUISM EXAMPLES

1. People should keep all the promises they make.

2. People should think before they make promises.

3. _____

Rumpelstiltskin

By the side of a wood, in a country a long way off, ran a fine stream of water; and upon the stream there stood a mill. The miller's house was close by, and the miller, you must know, had a very beautiful daughter. She was, moreover, very shrewd and clever; and the miller was so proud of her that he one day told the king of the land, who used to come and hunt in the wood, that his daughter could spin gold out of straw. Now this king was very fond of money; and when he heard the miller's boast, his greediness was raised, and he sent for the girl to be brought before him. Then he led her to a chamber in his palace where there was a great heap of straw, and gave her a spinning wheel, and said, "All this must be spun into gold before morning, as you love your life." It was in vain that the poor maiden said that it was only a silly boast of her father, for that she could do no such thing as spin straw into gold; the chamber door was locked, and she was left alone.

She sat down in one corner of the room, and began to bewail her hard fate when, on a sudden, the door opened and a droll-looking little man hobbled in, and said, "Good morrow to you, my good lass; what are you weeping for?" "Alas!" said she, "I must spin this straw into gold, and I know not how." "What will you give me," said the hobgoblin, "to do it for you?" "My necklace," replied the maiden. He took her at her word sat himself down to the wheel, and whistled and sang,

> "Round about, round about,
>
> Lo and behold!
>
> Reel away, reel away,
>
> Straw into gold!"

And round about the wheel went merrily; the work was quickly done, and the straw was all spun into gold.

When the king came and saw this, he was greatly astonished and pleased; but his heart grew still more greedy of gain, and he shut up the poor miller's daughter again with a fresh task. Then she knew not what to do and sat down once more to weep; but the dwarf soon opened the door and said, "What will you give me to do your task?" "The ring on my finger," said she. So her little friend took the ring and began to work at the wheel again, and whistled and sang,

> "Round about, round about,
>
> Lo and behold!
>
> Reel away, reel away,
>
> Straw into gold!"

Long before morning, all was done again.

The king was greatly delighted to see all this glittering treasure; but still, he had not enough. So he took the miller's daughter to a yet larger heap and said, "All this must be spun tonight; and if it is, you shall be my queen." As soon as she was alone that dwarf came in, and said, "What will you give me to spin gold for you this third time?" "I have nothing left," said she.

"Then say you will give me," said the little man, "the first little child that you may have when you are queen." "That may never be," thought the miller's daughter; and as she knew no other way to get her task done, she said she would do what he asked. Round went the wheel again to the old song, and the manikin once more spun the heap into gold. The king came in the morning, and, finding all he wanted, was forced to keep his word; so he married the miller's daughter, and she really became queen.

At the birth of her first little child, she was very glad and forgot the dwarf. But one day, he came into her room where she was sitting playing with her baby and put her in mind of it. Then, she grieved sorely at her misfortune and said she would give him all the wealth of the kingdom if he would let her off, but in vain; till at last, her tears softened him, and he said, "I will give you three days' grace, and if during that time, you tell me my name, you shall keep your child."

Now the queen lay awake all night, thinking of all the odd names that she had ever heard; and she sent messengers all over the land to find out new ones. The next day, the little man came, and she began with TIMOTHY, ICHABOD, BENJAMIN, JEREMIAH, and all the names she could remember; but to all and each of them he said, "Madam, that is not my name."

The second day she began with all the comical names she could hear of, BANDY-LEGS, HUNCHBACK, CROOK-SHANKS, and so on; but the little gentleman still said to every one of them, "Madam, that is not my name."

The third day, one of the messengers came back, and said, "I have traveled two days without hearing of any other names; but yesterday, I saw a little hut; and before the hut burnt a fire; and round about the fire a funny little dwarf was dancing upon one leg, and singing,

'Merrily the feast I'll make.

Today I'll brew, tomorrow bake;

Merrily I'll dance and sing,

For next day will a stranger bring.

Little does my lady dream

Rumpelstiltskin is my name!'"

When the queen heard this, she jumped for joy, and as soon as her little friend came, she sat down upon her throne. Then the little man cried out, "Now, lady, what is my name?" "Is it JOHN?" asked she. "No, madam!" "Is it TOM?" "No, madam!" "Is it JEMMY?" "It is not." "Can your name be RUMPELSTILTSKIN?" said the lady slyly. "Some witch told you that! Some witch told you that!" cried the little man and dashed his right foot in a rage so deep into the floor that he was forced to lay hold of it with both hands to pull it out.

Then he made the best of his way off, and all the court jeered at him for having had so much trouble for nothing!

Angelina Hernandez, 4th grade

(Using the Onion text structure)

1. People should always keep their promises.

2. I told my brother that he could have some of my Doritos and then I did not share them.

3. I told my brother that he could play on my tablet and then I did not share with him.

4. I told my brother that I would get him a game and I did not do it.

5. Even if I didn't, I still think people should always do what they say.

Julian Ponce, 6th grade

(Using the Story of My Thinking text structure)

1. I used to think that it's easy to keep promises.

2. I made promises to play games with my friends, to take the garbage out, to bring food for my friends on the last day of school. All of these promises I kept and it was easy. Well, it was easy for some of them, and a little harder for others.

3. But one day at home, my mom reminded me that I had forgotten that I promised to go outside and clean the stones on the sidewalk path. There was so much going on, I forgot all about it. I made up excuses (Oak pollen! And it's raining!) but I really just forgot the promise.

4. So now I think the more promises you make, the easier it is to forget about them. And you fail.

Katalina Luna, 5th grade

(Using the Story of My Thinking text structure)

My truism: Sometimes people make promises they'll regret.

1. I used to think it is easy to make a promise and keep it.

2. But then I made a promise to run with my mom Tuesday and Thursday and it was so tiring I knew I shouldn't have made that promise.

3. So now I think that next time before making a promise, I should consider what it would be like to fulfill it.

Kimberlie Gonzalez, 7th grade

(Using the 11-Minute Essay text structure)

Everyone has gone through the difficulty of keeping and making promises. The promises you make are the ones you have to keep close to your heart. Although keeping a promise may seem difficult, the outcome of keeping a promise might give you something quite lovely and pleasing in return.

A simple promise can be distinguished between two friends or perhaps two loved ones. Either it's keeping something between others or promising one to make a huge impact, it'll bring them far in life. In the movie *Up*, Carl promises Elle, his deceased wife, that he'll do anything it takes to get to Paradise Falls. With lots of dedication and patience during his quest, he arrives at Paradise Falls with the thought of Elle in his mind. As he arrived, he sees the beautiful waterfall gushing and spewing water as the gray rough rocks surrounded the peaceful waves. The remarkable journey surely brought him far in his life as the promise wielded love and happiness.

Fortunately for Hamilton, Laurens, Lafayette, and Mulligan, the promise they made brought them victory. In the Broadway musical, *Hamilton*, he and the rest of the abolitionists promised to fight in the war against the British forces, even if it meant sacrificing themselves. With the hard work and determination, they won the battle of Yorktown against the British troops. In the end, their promise brought them victory as they celebrated their victories against Britain.

In the end, their promises led them far in their life with many great outcomes. Sometimes the promises you keep that contain love and determination will bring you beneficial things such as victories or completion of goals that will bring you very far in life.

22 Gifts

Read the story.
Think about how other people bring us gifts, some good and some bad.
Write an essay about how even negative gifts can add to our lives.

MY TRUISM

HINDSIGHT REFLECTIONS

| This bad situation happened | How I should have reacted | How I did react | Now I know ... |

MY KERNEL ESSAY

1. _____

2. _____

3. _____

4. _____

_____

_____

TRUISM EXAMPLES

1. What goes around, comes around. _____

2. Not every friend wishes us well. _____

3. _____

The Sleeping Beauty

A king and queen once upon a time reigned in a country a great way off, where there were in those days fairies. Now this king and queen had plenty of money, and plenty of fine clothes to wear, and plenty of good things to eat and drink, and a coach to ride out in every day. But though they had been married many years, they had no children, and this grieved them very much indeed.

But one day the queen had a little girl, so very beautiful that the king could not cease looking on it for joy and said he would hold a great feast and make merry, and show the child to all the land. So he asked his kinsmen, and nobles, and friends, and neighbors. But the queen said, "I will have the fairies also, that they might be kind and good to our little daughter." Now there were thirteen fairies in the kingdom; but as the king and queen had only twelve golden dishes for them to eat out of, they were forced to leave out one of the fairies without asking her. So twelve fairies came, each with a long white wand in her hand; and after the feast was over they gathered round in a ring and gave all their best gifts to the little princess. One gave her goodness, another beauty, another riches, and so on till she had all that was good in the world.

Just as eleven of them had done blessing her, a great noise was heard in the courtyard, and word was brought that the thirteenth fairy was come into the dining hall. Now, as she had not been asked to the feast, she was very angry and scolded the king and queen very much and set to work to take her revenge. So she cried out, "The king's daughter shall, in her fifteenth year, be wounded by a spindle and fall down dead." Then the twelfth of the friendly fairies, who had not yet given her gift, came forward and said that the evil wish must be fulfilled, but that she could soften its mischief; so her gift was that the king's daughter, when the spindle wounded her, should not really die, but should only fall asleep for a hundred years.

However, the king hoped still to save his dear child altogether from the threatened evil; so he ordered that all the spindles in the kingdom should be bought up and burnt. But all the gifts of the first eleven fairies were in the meantime fulfilled; for the princess was so beautiful, and well behaved, and good, and wise, that everyone who knew her loved her.

It happened that, on the very day she was fifteen years old, the king and queen were not at home, and she was left alone in the palace. So she roved about by herself and looked at all the rooms and chambers, till at last, she came to an old tower to which there was a narrow staircase ending with a little door. The door sprang open, and there sat an old lady spinning away very busily. "Why, how now, good mother," said the princess; "what are you doing there?" "Spinning," said the old lady, and nodded her head, humming a tune, while buzz! went the wheel. "How prettily that little thing turns round!" said the princess and took the spindle and began to try and spin. But scarcely had she touched it before the fairy's prophecy was fulfilled; the spindle wounded her, and she fell down lifeless on the ground.

However, she was not dead, but had only fallen into a deep sleep; and the king and the queen, who had just come home, and all their court, fell asleep too; and the horses slept in the stables, the dogs in the court, the pigeons on the house-top.

A large hedge of thorns soon grew round the palace, and every year it became higher and thicker, till at last, the old palace was surrounded and hidden so that not even the roof or the chimneys could be seen. But there went a report through all the land of the beautiful sleeping Briar Rose: from time to time, several kings' sons came and tried to break through the thicket into the palace. This, however, none of them could ever do.

22 After many, many years there came a king's son into that land, and an old man told him the story of the thicket of thorns and how a beautiful palace stood behind it, and how a wonderful princess, called Briar Rose, lay in it asleep, with all her court. Then the young prince said, "All this shall not frighten me; I will go and see this Briar Rose."

Now that very day, the hundred years were ended and, as the prince came to the thicket, he saw nothing but beautiful flowering shrubs, through which he went with ease; and they shut in after him as thick as ever. Then he came at last to the palace, and there in the court lay the dogs asleep; and the horses were standing in the stables; and on the roof sat the pigeons fast asleep, with their heads under their wings.

Then he went on still farther, till at last, he came to the old tower and opened the door of the little room in which Briar Rose was; and there she lay, fast asleep on a couch by the window. She looked so beautiful that he could not take his eyes off her, so he stooped down and gave her a kiss. But the moment he kissed her, she opened her eyes and awoke and smiled upon him; and they went out together; and soon the king and queen also awoke, and all the court, and gazed on each other with great wonder.

And then the prince and Briar Rose were married, and the wedding feast was given; and they lived happily together all their lives long.

Jose Hernandez Martinez, 11th grade

Life is such a beautiful gift. The flowers bloom ever so bright, and the trees dance with delight. Birds sing endless songs, and insects shout. But with every Yang, there is also a Yin. Where there is life, death follows.

This was my situation. I was with high school seniors who once debated on whether or not they should end their chapter in the book of life. So many possible outcomes in this situation yet choosing one out of many saved a life that day. No one should have to go through these thoughts, but no matter who you are, eventually they'll catch up. That day I thought about myself, about how much I could benefit from these actions. And personally I am a very selfless person, but that day is agonizing to remember.

One night, I left my house with rage from a fight that broke out with my mother and me. We had been arguing like this for a while, and this was the last straw. I stormed out of the house and into my car, never wanting to see my mother again. So many thoughts ran through my mind, it seemed as if time was motionless. "She won't care if I'm gone; why would she?" I kept repeating this question endlessly. Negative thoughts clouded my mind, like heavy fog is to a captain's ship. The only difference was that there was no lighthouse for me.

Hesitation came first, doubt, then confidence. Shifting the vehicle into drive and slamming into the gas pedal as far as it will let me. Knowing that a sweet release was waiting for me, I headed straight toward a house, not caring who or what was on the other side of those walls. The house closed in on me when I slammed on the brakes, but fortunately I had stopped the car before a collision. In that moment, I realized that my selfish desire to end it all would have devastating effects on those I love. It even would alter the lives of people I didn't know. Attempting to end my life could have ruined the lives of others.

My head hit the windshield, but it was clear that I was alive. I sat in the car and looked out at the night. I realized that everyone I love and care about would have been left behind with the path I was taking.

Now I know I should have talked calmly to my mother. Knowing that my actions would have caused such pain was a burden I didn't want to carry. Now I know that life is a precious gift and it is short, but I must live it to the fullest.

NAME

Read the story.
Think about how people feel about making mistakes.
Write an essay about a bad choice that turned out well.

MY TRUISM

SURPRISE ENDING

| A big mistake someone made | What this caused | How it turned out | If the mistake had not happened | Truism |

MY KERNEL ESSAY

1.

2.

3.

4.

5.

TRUISM EXAMPLES

1. A mistake can have surprising results.

2. Some mistakes are punished, but others are rewarded.

3.

Snow White

Once upon a time in the middle of winter, when the flakes of snow were falling like feathers from the sky, a queen sat at a window sewing, and the frame of the window was made of black ebony. And whilst she was sewing and looking out of the window at the snow, she pricked her finger with the needle, and three drops of blood fell upon the snow. And she thought to herself, "Would that I had a child as white as snow, as red as blood, and as black as the wood of the window-frame."

Soon after that she had a little daughter, and her hair was as black as ebony; and she was called Little Snow White. And when the child was born, the Queen died. After a year had passed, the King took another wife. She was proud and haughty. She had a wonderful looking glass, and, when she stood in front of it and said,

> "Looking glass, Looking glass,
> on the wall,
>
> Who in this land is the fairest of all?"

the looking glass answered,

> "Thou, O Queen, art the fairest of all!"

Then she was satisfied, for the looking glass spoke the truth.

But when Snow White was seven years old she was as beautiful as the day. And once, when the Queen asked her looking-glass,

> "Looking glass, Looking glass,
> on the wall,
>
> Who in this land is the fairest of all?"

it answered,

> "Thou art fairer than all who are here,
> Lady Queen.
>
> But more beautiful still is Snow White,
> as I ween."

Then the Queen was shocked, and turned yellow and green with envy. From that hour, she hated Snow White so much. She called a huntsman, and said, "Take the child away into the forest. Kill her, and bring me back her heart." The huntsman took her away; but when he had drawn his knife, she began to weep, and said, "Ah, dear huntsman, leave me my life!" And the huntsman had pity on her and said, "Run away, then, you poor child." He stabbed a young boar and cut out its heart and took it to the Queen.

Snow White ran and she saw a little cottage. Everything in the cottage was small. There was a table on which were seven little plates, seven little knives and forks, and mugs. Against the wall stood seven little beds. Little Snow White was so hungry that she ate some from each plate. Then she laid herself down and went to sleep.

When it was quite dark the owners of the cottage came back; they were seven dwarfs who dug and delved in the mountains for ore. They lit their seven candles, and they saw that someone had been there. But the seventh, when he looked at his bed, saw little Snow White lying asleep. And the dwarfs did not wake her up.

When it was morning, little Snow White awoke, and was frightened when she saw the seven dwarfs. But they were friendly.

"My name is Snow White." She told them that her stepmother had wished to have her killed, and that she had found their dwelling. The dwarfs said, "If you will take care of our house, you can stay with us." "Yes," said Snow White and she stayed with them. The girl was alone the whole day, so the good dwarfs said, "Beware of your stepmother; be sure to let no one come in."

But the Queen went to her looking glass and said,

> "Looking glass, Looking glass,
> on the wall,
>
> Who in this land is the fairest of all?"

23 and the glass answered,

> "Oh, Queen, thou art fairest of all I see,
>
> But over the hills, where the
> seven dwarfs dwell,
>
> Snow White is still alive and well,
>
> And none is so fair as she."

Then she knew that little Snow White was still alive. And so she dressed herself like an old peddler woman. She went over the seven mountains to the seven dwarfs, and cried, "Pretty things to sell." Snow White unbolted the door and bought the pretty laces. "Child," said the old woman, "come, I will lace you properly for once." But the old woman laced so tightly that Snow White lost her breath and fell down as if dead. "Now I am the most beautiful," said the Queen to herself and ran away.

In the evening when the seven dwarfs came home, they cut the laces; then she came to life again. When the dwarfs heard what had happened they said, "The old peddler woman was the wicked Queen; let no one come in when we are not with you."

But the wicked woman reached home and asked,

> "Looking glass, Looking glass,
> on the wall,
>
> Who in this land is the fairest of all?"

and it answered as before,

> "Snow White is still alive and well,
>
> And none is so fair as she."

When she heard that, she made a poisonous comb. Then she disguised herself and went over the seven mountains to the seven dwarfs, knocked at the door, and cried, "Good things to sell," and pulled the poisonous comb out and held it up. It pleased the girl so well that she opened the door. The old woman said, "Put the comb in your hair," and the girl fell down senseless. The wicked woman said, "You are done for now," and she went away.

When the seven dwarfs came home, they saw Snow White lying as if dead. They found the poisoned comb. Scarcely had they taken it out when Snow White came to herself. Then they warned her once more to open the door to no one.

The Queen, at home, went in front of the glass and said,

> "Looking glass, Looking glass,
> on the wall,
>
> Who in this land is the fairest of all?"
>
> "Snow White is still alive and well,
>
> And none is so fair as she."

"Snow White shall die!" she cried.

Thereupon she made a poisonous apple. When the apple was ready she dressed herself up as a country woman, and went over the seven mountains to the seven dwarfs. She knocked at the door. Snow White said, "I cannot let anyone in; the seven dwarfs have forbidden me." "I shall soon get rid of my apples," the woman answered. "There, I will give you one."

"No," said Snow White, "I dare not take anything." "Are you afraid of poison?" said the old woman; "Look, I will cut the apple in two pieces." Snow White stretched out her hand and hardly had she a bit of it in her mouth than she fell down dead. The dwarfs found Snow White lying upon the ground; she breathed no longer; the poor child was dead. They laid her upon a bier and wept three days long. They had a transparent coffin of glass made, and they laid her in it, and wrote her name upon it in golden letters, and that she was a king's daughter.

It happened that a king's son came into the forest, and saw the coffin on the mountain, and Snow White within it. Then he said to the dwarfs, "Let me have the coffin. I will honor her as my dearest possession." The good dwarfs took pity upon him and gave him the coffin.

And now the King's son had it carried away by his servants. They stumbled over a tree stump, and with the shock, the poisonous piece of apple came out of her throat. She opened her eyes. "Where am I?" she cried. The King's son, full of joy, said, "You are with me," and said, "I love you more than everything in the world; come with me to my father's palace, you shall be my wife."

And Snow White was willing, and went with him, and their wedding was held with great show and splendor. But Snow White's wicked stepmother was also bidden to the feast. When she had arrayed herself in beautiful clothes, she went before the Looking glass, and said,

> "Looking glass, Looking glass,
> on the wall,
>
> Who in this land is the fairest of all?"

the glass answered,

> "Oh, Queen, of all here the fairest
> art thou,
>
> But the young Queen is fairer
> by far as I trow."

And when she went in, she knew Snow White; and she stood still with rage and fear, and could not stir. But iron slippers had already been put upon the fire, and they were brought in with tongs and set before her. Then she was forced to put on the red-hot shoes and dance until she dropped down dead.

Student Work Samples: Mistakes

Kaly Burciaga, 5th grade

1. My truism: Stay true to your beliefs.

2. I argued with my mom and stepdad.

3. Me and my mom and dad are not talking.

4. We're still not talking.

5. If we hadn't argued, we would be talking.

6. Some mistakes can affect your relationships with loved ones.

Vivian Sanchez, 6th grade

My truism: Sometimes, mistakes lead to success.

1. The queen tried to kill Snow White because she was jealous.

2. So she ordered the huntsman to kill Snow White.

3. The queen failed.

4. If the queen had not tried to kill Snow White, Snow White wouldn't have met the dwarfs who were kind to her.

5. Sometimes, jealousy can be overruled by kindness.

James Gaytan, 6th grade

1. The guard made a big mistake when he did not kill Snow White.

2. This caused Snow White to live.

3. In the end, the Queen died.

4. If the huntsman had not made his mistake, Snow White would not have been alive.

5. Sometimes a mistake is the right thing to do.

Allan Keyes, parent

1. I was trying to add a concert to our family calendar while I was on the rig. I wanted to see the Dirty River Boys.

2. Sarah rejected the event.

3. My phone binged. "What was that?" "My wife rejected the event." All my buddies laughed. She wanted to go to IKEA.

4. Now I still throw events on the family calendar, but if Sarah rejects it, then I know she has something else planned.

5. I just don't tell my buddies.

Notes

Kindness

NAME

Read the story.
Think about how much you value kindness in the world.
Write an essay about how people react to kindness in different ways.

MY TRUISM

WAYS TO DO SOMETHING

| Truism | A bad way (and why) | A better way (and why) | The best way |

MY KERNEL ESSAY

1. _____

2. _____

3. _____

4. _____

_____

_____

TRUISM EXAMPLES

1. Sometimes kindness is rewarded and sometimes it's not.

2. The kindness we send out always comes back.

3. _____

Snow White and Rose Red

A poor widow once lived in a little cottage. In front of the cottage was a garden, in which were growing two rose trees; one of these bore white roses, and the other red.

She had two children. One was called Snow White, and the other Rose Red; and they were as religious and loving, busy and untiring, as any two children ever were.

In the evening, when snow was falling, sitting by the hearth, the good widow would read aloud to them from a big book.

One evening, as they were all sitting cozily together like this, there was a knock at the door.

"Rose Red!" said her mother; "open the door; it is surely some traveler seeking shelter." But it was a bear that thrust his big, black head in at the open door. Rose Red cried out and sprang back, and Snow White hid herself behind her mother's bed. The bear said, "Do not be afraid; I am half-frozen."

"Poor bear!" the mother replied; "come in and lie by the fire." Then she called Snow White and Rose Red, telling them that the bear was kind and would not harm them.

"Children," begged the bear; "knock some of the snow off my coat." So they brought the broom and brushed the bear's coat quite clean.

After that, he stretched himself out in front of the fire, happy and comfortable. Before long, they were all quite good friends, and the children began to play with their visitor, pulling his thick fur, or placing their feet on his back, or rolling him over and over.

After this, every evening the bear came and lay by the fire, so they became quite fond of their curious playmate, and the door was not ever bolted in the evening until he had appeared.

When springtime came, one morning the bear said to Snow White, "Now I must leave you, and all the summer long I shall not be able to come back."

"Where, then, are you going, dear Bear?" asked Snow White.

"I have to go to the woods to protect my treasure from the bad dwarfs."

Snow White was very sad when she said good-bye to the good-natured beast, and unfastened the door; but in going out, he was caught by a hook in the lintel, and a scrap of his fur being torn, Snow White thought there was something shining like gold through the rent. Soon he was hidden among the trees.

One day the mother sent her children into the wood to pick up sticks. They found a big tree lying on the ground, and they noticed a dwarf, with a shriveled-up face and a snow-white beard in the tree trunk. The tiny fellow could not free himself. He stared at the children with his red, fiery eyes, and called out, "Why are you standing there? Come and help me!"

Despite the dwarf's bad temper, the girls took all possible pains to release him. Snow White took out her scissors and, in a moment, set the dwarf free by cutting off the end of his beard.

"Clumsy creatures, to cut off a bit of my beautiful beard." Then he swung a sack of gold across his shoulder and went off.

Not long afterward when the two sisters went to the brook to catch fish for dinner, they heard the same dwarf yell, "Don't you see that a wretch of a fish is pulling me in?"

The dwarf had been sitting angling from the side of the stream when, by ill-luck, a big fish taking the bait was dragging the dwarf after it.

The girls caught hold of him firmly. Again the scissors were taken out, and the tangled portion of his beard was cut off.

The dwarf exclaimed in a great rage, "Is this how you damage my beard?" Then he fetched a sack of pearls and hobbled off.

Soon after this, the poor widow sent her children to the town. On the way, they heard a heartrending cry, and they saw, with horror, that an eagle had seized the dwarf and was just about to carry him off. The kind children took a firm hold of the little man, and the eagle took to flight.

The little man squeaked, "See my little coat; you have damaged it, you clumsy, officious things!" Then he picked up a sack of jewels and slipped out of sight.

The maidens were quite used to his ungrateful ways; so they went on their way.

On their way home, once more they ran across their dwarf friend, admiring and counting the brilliant stones from his sack of jewels.

"What are you gazing at, making ugly faces?" cried the dwarf with rage. Suddenly with a great growl, a big black bear joined the party. The dwarf cried out in very evident anguish,

"Dear Mr. Bear, forgive me, I pray! I will render to you all my treasure. Grant me my life! I beg of you to take those two children, good Mr. Bear, and let me go!"

But the bear would not be moved by his speeches. He gave the ill-disposed creature a blow with his paw, and he lay lifeless on the ground.

Meanwhile, the maidens heard a well-known voice that called out, "Snow White, Rose Red, stay! Do not fear. I will accompany you."

Suddenly the bear-skin slipped to the ground, and there before them was standing a handsome man, completely garmented in gold, who said,

"I am a king's son, who was enchanted by the wicked dwarf lying over there. He stole my treasure, and compelled me to roam the woods transformed into a big bear until his death should set me free. Therefore he has only received a well-deserved punishment."

Some time afterward, Snow White married the Prince, and Rose Red his brother.

They shared between them the enormous treasure which the dwarf had collected in his cave.

The old mother spent many happy years with her children.

Natalie Lawinger, 11th grade

1. Kind-hearted people fix what needs fixing.

2. People help homeless victims.

3. People help tsunami victims.

4. People who care come together to fix things.

Thunder rolls in, lightning strikes, winds pick up, power goes out, buildings fall, people are trapped inside their own homes, and then the storm leaves. A hurricane collides with a country and wins. Neighboring countries, citizens of the world, refuse to allow the affected population to suffer more than they already have. When necessary, people are always willing to work with each other to fix what needs fixing. Regardless if it is an earthquake, hurricane, typhoon, tsunami, or just a war-torn territory, kind-hearted souls are here to lend a hand.

The water came in and washed away lives, picked away at hearts; a tsunami came to Japan and so did suffering. There was a plea. Orphans begging to go home, mothers calling for their children, tears, and that plea was heard by the world. Some packed their lives in a suitcase and took off to help people they'd never met. Others raised money, with songs, with lemonade stands, with heavy hearts, and a city was built again, with songs, with lemonade stands, and with smiles.

The world doesn't need a superhero. We've done well without one, and when it comes down to it, could a superhero really fix our problems? Could a superhero really prevent disaster? No, no one can prevent disaster (of the natural kind) and no single person can fix what's broken; but we can and do help ease the pain and loss. People aren't gods; we can't choose who gets hurt and who doesn't. We can only work with what we have. People can give their hearts and lives to a cause, and already do. People can make a difference together just by caring enough to try.

NAME _____

Read the story.

Think about the behavior of different guests you've seen in your home.

Write an essay about the importance of using good manners.

MY TRUISM _____

DESCRIPTION

| What it is | Kinds of it | Where you can find it | Parts of it | Truism about it |

MY KERNEL ESSAY

I. _____

2. _____

3. _____

4. _____

5. _____

TRUISM EXAMPLES

1. When someone has bad manners, they don't get a second invitation.

2. Knowing good manners doesn't mean you have to use them.

3. _____

The Story of the Three Bears

Once upon a time, there were Three Bears, who lived together in a house of their own, in a wood. One of them was a Little Wee Bear, and one was a Middle-sized Bear, and the other was a Great Big Bear. They had each a bowl for their porridge: a little bowl for the Little Wee Bear, and a middle-sized bowl for the Middle-sized Bear, and a great bowl for the Great Big Bear. And they had each a chair to sit in: a little chair for the Little Wee Bear, and a middle-sized chair for the Middle-sized Bear, and a great chair for the Great Big Bear. And they had each a bed to sleep in: a little bed for the Little Wee Bear, and a middle-sized bed for the Middle-sized Bear, and a great bed for the Great Big Bear.

One day, after they had made the porridge for their breakfast, they walked out into the wood while the porridge was cooling. And while they were away, a little girl called Goldilocks passed by the house and looked in at the window. And then she peeped in at the keyhole. Seeing nobody in the house, she lifted the latch. The door was not fastened because the Bears were good Bears, who did nobody any harm and never suspected that anybody would harm them. So Goldilocks opened the door and went in; and well pleased was she when she saw the porridge on the table. She was an impudent, rude little girl, and so she set about helping herself.

First she tasted the porridge of the Great Big Bear, and that was too hot for her. Next she tasted the porridge of the Middle-sized Bear, but that was too cold for her. And then she went to the porridge of the Little Wee Bear, and tasted it, and that was neither too hot nor too cold, but just right, and she liked it so well that she ate it all up, every bit!

Then Goldilocks sat down in the chair of the Great Big Bear, but that was too hard for her. And then she sat down in the chair of the Middle-sized Bear, and that was too soft for her. But when she sat down in the chair of the Little Wee Bear, that was neither too hard nor too soft, but just right. So she seated herself in it, and there she sat till the bottom of the chair came out, and down she came, plump upon the ground; and that made her very cross, for she was a bad-tempered little girl.

Now, being determined to rest, Goldilocks went upstairs into the bedchamber in which the Three Bears slept. And first she lay down upon the bed of the Great Big Bear, but that was too high at the head for her. And next she lay down upon the bed of the Middle-sized Bear, and that was too high at the foot for her. And then she lay down upon the bed of the Little Wee Bear, and that was neither too high at the head nor at the foot, but just right. So she covered herself up comfortably and lay there till she fell fast asleep.

By this time, the Three Bears came home to breakfast. Now careless Goldilocks had left the spoon of the Great Big Bear standing in his porridge.

"SOMEBODY HAS BEEN AT MY PORRIDGE!"

said the Great Big Bear in his great, rough, gruff voice.

Then the Middle-sized Bear looked at his porridge and saw the spoon was standing in it too.

"SOMEBODY HAS BEEN AT MY PORRIDGE!"

said the Middle-sized Bear in his middle-sized voice.

Then the Little Wee Bear looked at his, and there was the spoon in the porridge-bowl, but the porridge was all gone!

"SOMEBODY HAS BEEN AT MY PORRIDGE AND HAS EATEN IT ALL UP!"

said the Little Wee Bear in his little wee voice.

Upon this the Three Bears, seeing that someone had entered their house and eaten up the Little Wee Bear's breakfast, began to look about them. Now the careless Goldilocks had not put the hard cushion straight when she rose from the chair of the Great Big Bear.

"SOMEBODY HAS BEEN SITTING IN MY CHAIR!"

said the Great Big Bear in his great, rough, gruff voice.

And the careless Goldilocks had squatted down the soft cushion of the Middle-sized Bear.

"SOMEBODY HAS BEEN SITTING IN MY CHAIR!"

said the Middle-sized Bear in his middle-sized voice.

"SOMEBODY HAS BEEN SITTING IN MY CHAIR, AND HAS SAT THE BOTTOM THROUGH!"

said the Little Wee Bear in his little wee voice.

Then the Three Bears thought they had better make further search in case it was a burglar, so they went upstairs into their bedchamber. Now Goldilocks had pulled the pillow of the Great Big Bear out of its place.

"SOMEBODY HAS BEEN LYING IN MY BED!"

said the Great Big Bear in his great, rough, gruff voice.

And Goldilocks had pulled the bolster of the Middle-sized Bear out of its place.

"SOMEBODY HAS BEEN LYING IN MY BED!"

said the Middle-sized Bear in his middle-sized voice.

But when the Little Wee Bear came to look at his bed, there was the bolster in its place!

And the pillow was in its place upon the bolster!

And upon the pillow——?

There was Goldilocks's yellow head—which was not in its place, for she had no business there.

"SOMEBODY HAS BEEN LYING IN MY BED,—AND HERE SHE IS STILL!"

said the Little Wee Bear in his little wee voice.

Now Goldilocks awakened at once. Up she started, and when she saw the Three Bears on one side of the bed, she tumbled herself out at the other, and ran to the window. So naughty, frightened little Goldilocks jumped; and whether she broke her neck in the fall, or ran into the wood and was lost there, or found her way out of the wood and got whipped for being a bad girl, no one can say. But the Three Bears never saw anything more of her.

Madeline Caro, 5th grade

1. I don't always use my manners when I'm in public.

2. I sometimes burp out loud.

3. Especially when I'm drinking Coke.

4. And my mom gets mad at me and takes my Coke away.

5. So when people don't use their manners they get in trouble.

Mark Xin, 9th grade

1. Manners are quite simple actually when you really think about it, yet it seems that no one understands them. Manners can mean simply saying "Yes Ma'am," "No Ma'am," or "Yes, please."

2. You can be mannerly by being kind to others and knowing when it's appropriate to talk and when it isn't. For example, eating with your mouth open, or worse, talking while your mouth is full of food, are bad manners that a good number of people don't seem to recognize as bad.

3. You will see examples of good/bad manners throughout your life, oftentimes at school or work. It's not nice when you talk to people at lunch and they are chewing with their mouth open, or in the classroom having kids say "Yeah" instead of "Yes" or "Yes ma'am."

4. Part of having manners comes from being a good respectable human and the rest is being able to understand right from wrong.

5. People with bad manners are less respectable than people with good manners, and are oftentimes annoying and a pain to be around.

Ralph Stanford, 8th grade

1. What are manners? Manners are a certain type of etiquette you are taught growing up.

2. Example of manners are holding doors open for other people, using please and thank you, and using excuse me after releasing gas from mouth or rear end.

3. Nowadays older people use manners but we should be seeing it everywhere.

4. You use different manners for different settings, for example in public places, restaurants, parties, and many other places you can think of.

5. Manners are a lifestyle you should use all your life. It shows other people how you hold/care about and/or value yourself and others.

Part VI
Structures for Making an Argument

Bank of Text Structure Choices
For Making an Argument

CROSSING MY PATH

| Real life example | Truism | Example from story | How it relates to me today | Question about truism |

NOW AND LATER

| Problem | A shortcut solution | A long-term solution | How I would decide which is better |

FINDING THE TRUTH THROUGH EXPERIENCE

| I heard this | But I thought the opposite | Then I heard about this experience | Now I think this |

CURIOSITY

| I wondered ... | I figured out ... | Then I also figured out ... | Last I figured out ... | This all means that ... |

FIVE-PARAGRAPH ESSAY

| Truism | One way to tell (with example) | Another way to tell (with example) | Another way to tell (with example) | How this knowledge can help |

NAME

Read the story.

Think about how often we count on others in our circles of friends and family.

Write an essay about what causes groups to stick together or fall apart.

MY TRUISM

CROSSING MY PATH

Real life example	Truism	Example from story	How it relates to me today	Question about truism

MY KERNEL ESSAY

1. _____

2. _____

3. _____

4. _____

5. _____

_____

TRUISM EXAMPLES

1. Members in a group take care of each other.

2. One person's attitude can change a group.

3. _____

The Three Billy Goats Gruff

Once upon a time, there were three billy goats, who were to go up to the hillside to make themselves fat, and the name of all three was "Gruff."

On the way up was a bridge over a cascading stream they had to cross; and under the bridge lived a great ugly troll, with eyes as big as saucers, and a nose as long as a poker.

So first of all came the youngest Billy Goat Gruff to cross the bridge.

"Trip, trap, trip, trap!" went the bridge.

"Who's that tripping over my bridge?" roared the troll.

"Oh, it is only I, the tiniest Billy Goat Gruff, and I'm going up to the hillside to make myself fat," said the billy goat, with such a small voice.

"Now, I'm coming to gobble you up," said the troll.

"Oh, no! Pray don't take me. I'm too little, that I am," said the billy goat. "Wait a bit till the second Billy Goat Gruff comes. He's much bigger."

"Well, be off with you," said the troll.

A little while after came the second Billy Goat Gruff to cross the bridge.

"Trip, trap, trip, trap, trip, trap," went the bridge.

"Who's that tripping over my bridge?" roared the troll.

"Oh, it's the second Billy Goat Gruff, and I'm going up to the hillside to make myself fat," said the billy goat, who hadn't such a small voice.

"Now I'm coming to gobble you up," said the troll.

"Oh, no! Don't take me. Wait a little till the big Billy Goat Gruff comes. He's much bigger."

"Very well! Be off with you," said the troll.

But just then up came the big Billy Goat Gruff.

"Trip, trap, trip, trap, trip, trap!" went the bridge, for the billy goat was so heavy that the bridge creaked and groaned under him.

"Who's that tramping over my bridge?" roared the troll.

"It's I! The big Billy Goat Gruff," said the billy goat, who had an ugly hoarse voice of his own.

"Now I'm coming to gobble you up," roared the troll.

> "Well, come along! I've got two spears,
> And I'll poke your eyeballs out at your ears;
> I've got besides two curling-stones,
> And I'll crush you to bits, body and bones."

That was what the big billy goat said. And then he flew at the troll, and poked his eyes out with his horns, and crushed him to bits, body and bones, and tossed him out into the cascade, and after that he went up to the hillside. There the billy goats got so fat they were scarcely able to walk home again. And if the fat hasn't fallen off them, why, they're still fat; and so,

> Snip, snap, snout.
> This tale's told out.

Student Work Sample: Groups

Leia Barnett, 10th grade

For me, there was a time when few things appeared as inherently scary as a group project. I am an artist, and I have identified as such since middle school and I believed that that meant finding success alone. When I was fourteen, however, I discovered the importance behind working well with others, and the benefits of cooperative group-minded team work. At the time, I was just beginning to create well developed, presentable art pieces, occasionally displayed in The Art District of my hometown, in the windows of little trinket shops along the main thoroughfare that ran through The District. This area was my favorite part of town and I cherished creating pieces that the residents of my city could enjoy.

One day, my art teacher came to me with a unique and exciting opportunity. She was eager to tell me that she had just been presented with the opportunity to showcase the work of her top students downtown. There was, however, a catch to this scenario, that being, in order to create a piece, I was required to work with another student. It was, however, a way to get my early work into the community, so I begrudgingly accepted, with a bad attitude and a closed mind. The following week presented itself as challenging in a vast number of ways. My partner was loud, and I was quiet, I loved to work to the sound of eighties glam metal, and she preferred the likes of Ariana Grande and Sam Smith. Aside from the intense personality clashes, I began realizing that we were actually quite similar in the way we cherished and carefully crafted our artwork. Our piece began to look exquisite, and our initial differences started to lessen in importance. I realized that my initial reaction to the thought of working with a partner was unnecessary. The piece turned out to be one of my best and I realized that "it's the way a team plays as a whole that determines success. You may have the greatest bunch of individual stars in the world, but if they don't play together, the club won't be worth a dime" (Babe Ruth).

Notes

Cutting Corners

NAME _____

Read the story.

Think about how sometimes slower means better, but sometimes it doesn't.

Write an essay to discuss the benefits and/or dangers of taking shortcuts.

MY TRUISM _____

NOW AND LATER

| Problem | A shortcut solution | A long-term solution | How I would decide which is better |

MY KERNEL ESSAY

1. _____

2. _____

3. _____

4. _____

   _____

TRUISM EXAMPLES

1. Sometimes a temporary fix gives you time to plan a longer-term solution.

2. If you work too quickly, you can end up having to re-do the work.

3. _____

The Three Little Pigs

Once upon a time when pigs spoke rhyme

And monkeys chewed tobacco,

And hens took snuff to make them tough,

And ducks went quack, quack, quack, O!

There was an old sow with three little pigs, and as she had not enough to keep them, she sent them out to seek their fortune. The first that went off met a man with a bundle of straw, and said to him,

"Please, man, give me that straw to build me a house."

Which the man did, and the little pig built a house with it. Presently came along a wolf, and knocked at the door, and said,

"Little pig, little pig, let me come in."

To which the pig answered,

"No, no, by the hair of my chiny chin chin."

The wolf then answered to that,

"Then I'll huff, and I'll puff, and I'll blow your house in."

So he huffed, and he puffed, and he blew his house in, and ate up the little pig.

The second little pig met a man with a bundle of furze, and said,

"Please, man, give me that furze to build a house."

Which the man did, and the pig built his house. Then along came the wolf, and said,

"Little pig, little pig, let me come in."

"No, no, by the hair of my chiny chin chin."

"Then I'll puff, and I'll huff, and I'll blow your house in."

So he huffed, and he puffed, and he puffed, and he huffed, and at last he blew the house down, and he ate up the little pig.

The third little pig met a man with a load of bricks, and said,

"Please, man, give me those bricks to build a house with."

So the man gave him the bricks, and he built his house with them. So the wolf came, as he did to the other little pigs, and said,

"Little pig, little pig, let me come in."

"No, no, by the hair of my chiny chin chin."

"Then I'll huff, and I'll puff, and I'll blow your house in."

Well, he huffed, and he puffed, and he huffed and he puffed, and he puffed and huffed; but he could *not* get the house down. When he found that he could not, with all his huffing and puffing, blow the house down, he said,

"Little pig, I know where there is a nice field of turnips."

"Where?" said the little pig.

"Oh, in Mr. Smith's home field, and if you will be ready tomorrow morning I will call for you, and we will go together, and get some for dinner."

"Very well," said the little pig, "I will be ready. What time do you mean to go?"

"Oh, at six o'clock."

Well, the little pig got up at five, and got the turnips before the wolf came (which he did about six) and who said,

"Little Pig, are you ready?"

The little pig said, "Ready! I have been and come back again and got a nice potful for dinner."

The wolf felt very angry at this, but thought that he would be up to the little pig somehow or other, so he said,

"Little pig, I know where there is a nice apple tree."

"Where?" said the pig.

"Down at Merry garden," replied the wolf, "and if you will not deceive me I will come for you, at five o'clock tomorrow and get some apples."

Well, the little pig bustled up the next morning at four o'clock, and went off for the apples, hoping to get back before the wolf came; but he had further to go, and had to climb the tree, so that just as he was coming down from it, he saw the wolf coming, which, as you may suppose, frightened him very much. When the wolf came up he said,

"Little pig, what! Are you here before me? Are they nice apples?"

"Yes, very," said the little pig. "I will throw you down one."

And he threw it so far, that, while the wolf was gone to pick it up, the little pig jumped down and ran home. The next day the wolf came again, and said to the little pig,

"Little pig, there is a fair at Shanklin this afternoon, will you go?"

"Oh yes," said the pig, "I will go; what time shall you be ready?"

"At three," said the wolf. So the little pig went off before the time as usual, and got to the fair, and bought a butter churn, which he was going home with, when he saw the wolf coming. Then he could not tell what to do. So he got into the churn to hide, and by so doing turned it round, and it rolled down the hill with the pig in it, which frightened the wolf so much, that he ran home without going to the fair. He went to the little pig's house, and told him how frightened he had been by a great round thing which came down the hill past him. Then the little pig said,

"Hah, I frightened you, then. I had been to the fair and bought a butter churn, and when I saw you, I got into it, and rolled down the hill."

Then the wolf was very angry indeed, and declared he *would* eat up the little pig, and that he would get down the chimney after him. When the little pig saw what he was about, he hung on the pot full of water, and made up a blazing fire, and, just as the wolf was coming down, took off the cover, and in fell the wolf; so the little pig put on the cover again in an instant, boiled him up, and ate him for supper, and lived happy ever afterward.

Emmanuel Mendez, 11th grade

Coerced book assignments and book reports aren't the most venerated thing by students. For many, having to read a book for class can be a boring and dull task, especially when reading isn't your favorite thing to do and you have to stick to a meticulous and time-drenching reading schedule. It's always a recurring assignment that comes up every year, every semester, a fate that terrifies a multitude of pupils. The problematic dilemma gets exponentiated when there is the threat of an impending exam on the forced reading, riling up many people to think about what solution path they should take to understand the reading and pass the test. There are two possible solutions: the straightforward and simple one, which is reading the book, and then the easy path, which involves accessing chapter summaries online, which is usually done at the last minute and in a frantic manner.

When it comes to a shortcut solution, many peers are comfortable resorting to just going over the book chapter summaries online, while jeopardizing the profound reading experiences of the book. Just minutes before they enter the class, just minutes before the exam on the read gets placed before them, just minutes before and trepidation starts to settle in. To many, the mighty GradeSaver or Shmoop become their everlasting hope and destined deity. The children gather all the key points they may need. Cal goes to hospital and certain complexities are discovered. Perry and Dick commit their murders and head to Mexico. An ease and peace is found through the powers of short bullet points.

I could attempt to stick to the assigned reading schedule in order to truly comprehend the storyline of the book. I tend to find more ease and peace through this long-term solution method as I can reliably know the content, context, and inside drama cinematography elicited in my mind from reading page by page. Sometimes though, I can have trouble understanding a piece, but one must remember the usefulness of reading. Read too quickly and you won't understand well. You will understand well once you read more and thus begin to be able to read more quickly and fluently.

The long-term solution seems more effective compared to the shortcut as even though I might be a few chapters behind the reading schedule, I can still be able to enjoy the true emotions evoked by the piece of literature. I want to experience the true emotional connections given to society, the purposeful and creative work from renowned authors, not some bullet points on a website for the sleep deprived. If someone takes the time-saving shortcut, not only do they miss out on the drama, rhetoric, and sensational storyline, but also risk their grade in the end. If you work too quickly, you can end up having to re-do the work. It's better to go at one's pace and do it well the first time, in a reliable and self-fulfilling manner.

28 Information

Read the story.
Think about how people sometimes need a reality check.
Write an essay about the importance of knowledge.

MY TRUISM

FINDING THE TRUTH THROUGH EXPERIENCE

I heard this	But I thought the opposite	Then I heard about this experience	Now I think this

MY KERNEL ESSAY

1. _____

2. _____

3. _____

4. _____

_____

TRUISM EXAMPLES

1. When people reject provable information, they don't use the resources available to them.

2. Bad information can be dangerous.

3. _____

The Three Sillies

Once upon a time, when folk were not so wise as they are nowadays, there lived a farmer and his wife who had one daughter. Now every evening a young squire would stroll over to see her and stop to supper in the farmhouse, and every evening the daughter would go down into the cellar to draw the cider for supper.

So one evening in the cellar, she happened to look up at the ceiling, and she saw a big wooden mallet stuck in one of the beams. She had never noticed it before, and at once, she began thinking how dangerous it was to have the mallet just there.

"For," thought she, "supposing him and me was married, and supposing we was to have a son, and supposing he were to grow up to be a man, and supposing he were to come down to draw cider like as I'm doing, and supposing the mallet were to fall on his head and kill him, how dreadful it would be!"

And with that she began to cry. And she cried and cried.

Now, upstairs, they began to wonder why she was so long; so her mother went down to the cellar and found her, crying ever so hard, and the cider running all over the floor.

"Mercy me!" cried her mother, "Whatever is the matter?"

"O mother!" says she between her sobs, "It's that horrid mallet. Supposing him and me was married, and supposing we was to have a son, and supposing he was to grow up to be a man, and supposing he was to come down to draw cider like as I'm doing, and supposing the mallet were to fall on his head and kill him, how dreadful it would be!"

"Dear heart!" said the mother, seating herself beside her daughter and beginning to cry, "How dreadful it would be!"

So they both sat a-crying.

Now after a time, the farmer found them seated side by side, crying hard, and the cider running all over the floor.

"Zounds!" says he, "Whatever is the matter?"

"Just look at that horrid mallet up there, father," moaned the mother. "Supposing our daughter was to marry her sweetheart, and supposing they was to have a son, and supposing he was to grow to man's estate, and supposing he was to come down to draw cider like as we're doing, and supposing that there mallet was to fall on his head and kill him, how dreadful it would be!"

"Dreadful indeed!" said the father and started a-crying too.

Upstairs, the young squire lost patience and went into the cellar. And there he found them seated side by side a-crying, with their feet all a-wash in cider. So the first thing he did was to turn off the tap.

Then he said: "What are you three after?"

When they all three told him, the young squire burst out a-laughing. At last, he reached up to the old mallet and pulled it out, and put it safe on the floor, and said, "Never have I met with three such sillies as you. So I shall start on my travels, and if I can find three bigger sillies than you three, then I'll come back and be married—not otherwise."

So he wished them good-bye. One day, he came upon an old woman's cottage that had some grass growing on the thatched roof, and the old woman was trying her best to cudgel her cow into going up a ladder to eat the grass.

At last the young squire said, "It would be easier if you went up the ladder, cut the grass, and threw it down for the cow to eat."

Says the old woman, "I'll tie a rope round her neck. She can't fall off the roof without my knowing it. So mind your own business, young sir."

The old woman tied a rope round its neck, passed the rope down the chimney, and fastened t'other end to her wrist.

The young squire went on his way. But later he found that the cow had fallen off the roof and got strangled by the rope round its neck, while the weight of the cow had pulled the old woman by her wrist up the chimney, where she had got stuck half way and been smothered by the soot!

"That is one bigger silly," quoth the young squire. "So now for two more!"

Late one night at a little inn, he had to share a room with another traveler. Next morning, when they were dressing, what does the stranger do but carefully hang his breeches on the knobs of the tallboy!

"What are you doing?" asks young squire.

"I'm putting on my breeches," says the stranger; and with that, he goes to the other end of the room, takes a little run, and tried to jump into the breeches.

The stranger said, "It takes me the best part of an hour every morning before I get them on. How do you manage yours?"

Then young squire showed him how to put on his breeches. "So that," quoth young squire to himself, "is a second bigger silly."

But he traveled until one bright night, he saw round a pond a great crowd of villagers.

"What is the matter?" cried young squire.

"Aye! Matter enough," says they. "Can't 'ee see moon's fallen into the pond, an' we can't get her out nohow."

Then the young squire bade them look up over their heads where the moon was riding broad and full, but they wouldn't.

So the young squire said to himself, "I'll just go back and marry the farmer's daughter. She is no sillier than the rest."

So they were married, and if they didn't live happy ever after, that has nothing to do with the story of the three sillies.

Katalina Luna, 5th grade

1. My mom told me I was wearing my shirt correctly even when I thought I was wearing it backward.

2. Then my friends at school told me I was wearing it backward.

3. Now I think that my mom wasn't paying attention when I asked her.

4. When people pass on bad information, they are not using the resources available to them.

Michael Aguirre, 8th grade

1. My friend John once told me that if you hold a long metal pole in the air, there is a higher risk of getting shocked by lightning.

2. Then I thought the lightning wouldn't want to run into a pole so it would just go around it, right?

3. Then in science class the next day we learned that metal is a good conductor of electricity, therefore holding a metal pole in the air during a thunderstorm allows a higher risk of getting electrocuted by lightning.

4. Knowledge is very important. Knowledge can very well help you in life and death situations, but it's up to you to educate yourself.

29 Place

NAME _____

Read the story.

Think about how some places can make you happy while it is difficult to be happy in other places.

Write an essay about what it takes to be happy.

MY TRUISM _____

CURIOSITY

| I wondered ... | I figured out ... | Then I also figured out ... | Last I figured out ... | This all means that ... |

MY KERNEL ESSAY

1. _____

2. _____

3. _____

4. _____

5. _____

TRUISM EXAMPLES

1. You can't be happy if you're in the wrong place. _____

2. Everyone has the power to make themselves happy. _____

3. _____

Thumbelina

There was once a woman who wished very much to have a little child. She went to a fairy who said, "Oh, that can be easily managed. Here is a barleycorn. Put it into a flowerpot and see what will happen."

"Thank you," said the woman. Then she went home and planted it, and there grew up a large, handsome flower. Within the flower sat a very delicate and graceful little maiden, scarcely half as long as a thumb. They gave her the name of Thumbelina.

A walnut shell, elegantly polished, served her for a cradle; her bed was formed of blue violet leaves. One night, a large, ugly, wet toad crept through the window. "What a pretty little wife this would make for my son," said the toad, and she took up the walnut shell in which Thumbelina lay asleep, and jumped through the window with it. And the old toad swam out to a water lily leaf in the stream.

The tiny creature woke and began to cry bitterly when she found where she was. The toad said, "My son will be your husband." Then the toads swam away, leaving Thumbelina all alone.

The little fishes who swam beneath lifted their heads and saw Thumbelina. "No, it must never be!" So they gnawed the green stalk and the leaf floated down the stream, carrying Thumbelina far away.

During the whole summer, poor little Thumbelina lived quite alone in the wide forest. She wove herself a bed with blades of grass and drank the honey from the flowers every morning.

So passed away the summer and the autumn, and then came the winter—the long, cold winter. She felt dreadfully cold, for her clothes were torn, and she was herself so frail and delicate that she was nearly frozen to death.

She came to the door of a field mouse, who had a little den. There dwelt the field mouse in warmth and comfort, with a whole roomful of corn, a kitchen, and a beautiful dining room. Poor Thumbelina stood before the door, just like a little beggar girl.

"You poor little creature," said the field mouse, for she was really a good old mouse, "come into my warm room and dine with me."

She was pleased with Thumbelina, so she said, "You are quite welcome to stay with me all the winter, if you like." And Thumbelina found herself very comfortable.

"We shall have a visitor soon," said the field mouse one day. "If you could only have him for a husband, you would be well provided for indeed."

Thumbelina did not feel at all interested about this neighbor, for he was a mole. However, he came and paid his visit, dressed in his black velvet coat.

Thumbelina was obliged to sing to him, "Ladybird, ladybird, fly away home," and many other pretty songs. And the mole fell in love with her because she had so sweet a voice. The mole had dug a long passage under the earth, which led from the dwelling of the field mouse to his own, and here she had permission to walk with Thumbelina whenever she liked. But he warned them not to be alarmed at the sight of a dead bird. The mole went before them through the long, dark passage.

In the middle of the floor lay a swallow—the poor bird had evidently died of the cold. It made little Thumbelina very sad to see it, she did so love the little birds. But during the night, Thumbelina got out of bed and wove a large, beautiful carpet of hay. She spread some of it on each side of the bird, so that he might lie warmly in the cold earth.

"Farewell, pretty little bird," said she. Then she laid her head on the bird's breast, but it seemed as if something inside the bird went "thump, thump." It was the bird's heart; he was not really dead. She laid the wool more thickly over the poor swallow.

The next night, she again stole out to see him. He was alive, but very weak; he could only open his eyes for a moment. "Thank you, pretty little maiden," said the sick swallow; "I have been so nicely warmed that I shall soon regain my strength."

She brought the swallow some water in a flower leaf, and he told her that he had wounded one of his wings in a thorn bush and could not fly as fast as the others.

All winter, Thumbelina nursed him with care and love. Very soon the springtime came. Then the swallow bade farewell to Thumbelina and asked her if she would go with him. But she knew it would grieve the field mouse, so she said, "No, I cannot."

"Farewell, then, farewell, you good, pretty little maiden," said the swallow, and he flew out into the sunshine.

Thumbelina looked after him, and the tears rose in her eyes. She was very fond of the poor swallow.

"You are going to be married, little one," said the field mouse. "My neighbor has asked for you. What good fortune for a poor child like you!" But Thumbelina was not at all pleased, for she did not like the tiresome mole.

Every morning when the sun rose and every evening when it went down, she would creep out. She thought how beautiful and bright it seemed out there and wished so much to see her dear friend, the swallow, again. But he had flown far away into the lovely green forest.

When autumn arrived, the field mouse said, "In four weeks, the wedding must take place." Then she wept and said she would not marry the disagreeable mole.

"Nonsense," replied the field mouse. "You ought to be very thankful for such good fortune."

So the wedding day was fixed, on which the mole was to take her away to live deep under the earth, and never again to see the warm sun because he did not like it. "Farewell, bright sun," she cried, stretching out her arm toward it. "Greet the little swallow from me, if you should see him again."

"Tweet, tweet," sounded over her head suddenly. She looked up, and there was the swallow himself flying close by. She told him how unwilling she was to marry the ugly mole. And as she told him, she wept. Said the swallow, "Fly now with me, dear little one; you saved my life when I lay frozen in that dark, dreary passage."

"Yes, I will go with you," said Thumbelina; and she seated herself on the bird's back, and tied her girdle to one of his strongest feathers. The swallow rose in the air and flew where the air was fragrant with myrtles and orange blossoms.

At last the swallow flew down with Thumbelina and placed her on one of the broad leaves of a beautiful white flower. But how surprised she was to see in the middle of the flower a tiny little man with a gold crown on his head, and delicate wings at his shoulders, not much larger than was she herself. He was the angel of the flower, the king of all of the flowers.

"Oh, how beautiful he is!" whispered Thumbelina to the swallow.

When he saw Thumbelina he was delighted, and asked if she would be his wife and queen over all the flowers. She said yes to the handsome prince. Then all the flowers opened, and out of each came a little lady or a tiny lord with a present; but the best gift was a pair of beautiful wings, and they fastened them to Thumbelina's shoulders, so that she might fly from flower to flower.

Then there was much rejoicing.

"Farewell, farewell," said the swallow, with a heavy heart, as he left the warm countries, to fly back into Denmark. There he had a nest over the window of a house in which dwelt the writer of fairy tales. The swallow sang "Tweet, tweet," and from his song came the whole story.

Destiny Briseno, 5th grade

1. I always wondered why I was so upset when I moved to San Antonio.

2. Then I figured out I was out of my happy zone! So I needed to make San Antonio one of my happy places.

3. I soon figured out that it's not so bad here.

4. Last I figured out that even humans can learn to adapt.

5. This all means that everyone has the power make themselves happy. It's easy to be upset if you believe it's an upsetting place; but if you say everywhere is a good and happy place, you'll be happy.

Emilio Ramon, 4th grade

1. I wondered if I would be lonely in my room.

2. I figured out I wasn't lonely cause I had an imaginary friend.

3. I also figured out that it made me feel an emotion.

4. At last I figured out that that emotion was happiness.

5. The best happy places are secret.

Elias Baltierrez, 4th grade

1. I wondered what my cousin's house was going to look like.

2. I figured out it was nice.

3. I also figured out he had lots of Nerf guns.

4. Last I figured out he played my favorite game, Fortnite.

5. This all means that happy places make you have happy feelings.

30 Friendship

Read the story.

Think about how hard it is to tell if someone is a real friend.

Write an essay about the difficulty of trusting friendships.

MY TRUISM

FIVE-PARAGRAPH ESSAY

Truism	One way to tell (with example)	Another way to tell (with example)	Another way to tell (with example)	How this knowledge can help

MY KERNEL ESSAY

1.

2.

3.

4.

5.

TRUISM EXAMPLES

1. People act like your friends when you are successful.

2. Even real friends can have imperfections.

3.

The Tinderbox

A soldier came marching along the high road. One, two! One, two! He had been to the wars and he was on his way home now. He met an old witch on the road; she was so ugly, her lower lip hung right down on to her chin.

She said, "Good evening, soldier! What a nice sword you've got, and such a big knapsack! You shall have as much money as ever you like!"

"Thank you kindly, you old witch!" said the soldier.

"Do you see that big tree?" said the witch. "It is hollow inside! Climb up to the top and you can let yourself down! I will tie a rope round your waist so that I can haul you up again when you call!"

"What am I to do down under the tree?" asked the soldier.

"Fetch money!" said the witch. "When you get down to the bottom of the tree you will find yourself in a wide passage. You will see three doors. If you go into the first room, you will see a big box. A dog is sitting on the top of it, and he has eyes as big as saucers. I will give you my blue checked apron, which you can spread out on the floor; then take up the dog and put him on my apron, open the box and take out as much money as ever you like. It is all copper, but if you like silver better, go into the next room. There you will find a dog with eyes as big as millstones; put him on my apron and take the money. If you prefer gold, you go into the third room. But the dog sitting on that box has eyes each as big as the Round Tower. You only have to put him on to my apron, and you can take as much gold out of the box as you like!"

"That's not so bad!" said the soldier. "But what am I to give you, old witch?"

"I only want you to bring me an old tinderbox that my grandmother forgot the last time she was down there!"

"Well! Tie the rope round my waist!" said the soldier.

"Here it is," said the witch.

Then the soldier climbed up the tree, let himself slide down the hollow trunk, and found himself in the wide passage. Now he opened the first door. Ugh! There sat the dog with eyes as big as saucers staring at him.

He put the dog on to the witch's apron and took out as many pennies as he could cram into his pockets. Then he shut the box, put the dog on the top of it again, and went into the next room. Hallo! There sat the dog with eyes as big as millstones.

Then he put the dog on the apron, but when he saw all the silver in the box, he threw away all the coppers and stuffed his knapsack with silver. Then he went on into the third room. That dog really had two eyes as big as the Round Tower, and they rolled round and round like wheels.

He had never seen such a dog in his life; but then he lifted him down on to the apron and opened the chest. What a lot of gold! He could buy the whole of Copenhagen with it, and all the sugar pigs from the cake-women, all the tin soldiers, whips, and rocking-horses in the world! Now, he really had got a lot of money. He put the dog back on to the box, shut the door, and shouted up through the tree, "Haul me up, you old witch!"

"Have you got the tinderbox?"

"Oh!" said the soldier. "I had quite forgotten it." And he went back to fetch it. Then the witch hauled him up.

"What do you want the tinderbox for?" asked the soldier.

"That's no business of yours," said the witch.

"Rubbish!" said the soldier. "Tell me directly, or I will draw my sword and cut off your head."

"I won't!" said the witch.

Then the soldier cut off her head! But he tied all the money up in her apron, slung it on his back like a pack, put the tinderbox in his pocket, and marched off to the town.

He went straight to the finest hotel, because he was a rich man now. The people told him all about the grand things in the town, and about their king, and what a lovely princess his daughter was.

"Where is she to be seen?" asked the soldier.

"You can't see her at all!" they all said. "She lives in a great copper castle surrounded with walls. Nobody but the king dare go in and out, for it has been prophesied that she will marry a common soldier, and the king doesn't like that!"

He now led a very merry life; now he was rich and had a great many friends, who all said what a nice fellow he was—and he liked to be told that.

He at last found himself with only two pence left. Then he was obliged to move out of his fine rooms. He had to take a tiny little attic up under the roof, clean his own boots, and mend them himself with a darning needle. None of his friends went to see him because there were far too many stairs.

One dark evening, he got out the tinderbox with the candle end in it and struck fire, but as the sparks flew out from the flint, the door burst open and the dog with eyes as big as saucers said, "What does my lord command?"

"Get me some money," he said to the dog, and away it went.

It was back in a twinkling with a big bag full of pennies in its mouth. Now the soldier saw what a treasure he had in the tinderbox. If he struck once, the dog which sat on the box of copper came; if he struck twice, the dog on the silver box came, and if he struck three times, the one from the box of gold.

He now moved down to the grand rooms and got his fine clothes again, and then all his friends knew him once more and liked him as much as ever.

One day, he struck the flint, and, whisk, came the dog with eyes as big as saucers.

"I am very anxious to see the princess."

The dog was out of the door in an instant, and before the soldier had time to think about it, he was back with the princess. She was fast asleep on the dog's back, and she was so lovely that anybody could see that she must be a real princess! The soldier was obliged to kiss her.

Then the dog ran back again with the princess, but in the morning when the king and queen were having breakfast, the princess said that she had had such a wonderful dream about a dog and a soldier. She had ridden on the dog's back, and the soldier had kissed her.

Now the queen was a very clever woman; she made a pretty little bag which she filled with buckwheat. She then tied it onto the back of the princess, and she cut a little hole in the bag, so that the grains could drop out all the way wherever the princess went.

At night the dog came again, took the princess on his back, and never noticed how the grain dropped out all along the road.

In the morning, the king and the queen easily saw where their daughter had been, and they seized the soldier and threw him into the dungeons.

And they said to him, "Tomorrow, you are to be hanged." It was not amusing to be told that, especially as he had left his tinderbox behind him at the hotel.

In the morning, he could see through the bars in the little window that the people were hurrying to see him hanged.

"I say, you boy!" said the soldier. "If you will run to the house where I used to live, and fetch me my tinderbox, you shall have a penny!"

The boy was only too glad to have the penny, tore off to get the tinderbox, and gave it to the soldier.

Outside the town, a high scaffold had been raised, and the soldier mounted the ladder, but he said that a criminal was always allowed a harmless wish, and he wanted very much to smoke a pipe.

The king would not deny him this, so the soldier took out his tinderbox and struck fire, once, twice, three times, and there were all the dogs.

"Help me! Save me from being hanged!" cried the soldier.

And then the dogs rushed at the soldiers, and threw them up many fathoms into the air; and when they fell down, they were broken all to pieces.

The biggest dog took both the king and the queen and threw them after all the others. Then the people shouted, "Oh! good soldier, you shall be our king and marry the beautiful princess!"

The princess came out of the copper palace and became queen, which pleased her very much. The wedding took place in a week, and the dogs all had seats at the table, where they sat staring with all their eyes.

Danielle Mendez, 11th grade

People act like your friends when you are successful. This can mean financial or social success. It happens to everyone at least once in their friendship experiences.

One way to tell that you are being used in a friendship is noticing how your friend treats others compared to you. If they do things that make you feel bad, that should be the first sign to be wary of them. A friend speaking to you differently, showing disinterest, while they speak to their other friends politely and kindly that shows they do treat their real friends with care. Friends should not make each other feel bad. It is not fair for a friend to treat one friend fair and the other unfairly. That is a sign that that friend does not care about you. Friends should care about each other and be considerate of each other.

If someone asks you for certain things frequently, it can be another sign that they don't really care about you. If your "friend" often asks you for something, such as money and/or valuables, that should be a red flag. For instance, if you ask your "friend" to spend some time with you at the movies, and they refuse or make up excuses to decline several times, they are not a real friend. Real friends would want to spend time with each other to grow their friendship. If all a friend does is ask you for things, they are just taking advantage by using you for your successes, not appreciating who you truly are.

Another way to tell if a person is a real friend is to notice if they tell or encourage you to do bad things. Someone who makes you do something you normally would not do because you know it is wrong is not a real friend. If it is bad peer pressure, it is not a good thing to have in a friendship. Bad encouragement can get you into trouble. For example, if a friend encouraged you to steal when stealing is obviously wrong. Friends encouraging you to be a part of risky situations are not looking out for you but are instead looking for the results of your success. Bad friends do not look out for you; good friends always look out for you.

This knowledge can help you tell the difference between real friends from friends who only befriend you for your success.

Notes

Part VII
Structures for Content-Area Writing

Bank of Text Structure Choices

For Content-Area Writing

LEARNING FROM MISTAKES

One way I got in trouble	What happened after that	What I thought about my consequences	What I realize now

SOLVING A MYSTERY

What I know	What I don't know	Steps I took to find out	Successful?	Life lesson (truism)

SOMETHING CHANGED

What changed	How it used to be	How it is now	It helps me to know that ...

MAKING A CHANGE

I wanted to change this	But this was stopping me	So I did this	Truism

DISCOVERING THE TRUTH

Someone told me (or I read) ...	So I assumed ...	When actually ...	So now I understand ... (truism)

Read the story.

Think about how people are raised in different places and in different ways.

Write an essay about the meaning of "home."

MY TRUISM

LEARNING FROM MISTAKES

One way I got in trouble	What happened after that	What I thought about my consequences	What I realize now

---

MY KERNEL ESSAY

1. _____

2. _____

3. _____

4. _____

_____

TRUISM EXAMPLES

1. Home is wherever you feel most like yourself.

2. Everyone wants to go home sooner or later.

3. _____

Tom Thumb

A poor woodman sat in his cottage one night, smoking his pipe by the fireside, while his wife sat by his side spinning. "How lonely it is, wife," said he, "for you and me to sit here by ourselves." "How happy should I be if I had but one child!" said the wife, sighing. Now, odd as you may think it, not long afterward, she had a little boy, who was quite healthy and strong but was not much bigger than my thumb. So they said, "Little as he is, we will love him dearly." And they called him Thomas Thumb.

They gave him plenty of food, yet he never grew bigger, but kept just the same size as he had been when he was born. Still, he soon showed himself to be a clever little fellow.

One day, as the woodman was getting ready to go into the wood to cut fuel, he said, "I wish I had someone to bring the cart after me, for I want to make haste." "Oh, father," cried Tom, "I will take care of that." Then the woodman laughed and said, ''How?'' "Never mind that, father," said Tom; "I will get into the horse's ear and tell him which way to go." "Well," said the father, "we will try for once."

When the time came, the mother harnessed the horse and put Tom into his ear; and the little man told the beast, "Go on!" and "Stop!" and the horse went on well. It happened that two strangers came up. "What an odd thing that is!" said one. "There is a cart going along, and I hear a carter talking to the horse, but yet I can see no one." Said the other, "Let us follow the cart." So they went on into the wood, till at last they came to where the woodman was. Then Tom Thumb cried out, "See, father, here I am all right and safe! Now take me down!" So his father took his son out of the horse's ear and put him down upon a straw.

The two strangers were looking on in wonder. At last one said, "That little urchin will make our fortune." So they went up to the woodman and asked what he would take for the little man. "I won't sell him at all," said the father. But Tom crept up his father's coat and whispered in his ear, "Take the money, father, and let them have me; I'll soon come back to you."

So the woodman at last said he would sell Tom for a large piece of gold, and they paid the price. "Where would you like to sit?" said one of them. "Oh, put me on the rim of your hat." So they did as he wished; and when Tom had taken leave of his father, they took him away with them.

They journeyed on till it began to be dusky, and then the little man said, "Let me get down; I'm tired." So the man took off his hat and put him down on the side of the road. But Tom slipped into an old mouse hole. "Good night, my masters!" said he, "I'm off!" Then they ran at once to the place, but all in vain; and at last, it became quite dark, so that they were forced to go their way without their prize, as sulky as could be.

When Tom found they were gone, he came out of his hiding place. By good luck, he found a large empty snail shell. "This is lucky," said he. "I can sleep here very well" and in he crept.

Just as he was falling asleep, he heard two men passing by, and one said, "How can we rob that rich parson's house of his silver and gold?" "I'll tell you!" cried Tom. "Take me with you, and I'll soon show you how to get the parson's money." "But where are you?" said they. "Look about on the ground," answered he. At last, the thieves found him out and lifted him up in their hands. "You little urchin!" they said. "What can you do for us?" "Why, I can get between the iron window bars, and throw you out whatever you want." "That's a good thought," said the thieves.

When they came to the parson's house, Tom slipped through the window bars into the room and then called out as loud as he could bawl, "Will you have all that is here?" The thieves said, "Softly, softly! Speak low." But Tom bawled out again, "How much will you have? Shall I throw it all out?" Now the cook lay in the next room and heard this quite plain; so she sprang out of bed and ran to open the door. The thieves ran off as if a wolf was at their tails. Tom slipped off into the barn.

The little man crawled about in the hay loft, and laid himself down, meaning to sleep till daylight. But alas! How woefully he was undone! The cook got up early to feed the cows and carried a large bundle of hay, with the little man in the middle of it, fast asleep. He did not awake till he found himself in the mouth of the cow. At last down, he went into her stomach. More and more hay was always coming down. At last he cried out as loud as he could, "Don't bring me any more hay! Don't bring me any more hay!"

The maid was so frightened that she ran off to her master the parson, and said, "Sir, sir, the cow is talking!"

Tom called out, "Don't bring me any more hay!" Then the parson himself was frightened and told his man to kill her on the spot. So the cow was killed, and cut up; and the stomach, in which Tom lay, was thrown out upon a dunghill.

Soon a hungry wolf sprang out and swallowed up the whole stomach, with Tom in it, at one gulp, and ran away.

Tom called out, "My good friend, I can show you a famous treat," describing his own father's house. "You can crawl into the pantry, and there you will find cakes, ham, and everything that your heart can wish."

The wolf that very night went to the house and crawled into the pantry and ate and drank there to his heart's content. He wanted to get away; but he had eaten so much that he could not go out by the same way he came in.

This was just what Tom had reckoned upon; and now he began singing and shouting as loud as he could. The woodman and his wife, being awakened by the noise, peeped through a crack in the door; but Tom cried out, "Father, father! I am here; the wolf has swallowed me." And his father aimed a great blow, struck the wolf on the head, and killed him on the spot! And when he was dead, they cut open his body and set Tommy free. "Ah!" said the father, "What fears we have had for you!" "Yes, father," answered he. "I have traveled all over the world, I think, in one way or other, and now I am very glad to come home and get fresh air again."

"Well," said they, "you are come back, and we will not sell you again for all the riches in the world."

Then they hugged and kissed their dear little son. So Master Thumb stayed at home with his father and mother, in peace; for though he had done and seen so many fine things, and was fond enough of telling the whole story, he always agreed that, after all, there's no place like HOME!

Student Work Samples: Home

Gustavo Pineda, 4th grade

1. First Tom Thumb got into a horse's ear and people noticed.

2. Then he told his father to sell him and he'll come back.

3. After he had tricked so many people, he wanted to go home.

4. He realized that home is the place you go when you feel stressed. It's like your happy place. It's horrible to not have a home.

Janyce Parham, 9th grade

"Never judge a book by its cover" is something my mom said multiple times throughout the years of me growing up. When I first saw someone, I would automatically think of how they would act and talk. I used to think that by the way people looked, they would act a certain way. Highly attractive people acting snooty or cocky, "ugly" people acting way too nice. Sometimes also judging people just by what they wore. I never thought about the background stories that people might have that you can't read from their appearance. People come from different kinds of homes.

Then one day I was forced into a conversation with one of those very popular attractive kids while working on a class assignment. The first thing I thought was they were going to be rude and I would be doing all the work. Then the kid wanted to get to know me and told me about his family. I never thought that his background would be so complex.

That day I realized that people aren't exactly how you would think they are. There is a big personality inside. Everyone comes from a place where they feel at home.

NAME

Read the story.
Think about the powers of firsthand observation.
Write an essay about the importance of proof.

MY TRUISM

SOLVING A MYSTERY

| What I know | What I don't know | Steps I took to find out | Successful? | Life lesson (truism) |

MY KERNEL ESSAY

1. _____

2. _____

3. _____

4. _____

5. _____

_____

TRUISM EXAMPLES

1. Observations help you figure things out. _____

2. Sometimes tough cases can be cracked. _____

3. _____

The Twelve Dancing Princesses

There was a king who had twelve beautiful daughters. They slept in twelve beds all in one room; and when they went to bed, the doors were shut and locked up. But every morning their shoes were found to be quite worn through as if they had been danced in all night; and yet nobody could find out how it happened, or where they had been.

Then the king made it known to all the land, that if any person could discover the secret, and find out where it was that the princesses danced in the night, he should have the one he liked best for his wife and should be king after his death; but whoever tried and did not succeed, after three days and nights, should be put to death.

A king's son soon came. He was well entertained, and in the evening, was taken to the chamber next to the one where the princesses lay in their twelve beds. There he was to sit and watch where they went to dance; and, in order that nothing might pass without his hearing it, the door of his chamber was left open. But the king's son soon fell asleep; and when he awoke in the morning, he found that the princesses had all been dancing, for the soles of their shoes were full of holes. The same thing happened the second and third night: so the king ordered his head to be cut off. After him came several others; but they had all the same luck, and all lost their lives in the same manner.

Now it chanced that an old soldier, who had been wounded in battle and could fight no longer, passed through the country where this king reigned: and as he was travelling through a wood, he met an old woman who asked him where he was going. "I hardly know where I am going, or what I had better do," said the soldier. "But I think I should like very well to find out where it is that the princesses dance, and then in time, I might be a king." "Well," said the old dame, "that

is no very hard task: Only take care not to drink any of the wine which one of the princesses will bring to you in the evening; and as soon as she leaves, you pretend to be fast asleep."

Then she gave him a cloak and said, "As soon as you put that on, you will become invisible, and you will then be able to follow the princesses wherever they go." When the soldier heard all this good counsel, he determined to try his luck; so he went to the king and said he was willing to undertake the task.

He was as well received as the others had been, and the king ordered fine royal robes to be given him; and when the evening came he was led to the outer chamber. Just as he was going to lie down, the eldest of the princesses brought him a cup of wine; but the soldier threw it all away secretly, taking care not to drink a drop. Then he laid himself down on his bed, and in a little while, began to snore very loud as if he was fast asleep. When the twelve princesses heard this they laughed heartily; and the eldest said, "This fellow too might have done a wiser thing than lose his life in this way!" Then they rose up and opened their drawers and boxes, and took out all their fine clothes, and dressed themselves at the glass, and skipped about as if they were eager to begin dancing. But the youngest said, "I don't know how it is, while you are so happy, I feel very uneasy; I am sure some mischance will befall us." "You simpleton," said the eldest, "you are always afraid; have you forgotten how many kings' sons have already watched in vain? And as for this soldier, even if I had not given him his sleeping draught, he would have slept soundly enough."

When they were all ready, they went and looked at the soldier; but he snored on and did not stir hand or foot; so they thought they were quite safe. The eldest went up to her own bed and clapped her hands, and the bed sank into the floor and a trapdoor flew open. The soldier saw them going down through the trapdoor one after another, the eldest leading the way; and thinking he had no time to lose, he jumped up, put on the cloak which the old woman had given him, and followed them. But in the middle of the stairs, he trod on the gown of the youngest princess, and she cried out to her sisters, "All is not right; someone took hold of my gown." "You silly creature!" said the eldest, "It is nothing but a nail in the wall." Then down they all went, and at the bottom, they found themselves in a most delightful grove of trees. The leaves were all of silver and glittered and sparkled beautifully. The soldier wished to take away some token of the place; so he broke off a little branch, and there came a loud noise from the tree. Then the youngest daughter said again, "I am sure all is not right—did not you hear that noise? That never happened before." But the eldest said, "It is only our princes, who are shouting for joy at our approach."

Then they came to another grove of trees, where all the leaves were of gold; and afterward to a third, where the leaves were all glittering diamonds. And the soldier broke a branch from each; and every time there was a loud noise, which made the youngest sister tremble with fear. But the eldest still said, it was only the princes, who were crying for joy. So they went on till they came to a great lake; and at the side of the lake, there lay twelve little boats with twelve handsome princes in them, who seemed to be waiting there for the princesses.

One of the princesses went into each boat, and the soldier stepped into the same boat with the youngest. As they were rowing over the lake, the prince who was in the boat with the youngest princess and the soldier said, "I do not know why it is, but though I am rowing with all my might we do not get on so fast as usual, and I am quite tired: the boat seems very heavy today." "It is only the heat of the weather," said the princess. "I feel it very warm too."

On the other side of the lake stood a fine illuminated castle, from which came the merry music of horns and trumpets. There they all landed and went into the castle, and each prince danced with his princess; and the soldier, who was all the time invisible, danced with them too; and when any of the princesses had a cup of wine set by her, he drank it all up so that when she put the cup to her mouth, it was empty. At this, too, the youngest sister was terribly frightened, but the eldest always silenced her. They danced on till three o'clock in the morning, and then all their shoes were worn out so that they were obliged to leave off. The princes rowed them back again over the lake (but this time the soldier placed himself in the boat with the eldest princess); and on the opposite shore they took leave of each other, the princesses promising to come again the next night.

When they came to the stairs, the soldier ran on before the princesses and laid himself down; and as the twelve sisters slowly came up very much tired, they heard him snoring in his bed. So they said, "Now all is quite safe"; then they undressed themselves, put away their fine clothes, pulled off their shoes, and went to bed. In the morning, the soldier said nothing about what had happened, but determined to see more of this strange adventure, and went again the second and third night. And everything happened just as before; the princesses danced each time till their shoes were worn to pieces and then returned home. However, on the third night, the soldier carried away one of the golden cups as a token of where he had been.

As soon as the time came when he was to declare the secret, he was taken before the king with the three branches and the golden cup; and the twelve princesses stood listening behind the door to hear what he would say. And when the king asked him, "Where do my twelve daughters dance at night?" he answered, "With twelve princes in a castle underground." And then he told the king all that had happened and showed him the three branches and the golden cup which he had brought with him. Then the king called for the princesses and asked them whether what the soldier said was true. When they saw that they were discovered, and that it was of no use to deny what had happened, they confessed it all. And the king asked the soldier which of them he would choose for his wife; he answered, "I am not very young, so I will have the eldest." And they were married that very day, and the soldier was chosen to be the king's heir.

Student Work Samples: Mystery

Emilio Ramon, 4th grade

1. Mrs. Hover recommended the book *Loser*.

2. I didn't know if I could read it.

3. I read it.

4. Yes, in fact I read it in a week.

5. You never know until you try.

Katalina Luna, 5th grade

1. In math, I only knew how to count to at least 10.

2. What I didn't know was how to add, and that addition was a form of counting.

3. I had to learn step by step that if I count on from 1 number, I'll be able to add.

4. I was successful in finding out how to add using something I already knew.

5. Sometimes tough cases can be cracked with the knowledge you have.

Jayne Hover, teacher

1. I know how to crochet.

2. I didn't know how to figure out a very difficult pattern.

3. I went to several ladies who have crocheted for years to ask for their help.

4. No one could figure out the instructions, so I decided to use a different pattern.

5. Sometimes you have to know when to go with Plan B.

Notes

NAME

Read the story.

Think about how people mostly know that they are not perfect.

Write an essay about how our imperfections can become our strengths.

MY TRUISM

SOMETHING CHANGED

| What changed | How it used to be | How it is now | It helps me to know that ... |

MY KERNEL ESSAY

1. _____

2. _____

3. _____

4. _____

_____

_____

TRUISM EXAMPLES

1. Suffering can help a person feel for the suffering of others.

2. It's easy to remember what it's like to feel like an outcast.

3. _____

The Ugly Duckling

In a sunny spot down to the water's edge grew great burdocks, in the very center of the thick wood.

In this snug retreat sat a duck upon her nest, watching for her young brood to hatch.

At length, one shell cracked, and soon another, and from each came a living creature that lifted its head and cried "Peep, peep."

"Are you all out?" said the mother, rising to look. "No, not all; the largest egg lies there yet, I declare," so she sat down again.

At last the great egg broke, and the latest bird cried "Peep, peep," as he crept forth from the shell. How big and ugly he was! The mother duck stared at him and did not know what to think. "Well, we shall see when we get to the water."

On the next day, the weather was delightful, and the mother duck took her whole family down to the water and jumped in with a splash. "Quack, quack!" cried she, and one after another the little ducklings jumped in, and the ugly gray-coat was also in the water, swimming with them.

"Oh," said the mother. "See how well he uses his legs! He is my own child, and he is not so very ugly after all, if you look at him properly. Quack, quack! Come with me now. I will take you into grand society and introduce you to the farmyard, but you must keep close to me and, above all, beware of the cat."

When they reached the farmyard, the other ducks stared, and said, "We don't want him here"; and then one flew out and bit him in the neck.

"Let him alone," said the mother; "he is not doing any harm."

"Yes, but he is so big and ugly. He's a perfect fright," said the spiteful duck, "and therefore he must be turned out. A little biting will do him good."

"The others are very pretty children," said the old duck, "all but that one."

"He is not pretty," replied the mother, "but he has a very good disposition and swims as well as the others or even better. I think he will grow up pretty"; and then she stroked his neck and smoothed the feathers.

And so they made themselves comfortable; but the poor duckling who looked so ugly was bitten and pushed and made fun of, not only by the ducks but by all the poultry.

"He is too big," they all said; and the poor little thing did not know where to go and was quite miserable because he was so ugly as to be laughed at by the whole farmyard.

So it went on from day to day; even his brothers and sisters were unkind to him and would say, "Ah, you ugly creature, I wish the cat would get you" and his mother had been heard to say she wished he had never been born. The ducks pecked him, the chickens beat him, and the girl who fed the poultry pushed him with her feet. So at last he ran away, feeling very sorrowful.

"I believe I must go out into the world again," said the duckling. So the duckling left the cottage and soon found water on which it could swim and dive, but he was avoided by all other animals because of his ugly appearance.

Autumn came, and then winter approached. All this was very sad for the poor duckling.

The winter grew colder and colder; he was obliged to swim about on the water to keep it from freezing, but every night the space on which he swam became smaller and smaller. At length, it froze so hard that the ice in the water crackled as he moved, and the duckling had to paddle with his legs as well as he could, to keep the space from closing up. He became exhausted at last and lay still and helpless, frozen fast in the ice.

Early in the morning, a peasant who was passing by saw what had happened. He broke the ice in pieces with his wooden shoe and carried the duckling home to his wife. The warmth revived the poor little creature; but when the children wanted to play with him, the duckling thought they would do him some harm, so he started up in terror, but luckily he escaped.

It would be very sad were I to relate all the misery the poor little duckling endured during the hard winter; but one morning he felt the warm sun shining.

Then the young bird felt that his wings were strong, as he flapped them against his sides and rose high into the air. They bore him onward until he found himself in a large garden. Everything looked beautiful. From a thicket close by came three beautiful white swans, rustling their feathers and swimming lightly over the smooth water. The duckling had never seen any like them before. They curved their graceful necks, while their soft plumage shone with dazzling whiteness. The duckling saw these lovely birds and felt more strangely unhappy than ever.

"I will fly to these royal birds," he exclaimed, "and they will kill me because, ugly as I am, I dare to approach them. But it does not matter."

Then he flew to the water and swam toward the beautiful swans. The moment they espied the stranger, they rushed to meet him with outstretched wings.

"Kill me," said the poor bird and he bent his head down to the surface of the water and awaited death.

But what did he see in the clear stream below? His own image—no longer a dark-gray bird, ugly and disagreeable to look at, but a graceful and beautiful swan.

He now felt glad at having suffered sorrow and trouble because it enabled him to enjoy so much better all the pleasure and happiness around him; for the great swans swam round the newcomer and stroked his neck with their beaks, as a welcome.

Into the garden presently came some little children and threw bread and cake into the water.

"See," cried the youngest, "there is another swan come; a new one has arrived."

Then they threw bread and cake into the water and said, "The new one is the most beautiful of all."

Then he felt quite ashamed and hid his head under his wing, for he did not know what to do, he was so happy—yet he was not at all proud. He had been persecuted and despised for his ugliness. Then he rustled his feathers, curved his slender neck, and cried joyfully, from the depths of his heart, "I never dreamed of such happiness as this while I was the despised ugly duckling."

Samuel Rencher, 5th grade

1. I can tie my shoe.

2. When I was 7, I couldn't tie my shoe.

3. Now I can double-knot it in 15 seconds.

4. It's easy to remember what it's like to be an outcast.

Julian Ponce, 6th grade

1. I went from feeling bad to feeling better.

2. When I hurt my leg, and I walked funny like a chicken in the middle of laying an egg, people called me names and made me feel like a reject. I felt crippling depression.

3. Then at the end of the year, we played hide-n-go seek tag and became friends again.

4. When you see other people suffering or feeling like a reject, you know what to do because you know what it's like.

Christina Reimer, 7th grade

1. These days I think of myself as a reader a lot more than I used to.

2. In 4th grade, I only read about one book a year because I thought reading was boring. Then I only read what the teachers made us read. Compared to everyone else, I felt like a terrible reader and it was embarrassing, just like the ugly duckling felt when he compared himself to the other ducks.

3. Now I read about one book a week, once I discovered some genres that I really like: realistic fiction, historical fiction, and fantasy. I have confidence in my reading ability.

4. It helps me to know that sometimes people who think they are not good at something just haven't found the way that works for them.

Betlen Hernandez, 9th grade

My attitude has changed about peer pressure, when other people are pressuring you to do something that might have a negative effect in your future. Whether it's getting into college, or in job opportunities, I now think about myself first, not in doing what everyone is doing.

My experience when I went to Colombia the summer of 2017, I made poor choices because I was pressured by people, and frankly I didn't want to be the only one not doing what they were doing. After going to dinner with some old friends that I had not seen in months, they invited me to a party. At first I was hesitant, but they kept saying things like "Come on, it'll be fun," "You used to be the wild one, what happened to that girl?" or "Nothing bad will happen." I agreed, even though I knew deep down that it was a bad idea. There were a lot of people there. There were also drugs and alcohol.

It was around one in the morning when police came to shut it down. Multiple people got arrested for possession of illegal substances. I was arrested as well; I spent the night in jail; I was bailed out by my cousin.

It only took one poor decision, and being pressured by my "friends," that took away a scholarship to study for an entire summer, at the Galapagos, and Australia, and Oceania. I lost my chance to study marine biology with some of the best scientists. I learned my lesson the hard way, but now anytime I feel something is wrong, I think twice. Just because everyone is doing it, doesn't mean you should. Always think about your future.

Perseverance

Read the story.

Think about how people can do superhuman feats if it's for something they truly care about.

Write an essay to explain what perseverance looks like.

MY TRUISM

MAKING A CHANGE

I wanted to change this	But this was stopping me	So I did this	Truism

MY KERNEL ESSAY

1. _____

2. _____

3. _____

4. _____

_____

_____

TRUISM EXAMPLES

1. Sometimes you just have to keep going.

2. When something really matters, people will do the impossible.

3. _____

The Wild Swans

Far away, dwelt a king who had eleven sons and one daughter, named Eliza. Their father, the king, married a wicked sorceress. She told the king so many untrue things about the young princes that he gave himself no more trouble about them.

"Go out into the world and look after yourselves," said the queen to the princes. And they were turned into eleven beautiful wild swans.

With a strange cry, they flew through the windows far away to the seashore.

When the sun was about to set, Eliza saw eleven white swans, with golden crowns on their heads. The swans alighted quite close to her, flapping their great white wings. As soon as the sun had disappeared, the feathers of the swans fell off and eleven beautiful princes, Eliza's brothers, stood near her.

She uttered a loud cry. They laughed and wept and told each other how cruelly they had been treated by their stepmother.

"We brothers," said the eldest, "fly about as wild swans while the sun is in the sky, but as soon as it sinks behind the hills, we recover our human shape. Therefore, we must always be near a resting place before sunset; for if we were flying toward the clouds when we recovered our human form, we should sink deep into the sea."

"How can I break this spell?" asked the sister. And they talked about it nearly the whole night, slumbering only a few hours.

Eliza was awakened by the rustling of the wings of swans soaring above her. Her brothers were again changed to swans. Toward evening they came back, and as the sun went down, they resumed their natural forms. "Tomorrow," said one, "we shall fly away, not to return again till a whole year has passed. But we cannot leave you here. Have you courage to go with us? Will not all our wings be strong enough to bear you over the sea?"

"Yes, take me with you," said Eliza. They spent the whole night in weaving a large, strong net of willow and rushes. On this, Eliza laid herself down to sleep, and when the sun rose, the wild swans took up the net with their beaks and flew up.

They were far from the land when Eliza awoke. By her side lay a branch full of beautiful ripe berries; the youngest of her brothers had gathered them and placed them there. Onward the whole day they flew through the air like winged arrows. Eliza watched the sinking sun with great anxiety, for the little rock in the ocean was not yet in sight.

Presently, she caught sight of the rock just below them. Her brothers stood close around her with arms linked together, for there was not the smallest space to spare.

At sunrise the swans flew away from the rock, bearing their sister with them. At last she saw the real land to which they were bound. Long before the sun went down, she was sitting in front of a large cave, the floor of which was overgrown with delicate green creeping plants, like an embroidered carpet.

In her sleep, a fairy came out to meet her. "Your brothers can be released," said she, "if you have courage. Do you see the stinging nettle in my hand? These you must gather, even while they burn blisters on your hands. You must weave eleven coats with long sleeves; if these are then thrown over the eleven swans, the spell will be broken. But remember well, that from the moment you commence until your task is finished, you must not speak. The first word you utter will pierce the hearts of your brothers like a deadly dagger. Remember all that I have told you."

Eliza awoke. It was broad daylight, and she went forth from the cave to begin work with her delicate hands. The ugly nettles burned great blisters on her hands and arms, but she determined to bear the pain gladly if she could only release her dear brothers.

At sunset, her brothers returned, and when they saw her hands they understood what she was doing. The youngest brother wept, and where his tears touched her the burning blisters vanished. Eliza kept to her work.

One coat was already finished and she had begun the second, when she heard a huntsman's horn and was struck with fear. In a few minutes, all the huntsmen stood before the cave. The handsomest of them was the king of the country, who advanced toward her, saying, "How did you come here, my sweet child?"

Eliza shook her head. She dared not speak.

"Come with me," he said. Then he lifted her onto his horse. She wept and wrung her hands, but the king said, "I wish only your happiness."

Then the king declared his intention of making her his bride, but the archbishop whispered that the fair young maiden was only a witch. The king would not listen to him and led her through fragrant gardens and lofty halls, but not a smile appeared on her lips. She looked the very picture of grief. Then the king opened the door of a little chamber in which she was to sleep. On the floor lay the bundle of flax which she had spun from the nettles, and under the ceiling hung the coat she had made.

When Eliza saw all these things, the thought of her brothers and their release made her so joyful that she kissed the king's hand. Then he pressed her to his heart. She loved him with her whole heart.

At night she crept away into her little chamber and quickly wove one coat after another. But when she began the seventh, she found she had no more flax. She knew that the nettles she wanted to use grew in the churchyard and that she must pluck them herself.

With a trembling heart, Eliza crept into the garden in the broad moonlight till she reached the churchyard. She gathered the nettles, and carried them home with her.

Only the archbishop had seen her. Now he felt sure that his suspicions were correct; she was a witch and had bewitched the king and all the people. Secretly he told the king what he had seen and what he feared.

In the meantime, she had almost finished her task. Once more only must she venture to the churchyard and pluck a few handfuls. She went, and the king and the archbishop followed her. The king turned away his head and said, "The people must condemn her." Quickly she was condemned to suffer death by fire.

Away from the gorgeous regal halls, she was led to a dark, dreary cell. They gave her the ten coats which she had woven, to cover her, and the bundle of nettles for a pillow. But they could have given her nothing that would have pleased her more. She continued her task with joy and prayed for help.

Now all the people came streaming forth from the gates of the city to see the witch burned. An old horse drew the cart on which she sat, dressed her in a garment of coarse sackcloth. Even on the way to death, she would not give up her task. The ten finished coats lay at her feet; she was working hard at the eleventh, while the mob jeered her and said: "See the witch; she sits there with her ugly sorcery. Let us tear it into a thousand pieces."

At that moment, eleven wild swans flew over her and alighted on the cart. They flapped their large wings.

As the executioner seized her by the hand to lift her out of the cart, she hastily threw the eleven coats over the eleven swans, and they immediately became eleven handsome princes; but the youngest had a swan's wing instead of an arm, for she had not been able to finish the last sleeve of the coat.

"Now I may speak," she exclaimed. "I am innocent."

"Yes, she is innocent," said the eldest brother, and related all that had taken place. And a marriage procession, such as no king had ever before seen, returned to the castle.

Pablo Tello, 10th grade

1. The king's daughter Eliza wanted to cure her cursed brothers.

2. Their disease is incurable.

3. She takes difficult orders from a fairy for their cure.

4. People will do anything to get what they want.

Brandon Gallegos, 10th grade

Growing up, giving up is the simplest thing to do. It takes no skill; you don't lose anything, but nor do you gain anything. Perseverance is one of the hardest skills you can learn, but when you learn it, it can become the best thing in the world. When something really matters, people will do the impossible.

When I was in elementary, I was diagnosed with a little bit of ADHD which led to problems in learning and trying to pay attention. My main learning disability was in my reading comprehension and writing. For this, I was classified under "special needs" which wasn't bad but I always knew I was better and didn't have to belong in it any more.

After years of failed STAAR tests and other exams, I knew I needed to buckle down and really put in work despite my disabilities and other distractions. This wasn't easy, but little by little, I started paying closer attention to my classes and started doing better in my reading and writing as well as my other classes. At this point, I was already in middle school, ready for my freshman year of high school. I had gotten my report card for the whole school year. It was good, but I knew it could have been better. This killed me because it was frustrating that I worked so hard and got so little progress. I was at the point to where I just wanted to give up on all my hard work, but I knew I couldn't just give up. It wasn't about getting out of the "special needs" program. I wanted to do this for myself; I wanted to prove, that with a little hard work and a whole lot of dedication, anything is possible.

And it was. At my end of freshman year, I had my ARD meeting with my parents and some teachers. There they said how I've improved and I wouldn't need to be in the "special needs" program. It was the most exciting and emotional day of my life because I knew that all my hard work paid off.

When something really matters, people will do the impossible. With perseverance anything and everything is possible as long as you remember to never give up and try your hardest no matter what obstacles may be in your way.

Deception

NAME

Read the story.
Think about how people have to watch out for being scammed.
Write an essay about the dangers of ignoring warnings.

MY TRUISM

DISCOVERING THE TRUTH

| Someone told me (or I read) ... | So I assumed ... | When actually ... | So now I understand ... (truism) |

MY KERNEL ESSAY

1. _____

2. _____

3. _____

4. _____

_____

_____

TRUISM EXAMPLES

1. Young children need to be protected from harm.

2. As children grow into adults, they learn how to guard against deceit.

3. _____

The Wolf and the Seven Little Kids

There was once upon a time an old goat who had seven little kids and loved them with all the love of a mother for her children. One day, she wanted to go into the forest and fetch some food. So she called all seven to her and said, "Dear children, I have to go into the forest, so be on your guard against the wolf; if he comes in, he will devour you all, skin, hair, and all. The wretch often disguises himself, but you will know him at once by his rough voice and his black feet." The kids said, "Dear mother, we will take good care of ourselves; you may go away without any anxiety." Then the old one bleated, and went on her way with an easy mind.

It was not long before someone knocked at the house door and cried, "Open the door, dear children; your mother is here and has brought something back with her for each of you." But the little kids knew that it was the wolf by the rough voice; "We will not open the door," cried they, "thou art not our mother. She has a soft, pleasant voice, but thy voice is rough; thou art the wolf!" Then the wolf went away to a shopkeeper and bought himself a great lump of chalk, ate this, and made his voice soft with it. Then he came back, knocked at the door of the house, and cried, "Open the door, dear children, your mother is here and has brought something back with her for each of you." But the wolf had laid his black paws against the window, and the children saw them and cried, "We will not open the door, our mother has not black feet like thee: Thou art the wolf." Then the wolf ran to a baker and said, "I have hurt my feet, rub some dough over them for me." And when the baker had rubbed his feet over, he ran to the miller and said, "Strew some white meal over my feet for me." The miller thought to himself, "The wolf wants to deceive someone," and refused; but the wolf said, "If thou wilt not do it, I will devour thee." Then the miller was afraid and made his paws white for him. Truly men are like that.

So now the wretch went for the third time to the house door, knocked at it and said, "Open the door for me, children, your dear little mother has come home and has brought every one of you something back from the forest with her." The little kids cried, "First show us thy paws that we may know if thou art our dear little mother." Then he put his paws in through the window, and when the kids saw that they were white, they believed that all he said was true and opened the door. But who should come in but the wolf! They were terrified and wanted to hide themselves. One sprang under the table, the second into the bed, the third into the stove, the fourth into the kitchen, the fifth into the cupboard, the sixth under the washing bowl, and the seventh into the clock case. But the wolf found them all; one after the other he swallowed them down his throat. The youngest in the clock case was the only one he did not find. When the wolf had satisfied his appetite, he laid himself down under a tree in the green meadow outside and began to sleep. Soon afterward, the old goat came home again from the forest. Ah! What a sight she saw there! The house door stood wide open. The table, chairs, and benches were thrown down, the washing bowl lay broken to pieces, and the quilts and pillows were pulled off the bed. She sought her children, but they were nowhere to be found. She called them one after another by name, but no one answered. At last, when she came to the youngest, a soft voice cried, "Dear mother, I am in the clock case." She took the kid out, and it told her that the wolf had come and had eaten all the others. Then you may imagine how she wept over her poor children.

At length, in her grief she went out, and the youngest kid ran with her. When they came to the meadow, there lay the wolf by the tree and snored so loud that the branches shook. She looked at him on every side and saw that something was moving and struggling in his gorged body. "Ah, heavens," said she, "is it possible that my poor children can be still alive?" Then the kid had to run home and fetch scissors, and a needle and thread, and the goat cut open the monster's stomach, and hardly had she made one cut, than one little kid thrust its head out, and when she cut farther, all six sprang out one after another and were all still alive, and they had suffered no injury whatever, for in his greediness, the monster had swallowed them down whole. What rejoicing there was! Then they embraced their dear mother who said, "Now go and look for some big stones, and we will fill the wicked beast's stomach with them while he is still asleep." Then the seven kids dragged the stones thither with all speed and put as many of them into his stomach as they could get in; and the mother sewed him up again in the greatest haste so that he was not aware of anything and never once stirred.

When the wolf at length had had his sleep out, he got on his legs, and as the stones in his stomach made him very thirsty, he wanted to go to a well to drink. But when he began to walk and to move about, the stones in his stomach knocked against each other and rattled. Then cried he,

> "What rumbles and tumbles
>
> Against my poor bones?
>
> I thought it was six kids,
>
> But it's naught but big stones."

And when he got to the well and stooped over the water and was just about to drink, the heavy stones made him fall in and, as there was no help, he had to drown miserably. When the seven kids saw that, they came running to the spot and cried aloud, "The wolf is dead! The wolf is dead!" and danced for joy round about the well with their mother.

Jazlyn Garcia, 5th grade

1. Our friends entered a drawing to win a house.

2. When they were told they won, they had to pay 500 dollars to be able to get the house.

3. When they went to the area where their house was, there was no house there and that meant that they got scammed.

4. Now they know that they should never trust what people say because not everybody tells the truth.

Katalina Luna, 5th grade

1. My sister told me that someone said something bad to her.

2. I thought he was just flat out being rude to my sister.

3. Then I found out she had called him a midget first.

4. So now I know that sometimes children don't tell you the whole truth.

Destiny Briseno, 5th grade

1. Someone once told me I could win a free puppy if I had given my information.

2. So I assumed I would get a free puppy.

3. But actually it was a lie. We never got the puppy.

4. So now I understand. Don't believe everything you read or hear.

Julian Ponce, 7th grade

1. Someone online told my friend that they would give him the newest model of Beats for $150. He wanted to get them.

2. Since he assumed that it was a good price for a good pair of headphones, he ordered them.

3. Actually, it was a scam. When they arrived, they were broken. They weren't the same thing that he had seen in the picture. He tried to get a refund, but the seller said no.

4. So now he understands not to get scammed. Only some people tell the truth, and someone's lies can make us suffer.

Olivia Keyes, Kindergarten

1. Tatum said, "Olivia hurt me!" when I didn't.

2. "Is this true, Olivia?" I said, "No, I just wanted to play with Barbie."

3. "I believe my child more than you."

4. So now Tatum is still my friend, but I know that sometimes she doesn't tell the truth. But sometimes her do.

Appendices

Complete Text Structures Collection

Structures for Writing About Life Themes

STORY OF MY THINKING

I used to think (truism)	But this happened	So now I think ... (truism)

PARTS OF A WHOLE

The whole	One part	Another part	Truism

TYPE OF SOMETHING

One kind	Another kind	The worst kind	Truism

SHORT- AND LONG-TERM EFFECTS

What someone said	What surprised me about that	The effect it had at first	The effect it had later	How this will help me later

WHAT THE CHARACTERS KNOW ABOUT _____

What it means to most people	One thing she or he knows (and how)	Another thing she or he knows (and how)	What this adds up to for the characters

Structures for Explaining a Concept

CASE STUDY

Question	My (or someone else's) experience	What that shows	Truism

COMPARING NOTES

Some people think ...	Other people think ...	But I think ...	So I will ...

THE ONION

Truism	How do I know this? (one way)	If that had not happened, how else would I know this?	If that had not happened, how else would I know this?	Truism

RECONSIDERING A BELIEF

Most people think ...	... because (one way it's good)	But ... (one way it's bad)	So ... (truism)

LIFE LESSON

Truism	How it's true in the story	How it's true in life	How this will help me

Structures for Character Analysis

EVOLUTION OF A TERM

| What the word meant to me when I was little | What it meant when I was a little older | What it means to me now | What it will mean to me later in my life | What all this says to me |

CHAIN REACTION

| One thing that happened | What that caused | What else that caused | How it turned out | Truism |

DOUBLE TAKE

| What happened | A negative way to view this | A positive way to view this | Which way I think is stronger | Truism |

NEWS/GOSSIP: TELL ME, TELL ME

| At the time ... | All of a sudden ... | This was surprising because ... | People said ... | It just goes to show you: |

CHANGE OF PLANS

| Where I was going (and why) | Something unexpected that happened | How my plans changed | What I think (truism) |

Structures for Analyzing a Theme in Literature

WRONG ASSUMPTIONS

I made this wrong assumption	... happened as a consequence	I learned this truth	So now I believe ...

FINDING OUT FOR SURE

I've never been sure if ...	But I've always suspected that ...	Because once I experienced ...	Which made me think that ...	And finally I realized that ...

DEFINITION

Definition of something	How to tell if something fits this definition	One example that fits	Truism

THE 11-MINUTE ESSAY

Truism	How it's true in a story	How it's true in a movie	How it's true in my life	I wonder ...

TEVYE'S DEBATE

On one hand ...	On the other hand ...	But on the other hand ...	But on the other hand ...	So ...

Structures for Commentary About Plot

STORY OF MY THINKING

I used to think (truism)	But this happened	So now I think ... (truism)

HINDSIGHT REFLECTIONS

This bad situation happened	How I should have reacted	How I did react	Now I know ...

SURPRISE ENDING

A big mistake someone made	What this caused	How it turned out	If the mistake had not happened	Truism

WAYS TO DO SOMETHING

Truism	A bad way (and why)	A better way (and why)	The best way

DESCRIPTION

What it is	Kinds of it	Where you can find it	Parts of it	Truism about it

Structures for Making an Argument

CROSSING MY PATH

| Real life example | Truism | Example from story | How it relates to me today | Question about truism |

NOW AND LATER

| Problem | A shortcut solution | A long-term solution | How I would decide which is better |

FINDING THE TRUTH THROUGH EXPERIENCE

| I heard this | But I thought the opposite | Then I heard about this experience | Now I think this |

CURIOSITY

| I wondered ... | I figured out ... | Then I also figured out ... | Last I figured out ... | This all means that ... |

FIVE-PARAGRAPH ESSAY

| Truism | One way to tell (with example) | Another way to tell (with example) | Another way to tell (with example) | How this knowledge can help |

Structures for Content-Area Writing

LEARNING FROM MISTAKES

One way I got in trouble	What happened after that	What I thought about my consequences	What I realize now

SOLVING A MYSTERY

What I know	What I don't know	Steps I took to find out	Successful?	Life lesson (truism)

SOMETHING CHANGED

What changed	How it used to be	How it is now	It helps me to know that ...

MAKING A CHANGE

I wanted to change this	But this was stopping me	So I did this	Truism

DISCOVERING THE TRUTH

Someone told me (or I read) ...	So I assumed ...	When actually ...	So now I understand ... (truism)

25 More Things to Do With These Lessons

1. Write an original fairy tale using one of the truisms or themes.

2. Rewrite a fairy tale in a contemporary setting using a truism and theme.

3. Write an original fairy tale using your truism or fairy tale theme.

4. Make an illustrated copy of your writing for a class book or personal book.

5. Form a group to do Reader's Theatre with one of the fairy tales.

6. Make a shoebox diorama or a scrapbook of artifacts from a fairy tale.

7. Do a multigenre book in the style of *The Jolly Postman*.

8. Write a parody of a fairy tale in story form or in a script to be performed.

9. Make a glossary of the fairy tale themes with illustrations or icons for each.

10. Make a comic book strip from your fairy tale, kernel, or complete essay.

11. Make a list of humorous or sarcastic truisms for a fairy tale.

12. Write a "Simpsons"–style synopsis or theme from a fairy tale.

13. Make a journal pocket and collect truisms or themes for future writing.

14. Write a first-person essay as a character, explaining your truism and using details from your fairy tale.

15. Research and compare/contrast other versions of a fairy tale.

16. List your ten favorite words from a fairy tale and use them in a new essay.

17. Choose your favorite "old-timey" words or phrases from a fairy tale and research their origins.

18. "Who am I?" Using details from the stories, write riddles based on fairy tale characters and have classmates guess who is speaking.

19. Pick your favorite scene from a fairy tale and rewrite it as a script. Assign parts to classmates and be prepared to perform it.

20. Use three of the "One-Pager" craft lessons to revise and share your completed essay.

21. Do a cubing activity for a fairy tale summary: characters, setting, problem, solution, theme, truism.

22. "In other words ..." Retell your fairy tale or personal essay to a partner, small group, or class without using the written version.

23. Design a poster with a selection of your favorite fairy tales and themes, including illustrations.

24. Draw characters from your fairy tale or essay and put truisms in thought bubbles over their heads.

25. Take a truism and make it part of the chorus for an original song you write.

Blank Student Planning Page

NAME _____

Read the story.

Think about

Write an essay about

MY TRUISM

_____

MY TEXT STRUCTURE _____

MY KERNEL ESSAY

1. _____

2. _____

3. _____

4. _____

5. _____

TRUISM EXAMPLES

1. _____

2. _____

3. _____

Text Chunkyard

Use these pieces to create your original text structure.

| This is true. | I know this. | I like this. | |

| I saw this. | I thought this. | I heard this. | A conversation |
| | | | A sight |

| This is happening. | This happened. | This happens. | This could happen. | This should happen. |

for
and
nor
but
or
yet
so
also
because
if
since
whenever
unless
instead
until
in one case
one time
however
at the same time
even so
by contrast,
in other words
then
gradually
meanwhile
overnight
simultaneously
in fact
particularly
above all
as a result
therefore

Get Student Writers Talking: Conversation Strategies

Sometimes writers need to talk to get their juices flowing and to make decisions about their writing.

Use these Conversation Strategies to help student writers start talking!

Afterward, ask students to reflect and debrief:

What kind of thinking did you do during this conversation?

How can you do that same kind of thinking when you are writing on your own?

GUIDELINES FOR BRAINSTORMING

✓ Produce as many ideas as possible.

✓ Say your ideas aloud and/or write them down as soon as you think of them.

✓ Don't judge, censor, or criticize ideas while brainstorming.

✓ Think of unusual ideas.

✓ Riff off the ideas of others; combine ideas to form new ones.

✓ Don't stop too soon—allow quiet/thinking time.

WHEN YOU'RE TRYING TO …	TRY THIS KIND OF CONVERSATION …	HERE'S HOW IT WORKS …	IT WORKS BEST WITH …
Brainstorm ideas based on the theme or the "Think about …" statement.	Idea Storm	1. Put chart paper around the room (one poster per 5–7 students). In the center of each poster, write the theme word or the "Think about …" statement. 2. Review the Guidelines for Brainstorming. 3. Students use markers and create a web of ideas in response to the theme or "Think about …" prompt. 4. After a few minutes, groups rotate; students read what's written on the next chart paper and continue adding. 5. After a few rotations, students jot down ideas from around the room that they want to think about using in their own essays.	ALL
Brainstorm ideas in response to a prompt.	Café Conversations	1. Arrange tables or groups of desks for groups of 5–6 students to sit together. 2. In the center of a piece of chart paper covering each table, rewrite the prompt in the form of a question. 3. Students gather in groups at each table and discuss the prompt for a few minutes. 4. Students make notes of their ideas on the chart paper. 5. When it's time to rotate, one student stays behind to recap the conversation for the next group who picks up the conversation and continues. 6. Repeat and rotate for a few rounds of conversation.	ALL
Decide how to respond to a prompt that asks you to choose a side.	Conversation Strategies	1. Turn the prompt into a yes/no question. Examples: Is it better to try to achieve more rather than to be happy with what you have? (Lesson 7) Is stealing ever justifiable? (Lesson 13) 2. Working in pairs or trios, students develop reasons to support BOTH "yes" and "no." 3. Pairs or trios combine to form groups of 4–6. Students share their reasons with each other. 4. Groups decide on ONE answer and decide which reason provides the best support. 5. Spokespeople report out to the whole class. 6. Each student individually writes his or her own conclusion, using the support she or he finds most compelling.	7. The Fisherman and His Wife (Greed), Comparing Notes 13. Jack and the Beanstalk (Stealing), Double Take

WHEN YOU'RE TRYING TO ...	TRY THIS KIND OF CONVERSATION ...	HERE'S HOW IT WORKS ...		IT WORKS BEST WITH ...
Choose a truism.	Opinion Continuum	1.	As a class, brainstorm a few truisms.	ALL
		2.	Put a line on the floor; label one end "strongly agree" and the other end "strongly disagree."	
		3.	Read each truism aloud (and write or project on board).	
		4.	Students stand on the line to show how they feel about that truism, then turn and talk with others around them about why they feel the way they do.	
		5.	Volunteers share their reasons with the whole class.	
		6.	Students are free to move if they change their minds after hearing their classmates' reasons.	
		7.	Students make a note of which truisms they agree with most strongly and why.	
Experiment with text structures that draw on personal experiences.	Tell Me More About That ...	*One of the most effective questions interviewers can ask someone they're interviewing is simply, "Tell me more about that ..."*		1. Beauty and the Beast (Appearances), Story of My Thinking
		1.	Give students a prompt and a menu of text structures that ask them to draw on personal experiences.	4. Diamonds and Toads (Power of Words), Short- and Long-Term Effects
		2.	Individually, students choose a truism and 2 or 3 text structures to try out through conversation before choosing one to try out on paper.	6. The Emperor's New Clothes (Peer Pressure), Case Study
		3.	With a partner, students take turns being the interviewer and the writer being interviewed.	8. The Frog Prince (Selfishness), The Onion
		4.	The writer shares the truism she or he has chosen.	11. Hansel and Gretel (Listening), Evolution of a Term
		5.	The interviewer uses the first box of the text structure to ask a question. Example: Text structure box: "What the word meant to me when I was little" (Lesson 11) Interviewer's question: "What did the word mean to you when you were little?"	12. Henny Penny (Fear), Chain Reaction
				14. The Little Red Hen (Generosity), News/Gossip: Tell Me, Tell Me
				15. Little Red Riding Hood (Distractions), Change of Plans
				16. The Nightingale (Love), Wrong Assumptions
		6.	The writer answers.	17. One-Eye, Two-Eyes, and Three-Eyes (Humiliation), Finding Out for Sure
		7.	The interviewer asks, "Can you tell me more about that ... ?"	21. Rumpelstiltskin (Promises), Story of My Thinking
		8.	The writer responds.	22. The Sleeping Beauty (Gifts), Hindsight Reflections
		9.	Repeat this process with the rest of the boxes in the text structure.	23. Snow White (Mistakes), Surprise Ending
		10.	Students change roles and repeat.	29. Thumbelina (Place), Curiosity
		11.	After talking through 2 or 3 text structures, student writers choose one to try out in writing.	31. Tom Thumb (Home), Learning From Mistakes
				32. The Twelve Dancing Princesses (Mystery), Solving a Mystery
				33. The Ugly Duckling (Humility), Something Changed
				34. The Wild Swans (Perseverance), Making a Change

(Continued)

WHEN YOU'RE TRYING TO ...	TRY THIS KIND OF CONVERSATION ...	HERE'S HOW IT WORKS ...	IT WORKS BEST WITH ...
Brainstorm ideas when using a text structure that asks you to define, describe, or analyze something.	Yes, and ...	*One of the rules for participating in an improv comedy sketch is that the performers must always say, "Yes, and ..." and go along with what the person before them said or did.* 1. Give students the prompt and text structure. 2. Students form small groups, and sit facing each other. 3. Each group appoints a scribe who creates a large chart, using each box from the text structure as a column heading. 4. Review the Guidelines for Brainstorming. 5. Students brainstorm ideas for each box of the text structure, taking turns, and saying "Yes, and ..." before adding another idea. Students brainstorm for several rounds before moving on to the next box in the text structure. The scribe adds all ideas to the chart. 6. Students choose ideas from the group chart that work best with the truism they want to use in their writing.	2. The Bremen Town Musicians (Family), Parts of a Whole 3. Cinderella (Hardships), Type of Something 18. The Princess and Pea (Tests), Definition 25. The Story of the Three Bears (Manners), Description
Think of lots of different examples (from life, literature, etc.) that can be used to explain a truism.	The Wisdom of the Room	1. As a class, brainstorm a few truisms in response to the prompt. 2. Post truisms around the room. Each student moves to the truism she or he wants to use in his or her writing. 3. Students form small groups focused on the same truism and text structure. 4. Students create a large chart, using each box from the text structure as a column heading. 5. Review the Guidelines for Brainstorming. 6. Individually, students jot down ideas on sticky notes then post to the chart. 7. Students continue to brainstorm, inspired by one another's ideas to think of more and more examples.	5. The Elves and the Shoemaker (Gratitude), What the Characters Know About _____ 10. The Golden Goose (Laughter), Life Lesson 19. Puss in Boots (Reputation), The 11-Minute Essay 24. Snow White and Rose Red (Kindness), Ways to Do Something 26. The Three Billy Goats Gruff (Groups), Crossing My Path 27. The Three Little Pigs (Cutting Corners), Now and Later 30. The Tinderbox (Friendship), Five-Paragraph Essay

WHEN YOU'RE TRYING TO …	TRY THIS KIND OF CONVERSATION …	HERE'S HOW IT WORKS …		IT WORKS BEST WITH …
Create a kernel essay using a text structure that looks at two sides of the same coin.	Yes, but …	1.	Give students the prompt and text structure.	9. The Gingerbread Boy (Confidence), Reconsidering a Belief
		2.	As a class, brainstorm a few truisms in response to the prompt.	20. Rapunzel (Companionship), Tevye's Debate
		3.	Post truisms around the room. Each student moves to the truism she or he wants to use in his or her writing.	28. The Three Sillies (Information), Finding the Truth Through Experience
		4.	Students form small groups (3 or 5 works best) focused on the same truism, and sit facing each other.	35. The Wolf and the Seven Little Kids (Deception), Discovering the Truth
		5.	Review the Guidelines for Brainstorming.	
		6.	One student starts the conversation by agreeing with the statement and explaining why or giving an example.	
		7.	The next student says "Yes, but …" and gives an example or explanation to contradict or disagree with the truism.	
		8.	Repeat, repeat, repeat.	
		9.	Students jot notes to capture ideas for both sides of the issue.	
Think of details to add to a kernel essay.	Tell Me More About This	1.	Students write kernel essays.	ALL
		2.	Students share kernel essays with a partner, then take turns being the interviewer and the writer being interviewed.	
		3.	The writer rereads his or her first sentence then pauses.	
		4.	The interviewer asks, "Can you tell me more about [identifies something specific from the sentence] … ?"	
		5.	The writer answers then decides what kind of detail it was. (The interviewer can help with this.)	
		6.	The writer jots an icon in the "My ICONS for details" box as a reminder to add that kind of detail to his or her writing.	
		7.	Students change roles and repeat.	

Source: Developed by Honor Moorman.

Steps for the Truism Braid Essay

1. Start with a simple truism at the top.

2. In the green (left) heart, write a title of a book or movie you love.

3. Next to the heart, explain how that title illustrates your truism.

4. In the green (left) box, write a heart truism, telling a specific truism that relates to that character's situation.

5. Switch sides.

6. In the pink (right) heart, write the title of another book or movie you love.

7. Next to that heart, explain how that title illustrates your truism.

8. In the pink (right) box, write a heart truism, telling a specific truism that relates to this character's situation.

9. For the conclusion, add together the simple truism on top and phrases from your heart truisms.

See examples below.

See the simple truism at the top.

Green (left) heart: *Forrest Gump*.

Pink (right) heart: *Beauty and the Beast*.

Read the short explanations for each.

Heart truisms: Notice how the green (left) and pink (right) heart truisms are related but different from the simple truism at the top.

See how a phrase from each of the heart truisms is added to the yellow truism to make an improved conclusion.

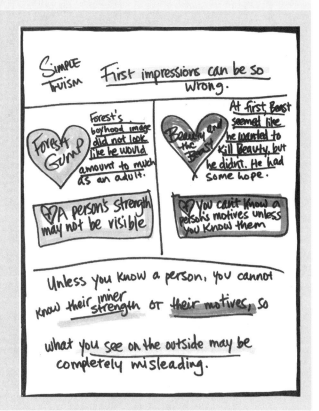

Finished example #1

decoded

Everyone has gone through the difficulty of keeping and making promises. The promises you make are the ones you have to keep close to your heart. Although keeping a promise may seem difficult, the outcome of keeping a promise might give you something quite lovely and pleasing in return.

A simple promise can be distinguished between two friends or perhaps two loved ones. Either it's keeping something between others or promising one to make a huge impact, it'll bring them far in life. In the movie Up, Carl promises Elle, his deceased wife, that he'll do anything it takes to get to Paradise Falls. With lots of dedication and patience during his quest, he arrives at Paradise Falls with the thought of Elle in his mind. As he arrived, he sees the beautiful waterfall gushing and spewing water as the gray rough rocks surrounded the peaceful waves. The remarkable journey surely brought him far in his life as the promise wielded love and happiness.

Fortunately for Hamilton, Laurens, Lafayette, and Mulligan, the promise they made brought them victory. In the Broadway Musical, Hamilton and the rest of the abolitionists promised to fight in the war against the british forces, even if it meant sacrificing themselves. With the hard work and determination, they won the battle of Yorktown against the british troops. In the end, their promise brought them victory as they celebrated their victories against Britain.

In the end, their promises led them far in their life with many great outcomes. Sometimes the promises you keep that contain love and determination will bring you beneficial things such as victories or completion of goals that will bring you very far in life.

Kimberlie Gonzalez, grade 7

Finished example #2

decoded

Everyone has problems in life, whether they are very insignificant or terrifyingly dismal. In turn, we all strive to solve these crisises by reaching for something better. We hope and dream for these brighter futures to come true, and fight as hard as we can to make them happen. These dreams are also known as our goals, and they help us see the world from a better perspective.

Even great historical figure faced hardships that required them to make goals for their future. Take Martin Luther King Junior for example. He grew up in a world that was not only unfair but also unjust. However, instead of getting discouraged, he saw his difficulties as opportunities to change his life and the lives of those around him. He dreamed for a better future and made it come true.

Another awe-inspiring historical figure is Harriet Tubman. As a child, she was raised into a life of slavery that she was told was inevitable. However, instead of accepting her fate, she found a way to free hundreds of slaves including herself, and lead them to a life where they could have a hope and a future. She fought for her own dream, and never stopped hoping for a life where she could be free.

The world will always be there to weigh you down. There will always be another hardship. Just around the corner. Most people believe that there is no way to change that. However, the few that hope for something better and are willing to fight for it are the few that can accomplish any goal that they wish to see happen.

Reader Rubric With Words and Faces

Reader Rubric for STAAR

	Organization Chunkability; kernelizability	Central Idea; Logical Progression Clarity of flow	Originality Truism/thought- provoking quality argument/depth	Craft Word choice/ devices/figurative language	Conventions Correctness; syntax
1 Huh?	You can't kernelize this.	Unclear main idea/ confusing/ unfocused	Obvious thoughts/ everyone already agrees	Not many identifiable icons/ lots of general words	Barely any punctuation/ lots of mistakes/ choppy sentences/ hard to read aloud
2 Ok …	You can almost kernelize this.	Kind of clear/ some focus	Pretty obvious	Not much craft to find	Some mistakes/you can read this aloud
3 Ahh.	Kernelizes pretty easily	Clear, consistent point/very focused	Not completely boring	Some specifics/ some choices	Mostly correct/ some sentence variety/easy to read aloud
4 Oh yes.	Practically kernelizes itself at a glance, including transitions	Completely focused and moves/ideas connected in interesting ways	Thought-provoking or unusual perspective	Many specifics; icons/multiple colors/bookends/ devices/powerful diction	Varied and sophisticated syntax/ pitchforks/a pleasure to read aloud
What would fix this	Kernel essays Transitions Daily writing	Truisms The arguer QA12345 Dead giveaways Daily writing	Levels Walk of 4s Daily writing	Sparkling sentences Icons Pitchforking Dead giveaways Daily writing	Grammar Keepers Pitchforking Sentence wringer Daily writing

Reader Rubric for STAAR

	Organization	Central Idea; Logical Progression	Originality	Craft	Conventions
	Chunkability; kernelizability	Clarity of flow	Truism/thought-provoking quality argument/depth	Word choice/ devices/figurative language	Correctness; syntax
1 Huh?	(sad face)	(sad face)	(sad face)	(sad face)	(sad face)
2 Ok ...	(neutral face)	(neutral face)	(neutral face)	(neutral face)	(neutral face)
3 Ahh.	(smiling face)	(smiling face)	(smiling face)	(smiling face)	(smiling face)
4 Oh yes.	(star-eyed face)	(star-eyed face)	(star-eyed face)	(star-eyed face)	(star-eyed face)
What would fix this	Kernel essays Transitions Daily writing	Truisms The arguer QA12345 Dead giveaways Daily writing	Levels Walk of 4s Daily writing	Sparkling sentences Icons Pitchforking Dead giveaways Daily writing	Grammar Keepers Pitchforking Sentence wringer Daily writing

Intensity Scale

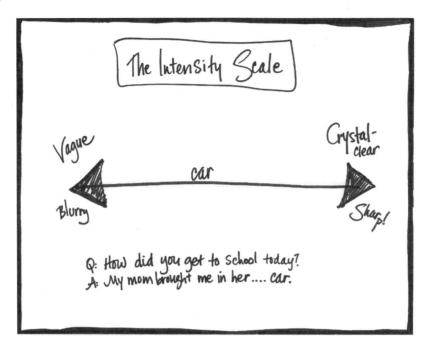

Vague language? Why does it matter? Here's why

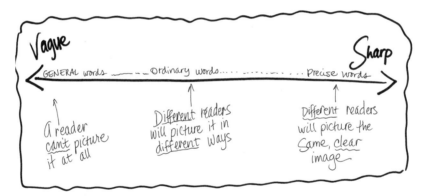

So put an ordinary word in the middle of a line . . . and fill in the rest of the scale.

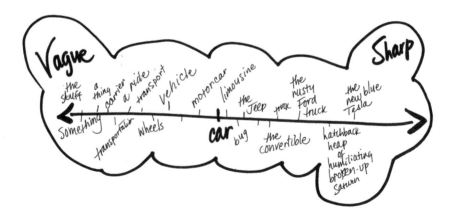

You'll get really good at sharpening up vague language.

Try one. Pick out a plain word and put it in the middle of a line.

What's Better ... This? Or That?

Working independently or working as a team?
Living in the city or living in a small town?
The life of a grownup or the life of a child?
Having pets or having a clean house?
War or peace?
Conforming or being an individual?
Driving a car or staying fit by walking?
Sports or music?
Staying single or getting married?
Having children or living as an adult with no children?
Having a secure job or an adventurous job?
Owning a home or renting and being free to move around?
Getting an advanced education or working right after high school?
Asking for help or doing things on your own?
Taking risks or choosing a safe path?
Marrying young or later in life?
Buying what you want or saving money?
Minding your own business or getting involved in friends' difficulties?
Living in a house or an apartment?
Living alone or living with others?
Buying a lot of small meals or one big meal?
Glasses or contact lenses?
Pen or pencil?
Seeing the glass half full or half empty?
Clinging to things or letting things go?
Tennis shoes or dress shoes?
Reading or watching TV?
Pool or hot tub?
Being organized or being messy?
Color or black and white?
Living in a one-story or a two-story house?
Long hair or short hair?
A car or a truck?
Chips or fries?
Sun or snow?
Left or right?
Superhero or villain?
Being tall or short?
Having straight or curly hair?
Fake or real?

Source: Developed by a sixth-grade class.

Ms. Kern's Final Exam Project and Timetable

Rubric and Schedule: Fairytale Final (AP Lang)

For your final for AP Lang, you will be commissioned by Ms. Bernabei to write a piece that can appear as an example of student writing to be published in her new book *Text Structures From Fairy Tales*. We will start by talking to her about the project and her specific needs and then you will spend two days planning, constructing, and refining your commissioned work. On the third day, we will hand your work over to Ms. Bernabei for publication consideration.

Schedule:

Friday 5/18: Choose three kernel structures that inspire you, read the source text (fairytales), and draft your three kernel essays.

Tuesday 5/22: Write and refine your essay from one of the kernel structures, check your work against the rubric, and refine.

Thursday 5/24: Submit work to Ms. Kern and Ms. Bernabei. Celebrate!!

STANDARD: E3.13 WRITING/WRITING PROCESS. STUDENTS USE ELEMENTS OF THE WRITING PROCESS (PLANNING, DRAFTING, REVISING, EDITING, AND PUBLISHING) TO COMPOSE TEXT.	4 WOW!	3 CLOSE	2 REVISION NEEDED	1 INCOMPLETE
Planning—Student has planned and submitted three kernel structures.				
Drafting—Final essay draft stems from one of the chosen kernel structures.				
Organization—Final essay is kernelizable (can be separated into and read as its separate parts).				
Craft—Author includes and identifies at least three pieces of writers' craft (literary devices, rhetorical devices, literary schemes, and tropes).				
Truism—The truism that the essay is meant to convey is clear and compelling.				
Conventions—Final essay observes standard written conventions.				

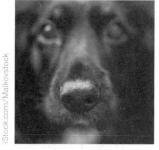

1 Even sad things are important.

2 Sometimes good things don't last very long.

3 Nothing is as precious as an innocent child.

4 Our families help make us who we are.

Truisms
Life Lessons, Thematic Statements

I've learned that you can tell a lot about a person by the way he/she handles these three things: a rainy day, lost luggage, and tangled Christmas tree lights.

I've learned that regardless of your relationship with your parents, you miss them terribly after they die.

I've learned that making a living is not the same thing as making a life.

I've learned that life sometimes gives you a second chance.

I've learned that you shouldn't go through life with a catcher's mitt on both hands. You need to be able to throw something back.

I've learned that whenever I decide something with kindness, I usually make the right decision.

I've learned that even when I have pains, I don't have to be a pain.

I've learned that every day you should reach out and touch someone. People love that human touch—holding hands, a warm hug, or just a friendly pat on the back.

I've learned that I still have a lot to learn.

—Selections from *The Complete Live and Learn and Pass It On*, edited by H. Jackson Brown, Jr.

14 We are guided by all those who have gone before us.

13 There's no such thing as undignified work.

12 Adults make friends in different ways than children do.

11 People pay attention to different things.

10 Life is so fragile.

9 Pretending starts with wishes that haven't come true yet.

5 A person's dreams can come true.

6 Nobody can tell someone else how to grow up.

7 Nobody gets along all the time.

8 Standing in the light means you cast a shadow.

Source: Lightning in a Bottle, Gretchen Bernabei © 2010

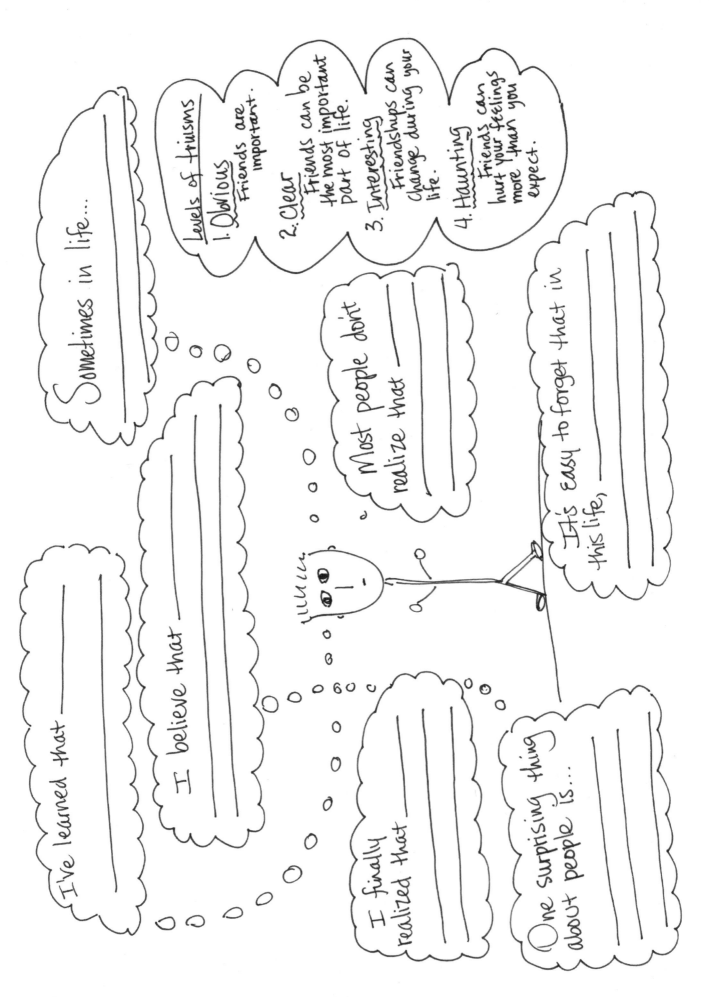

ADDING DETAILS

Three Useful Methods for...

to the sentences in a kernel essay

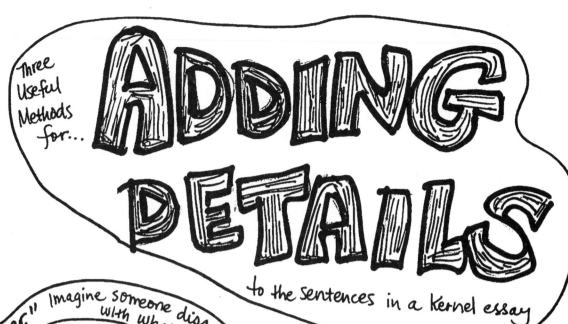

Use "the arguer." Imagine someone disagreeing with what you say.

My mom was mad.

No way.

I don't think so.

Prove that.

You made that up.

Use intentional strokes, in any combinations

Writer's Craft

- ☑ action
- ☑ snapshots
- ☑ thoughtshots
- ☑ dialogue
- ☑ pitchforking
- ☑ smells
- ☑ onomatopeia
- ☑ metaphors/similes
- ☑ renaming
- ☐ (add all year)

QA12345. Just put the sentence in "A" and delete "Q."

Q. —————————
A. —————————
1. How do you know?
2. Huh? What's that?
3. How ELSE do you know?
4. Huh? What's that?
5. So...the answer is...?

BEFORE (write a plain sentence from your kernel essay here)

green- action
blue- snapshots
yellow- thoughtshots
red- dialogue
purple- pitchforks

Add details here →

AFTER (Using any details, in any order, write your new sentence(s) here ↓)

Details ↗

Snapshot Challenge

1. Look at your sentence.
2. Imagine that you're looking at a photograph (or snapshot) taken at that moment.
3. Use words to describe everything you can see in the snapshot.

Hints: What was each person wearing? What expressions were on their faces? Where were they sitting? Standing? What was in their hands? What was the weather like? How much light was in the room? What things could you see? What details were there? Imagine looking at the images from top to bottom, or from left to right….What's in the background? What were people saying? What are they not saying? What do their faces look like they are about to say? What did you see? What did you not see? What were you afraid to see? What did you stare at? What were you amazed to see? What caught your eye first? Who else was there? What could you see out the corner of your eye? What did that tell you? What worries did you have? What did you already know about what you saw? What did you NOT know about what you saw?

Thoughtshot Challenge

1. Look at your sentence.
2. Imagine that people could hear everything you were thinking at that moment.
3. Write down everything that went through your head, everything you thought right then.

Hint: Draw a stick figure. Draw ten thought bubbles over the stick figure's head. Imagine that the stick figure is you. Fill in the ten thought bubbles with thoughts you were having right then.

Another hint: What did you think? What went through your mind? What did you think when you looked around? What did you wonder? What did you know for sure? What never occurred to you? What's one thing that you did NOT know then? What did you wish? What did you know? What did you think would happen? What did you believe? What were you waiting for? How fast was your heart beating? What were you sure about? What do you think the other people in the room were thinking? When you heard something, what did that mean? What doubts did you have? What worries did you have? What did you know? Not know? What did you tell yourself? What did you answer yourself? What did you answer yourself back?

Senses Challenge

1. Look at your sentence.
2. Write details to show every one of the senses:
    ➢ What did you see?
    ➢ What did you hear?
    ➢ What did you smell?
    ➢ What did you feel?
    ➢ What did you taste?

What smells could you notice? Could you smell any food smells? Could you smell any animal smells? What perfumes or colognes or soap smells could you recognize? What did the air smell like? What feelings could you smell in the air? What could you hear clearly? What could you just barely hear? What background noises could you hear? Did anyone's voice remind you of anything? What did your breathing sound like? Was there any music in the background? Was there any music running through your mind? What noise did you expect to hear? What noise did you not expect to hear? What were you hoping to hear? What were you hoping not to hear? What were your fingers touching? What did anything feel like? Did the feel of anything remind you of something? What taste was in your mouth? What had you eaten recently?

Hint: Try to add variety to your sentences so they don't all start with "I." You don't have to use every sense, but the more you can add, the better!

Dialogue Challenge

1. Look at your sentence.
2. Imagine all of the conversation that went on at that moment.
3. Write down everything everyone said.

Hints: Dialogue is more than just words. It's also looks and silences. Pauses. Stares. Short bursts!

What did you say out loud? What did you whisper? What did someone else say? What did you say back? What did you stop yourself from saying? What did someone say under their breath? What voices were in the background? What did you hear them say? What were people saying? Not saying? About to say? What did you wish out loud? What song was anyone singing? What did anyone shout? What did you want to shout? What do you wish someone would have said? What's one thing you're glad nobody said? What question did you ask? What answer did you get?

Ba-da-bing Challenge

1. Look at your sentence.
2. Write one ba-da-bing sentence for that moment, with these three parts:

Pitchforking Challenge

1. Look at your sentence.
2. Underline anything pitchforkifiable.
3. Draw lines and pitchfork at least one place.

Need some help finding something pitchfork-worthy? Try using the AAAWWWUBIS!
(After Although As When Where While Until Because If Since)

Can you pitchfork the AAAWWWUBIS to tell more of the truth?
Like these: After this, this, and this…
Or … Not when this, or this, or this…
Or … If this, and this, and this…

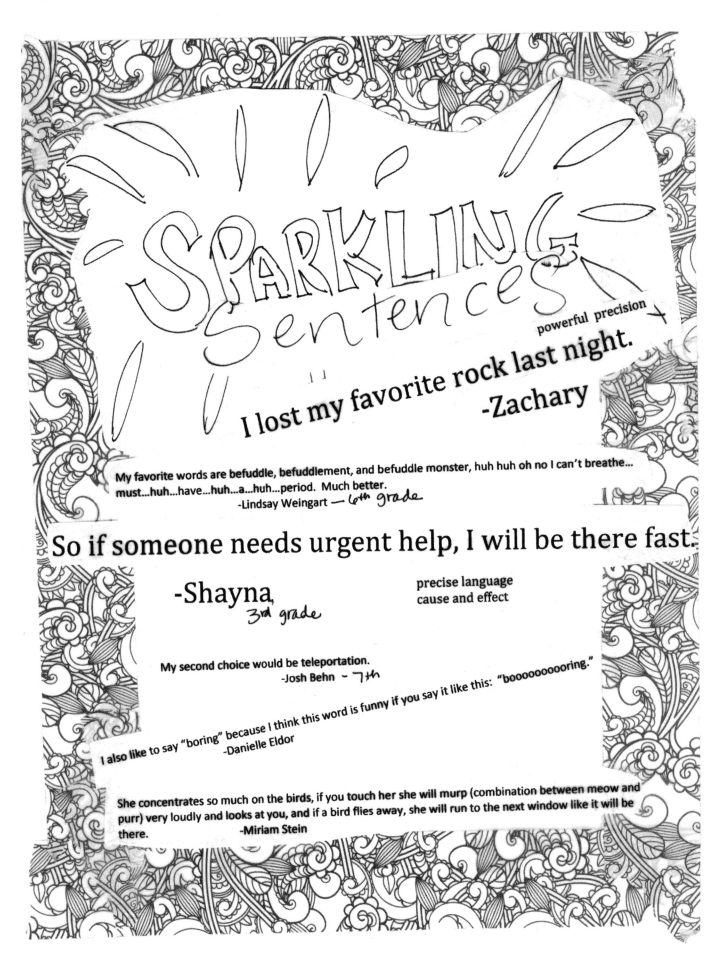

SPARKLING Sentences

powerful precision

I lost my favorite rock last night.

-Zachary

My favorite words are befuddle, befuddlement, and befuddle monster, huh huh oh no I can't breathe... must...huh...have...huh...a...huh...period. Much better.
-Lindsay Weingart — 6th grade

So if **someone** needs urgent help, I will be there fast.

-Shayna,
3rd grade

precise language
cause and effect

My second choice would be teleportation.
-Josh Behn ~ 7th

I also like to say "boring" because I think this word is funny if you say it like this: "booooooooring."
-Danielle Eldor

She concentrates so much on the birds, if you touch her she will murp (combination between meow and purr) very loudly and looks at you, and if a bird flies away, she will run to the next window like it will be there.
-Miriam Stein

Q: Can you give me a definition of sparkling sentences?
  —Desiree Stone, Killeen, TX
   Teacher, 4th grade

A: ↓

You put one of their sentences up on the board or overhead and have everyone read it. "Let's look for what this writer did to make this sentence so powerful," you say.

Listen to the children as they look to see what's good about the writing, and as they tell you what the writer did. "He put a period." "He started with a capital letter." Those will come first, if they're used to DOL. "I like the way he used this word." someone will say, and you're off and running.

You don't have to tell them anything about what sparkling sentences are, just show them. You just look at individual sentences, maybe two a day, admire them, name the parts of them ("Oh look! This is called an appositive…") if they don't know them, and post them on the wall, with the students' names on them.

Does this help?
Gretchen

★This one strategy may be the single most powerful change-agent of all the tricks in my writing book. —GB

Make sure to:

Weeping, she fell on her knees in the soft grass of the forest and prayed. —Marie
"Sir, our Air Force has been taken down!" said one toy soldier. —Isaiah
He craned his neck to see a small hand holding him down. —Fina

9th grade examples

"Dang, this is harder than I thought," I told my sister. —Christopher
I wonder why the earth moves and we don't feel it. —Gaby
"What's this?" I asked as I picked up the mysterious cup. —Rachel
Her hair was soft and smooth, and her perfume smelled like cherry. —Brandon
What? You expect me to baby-sit on a Saturday! —Joseph
I could feel the air piercing my face. —Preston

MAKE SURE NOT TO:

Notes:

Brought to you by Gretchen Bernabei

For more information, see Crunchtime, p. 84-87 and Reviving the Essay

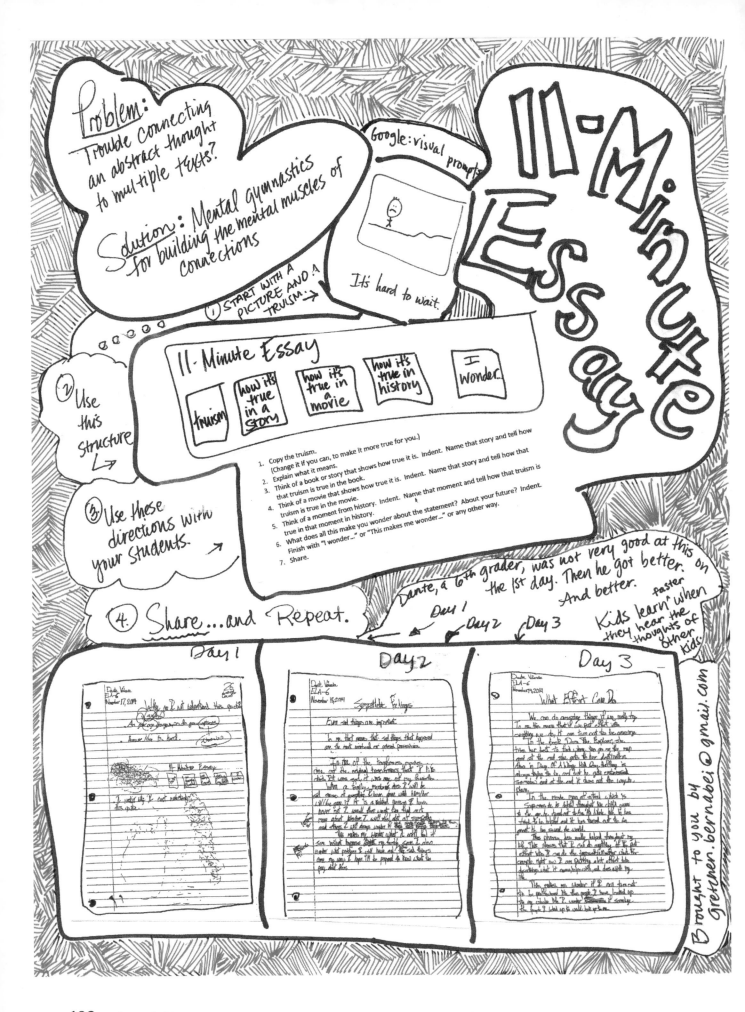

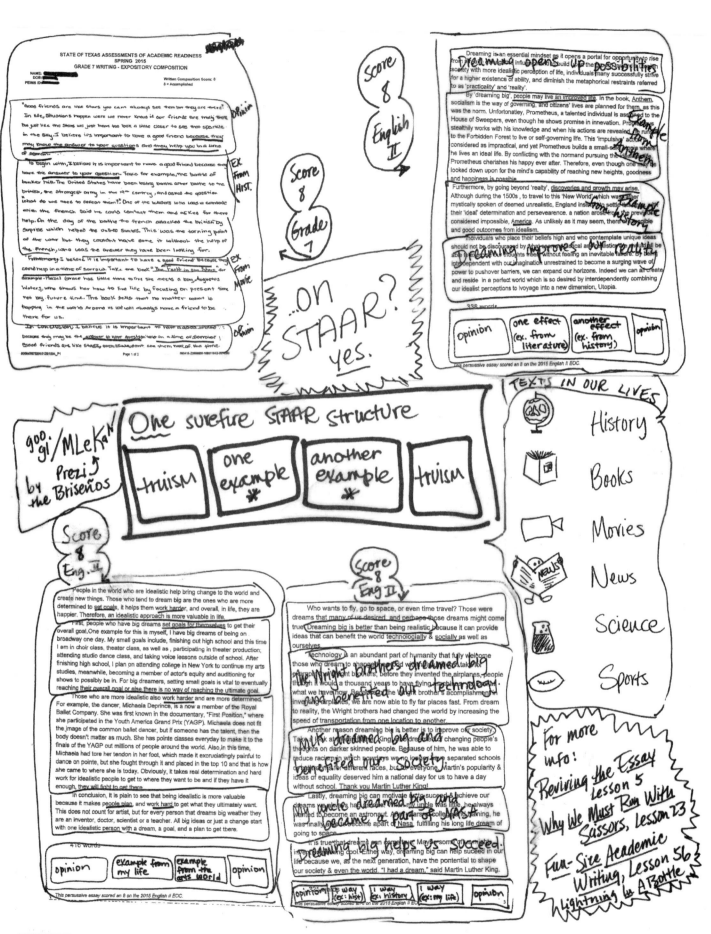

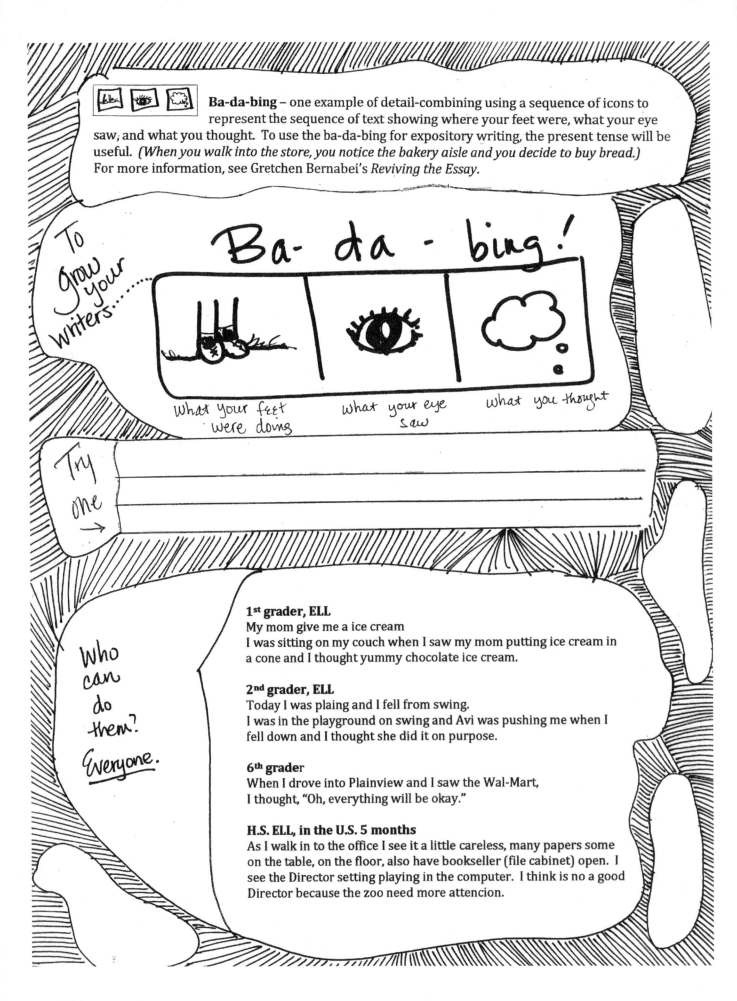

Ba-da-bing – one example of detail-combining using a sequence of icons to represent the sequence of text showing where your feet were, what your eye saw, and what you thought. To use the ba-da-bing for expository writing, the present tense will be useful. *(When you walk into the store, you notice the bakery aisle and you decide to buy bread.)* For more information, see Gretchen Bernabei's *Reviving the Essay*.

To grow your writers.....

Ba-da-bing!

What your feet were doing   What your eye saw   What you thought

Try one →

Who can do them? Everyone.

1st grader, ELL
My mom give me a ice cream
I was sitting on my couch when I saw my mom putting ice cream in a cone and I thought yummy chocolate ice cream.

2nd grader, ELL
Today I was plaing and I fell from swing.
I was in the playground on swing and Avi was pushing me when I fell down and I thought she did it on purpose.

6th grader
When I drove into Plainview and I saw the Wal-Mart,
I thought, "Oh, everything will be okay."

H.S. ELL, in the U.S. 5 months
As I walk in to the office I see it a little careless, many papers some on the table, on the floor, also have bookseller (file cabinet) open. I see the Director setting playing in the computer. I think is no a good Director because the zoo need more attencion.

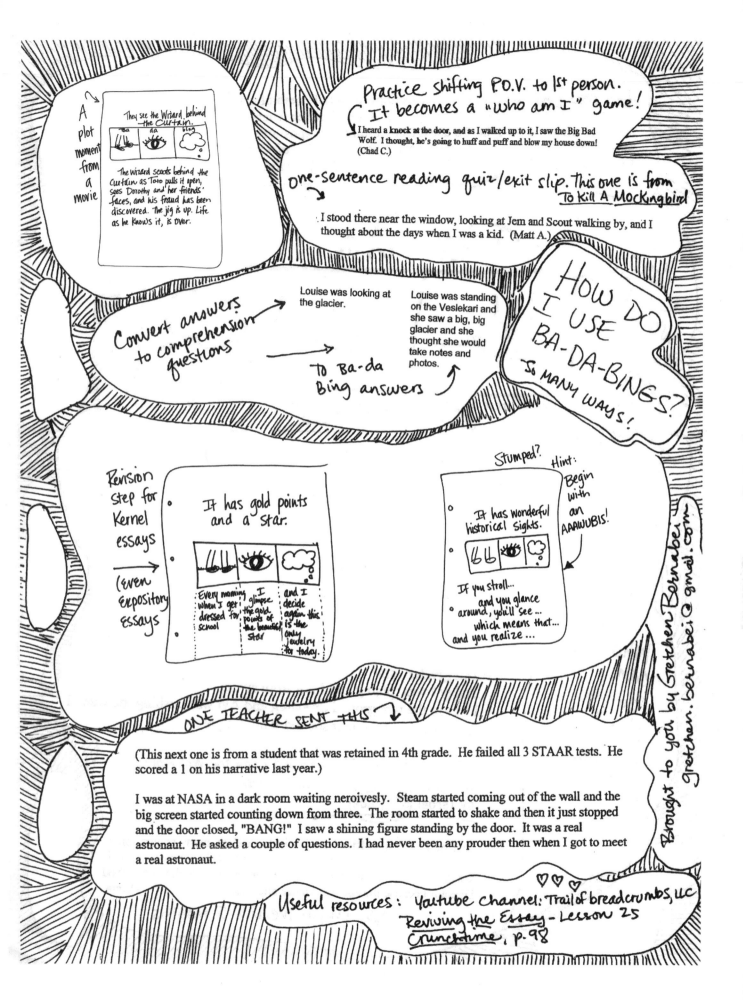

A plot moment from a movie

They see the Wizard behind the Curtain.

Ba | da | bing

The Wizard scoots behind the curtain as Toto pulls it open, sees Dorothy and her friends' faces, and his fraud has been discovered. The jig is up. Life as he knows it, is over.

Practice shifting P.O.V. to 1st person. It becomes a "who am I" game!

I heard a knock at the door, and as I walked up to it, I saw the Big Bad Wolf. I thought, he's going to huff and puff and blow my house down! (Chad C.)

One-sentence reading quiz/exit slip. This one is from To Kill A Mockingbird

I stood there near the window, looking at Jem and Scout walking by, and I thought about the days when I was a kid. (Matt A.)

Convert answers to comprehension questions

Louise was looking at the glacier.

Louise was standing on the Veslekari and she saw a big, big glacier and she thought she would take notes and photos.

To Ba-da Bing answers

HOW DO I USE BA-DA-BINGS! So many ways!

Revision step for Kernel essays → (even Expository essays

It has gold points and a star.

Every morning when I get dressed for school | I glimpse the gold points of the beautiful star | and I decide again this is the only jewelry for today.

Stumped? Hint: Begin with an AAAWWUBIS!

It has wonderful historical sights.

bb

If you stroll... and you glance around, you'll see ... which means that... and you realize ...

ONE TEACHER SENT THIS

(This next one is from a student that was retained in 4th grade. He failed all 3 STAAR tests. He scored a 1 on his narrative last year.)

I was at NASA in a dark room waiting neroively. Steam started coming out of the wall and the big screen started counting down from three. The room started to shake and then it just stopped and the door closed, "BANG!" I saw a shining figure standing by the door. It was a real astronaut. He asked a couple of questions. I had never been any prouder then when I got to meet a real astronaut.

♡♡♡
Useful resources: Youtube channel: Trail of breadcrumbs, LLC
Reviving the Essay - Lesson 25
Crunchtime, p. 98

Brought to you by Gretchen Bernabei, Gretchen.bernabei@gmail.com

Writer's Toolbox With Dead Giveaways

DEAD GIVEAWAYS THE BAD

AUTHOR'S CRAFT THE GOOD ✓

MAKES WRITING WEAKER

- Vague writing
- Repetition
- Throwaway writing
- Words in weird order
- Crazy logic

Makes writing stronger

Images

Sensory Details

Pitchforks

Action

Similes/Metaphors

Vocabulary

Thoughtshots

Dialogue

Personification

REVISION: Finding something from here and improving it with something from here

Explanations of Terms

Revision: Find the bad writing.

       Replace it with good writing.

Example sentence: **The waiter was angry.**

DEVICE	EXAMPLE
Images What you could see	*His face was scarlet with fury.*
Sensory details What you could hear, smell, taste	*We could hear his stomping feet. We caught the whiff of tension in the air.*
Pitchforks Embedded lists	*We couldn't tell what was worse, the food or his angry service.*
Action Replace the "to be" verbs	*Blazing to our table, he glared at us.*
Metaphors Describe it as something concrete (like a land form or life form)	*He was a volcano of anger, serving hot destruction with the menus.*
Similes Compare it to something way different	*He handed us our bill like a sour boyfriend breaking up.*
Vocabulary Use some of those words you have been learning	*This guy was definitely not benevolent enough to work in the service industry.*
Thoughtshots What might occur to you, in your head	*I wondered if he might snap.*
Dialogue Write the talking	*"What!?" he snarled. "Could I have some more tea?" "Again?"*
Personification Make an object act like a person	*His pen groaned resentfully as he wrote our order.*

PROBLEM	EXAMPLES
Vague General; blurry nonspecific	*There was something wrong with the guy.*
Repetition Same words or ideas, not for intentional effect	*He was mad, and also he was angry. He was very mad.*
Throwaway writing Telling the reader about your writing and your plans for later	*This is the part where I'm going to tell you about the waiter's mood. (I hope you like it.) And then we're going to take a walk on the beach.*
Weird order words of Words that have not read aloud been	*Mad this guy walking in was.* *My tacos he didn't even remember me.*
Crazy logic The words do not mean what the writer is trying to say	*Putting her lipstick on, the waiter yelled at the lady.*

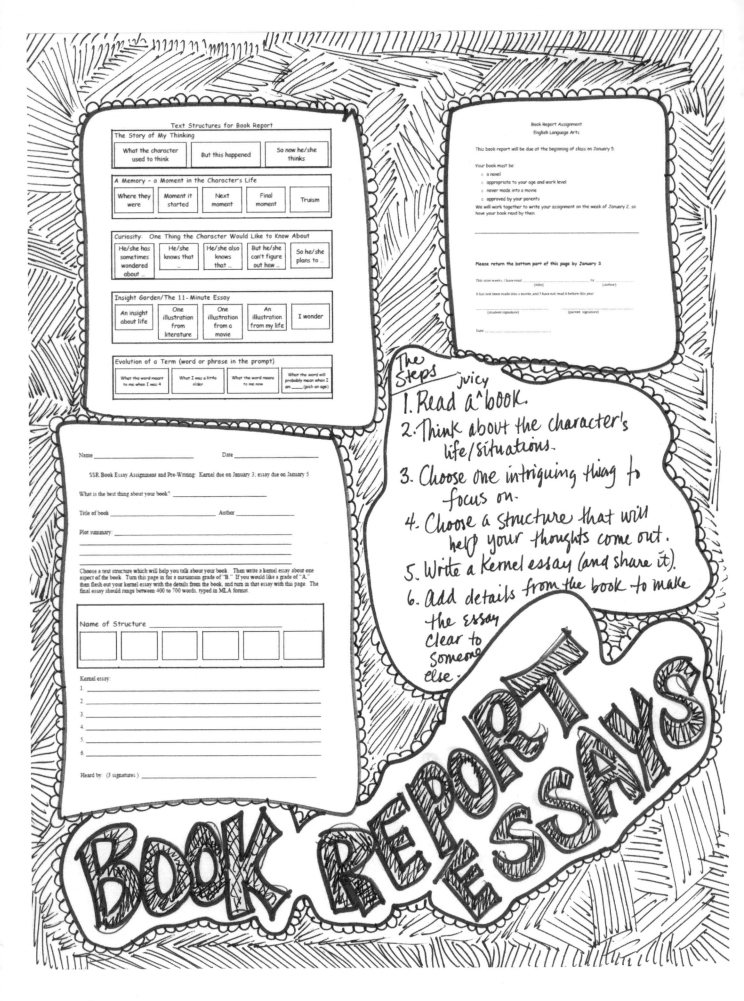

Text Structures for Book Report

The Story of My Thinking

What the character used to think	But this happened	So now he/she thinks

A Memory - a Moment in the Character's Life

Where they were	Moment it started	Next moment	Final moment	Truism

Curiosity: One Thing the Character Would Like to Know About

He/she has sometimes wondered about ...	He/she knows that ...	He/she also knows that ...	But he/she can't figure out how ...	So he/she plans to ...

Insight Garden/The 11-Minute Essay

An insight about life	One illustration from literature	One illustration from a movie	An illustration from my life	I wonder

Evolution of a Term (word or phrase in the prompt)

What the word meant to me when I was 4	What I was a little older	What the word means to me now	What the word will probably mean when I am _____ (pick an age)

Book Report Assignment
English Language Arts

This book report will be due at the beginning of class on January 5.

Your book must be:
- a novel
- appropriate to your age and work level
- never made into a movie
- approved by your parents

We will work together to write your assignment on the week of January 2, so have your book read by then.

_____

Please return the bottom part of this page by January 3.

This nine weeks, I have read _____ (title) by _____ (author)
It has not been made into a movie, and I have not read it before this year

_____ (student signature)   _____ (parent signature)

Date _____

The
Steps

juicy

1. Read a ^book.
2. Think about the character's life/situations.
3. Choose one intriguing thing to focus on.
4. Choose a structure that will help your thoughts come out.
5. Write a kernel essay (and share it).
6. Add details from the book to make the essay clear to someone else.

Name _____   Date _____

SSR Book Essay Assignment and Pre-Writing: Kernel due on January 3; essay due on January 5

What is the best thing about your book? _____

Title of book _____   Author _____

Plot summary: _____
_____
_____

Choose a text structure which will help you talk about your book. Then write a kernel essay about one aspect of the book. Turn this page in for a maximum grade of "B." If you would like a grade of "A," then flesh out your kernel essay with the details from the book, and turn in that essay with this page. The final essay should range between 400 to 700 words, typed in MLA format.

Name of Structure _____

Kernel essay:
1. _____
2. _____
3. _____
4. _____
5. _____
6. _____

Heard by: (3 signatures) _____

BOOK REPORTS ESSAYS

For more information about the values of self-selected reading
→ see →
BOOK LOVE by Penny Kittle
The Book Whisperer by Donalyn Miller

Or...

A Graphic book report/ book review for posting

→

Batya Katz - Grade 8   51

"Frankie White" Case Finally Solved!

★★★★

MISSION ROAD

(Lesson 51 in Fun-Size Academic Writing)

Name _____   Book title _____

Checking your essay:

Look over your essay and comment about its strengths and weaknesses in this self-assessment.

Organization and structure	Kernel essay attached and developed well?		40 points
Book knowledge	Is it clear you read your book?		20 points
Form	MLA format complete?		20 points
Mechanics	Capitals? Periods? Spelling?		20 points
			Total

Your comments here:

← How do I grade this? Maybe like this?

Brought to you by Gretchen Bernabei (gretchen bernabei @ gmail.com

This assignment is downloadable at www. trail of breadcrumbs. net.

References

Andersen, H. C. (1837). The emperor's new clothes. In H. C. Andersen, *Fairy tales told for children*. Retrieved from https://www.worldoftales.com/fairy_tales/Hans_Christian_Andersen/THE%20EMPEROR%27S%20NEW%20CLOTHES.html

Andersen, H. C. (1843). The nightingale. In H. C. Andersen, *New fairy tales*. Retrieved from https://www.worldoftales.com/European_folktales/European_folktale_2.html

Andersen, H. C. (1914). Little Thumbelina. In J. H. Stickney (Ed.), *Hans Andersen's fairy tales*. Boston, MA: Ginn. Retrieved from https://www.worldoftales.com/fairy_tales/Hans_Christian_Andersen/Andersen_fairy_tale_6.html

Andersen, H. C. (1914). The ugly duckling. In J. H. Stickney (Ed.), *Hans Andersen's fairy tales*. Boston, MA: Ginn. Retrieved from https://www.worldoftales.com/fairy_tales/Hans_Christian_Andersen/Andersen_fairy_tale_3.html

Andersen, H. C. (1915). The princess and the pea. In J. H. Stickney (Ed.), *Hans Andersen's Fairy Tales* (2nd series). Boston, MA: Ginn. Retrieved from https://www.worldoftales.com/fairy_tales/Hans_Christian_Andersen/Andersen_fairy_tale_47.html

Andersen, H. C. (1915). The wild swans. In J. H. Stickney (Ed.), *Hans Andersen's fairy tales*. Boston, MA: Ginn. Retrieved from https://www.worldoftales.com/fairy_tales/Hans_Christian_Andersen/Andersen_fairy_tale_25.html

Asbjornsen, P. C., & Moe, J. (2001). The three billy goats gruff. In P. C. Asbjornsen & J. Moe, *Norske Folkeeventyr* (G. W. Dasent, Trans., in *Popular tales from the Norse*; London, England: Routledge, pp. 275–276). Retrieved from http://www.pitt.edu/~dash/type0122e.html#gruff

Busch, W. (1910). The soldier and the tinderbox. In W. Busch, *Ut ôler Welt: Volksmärchen, Sagen, Volkslieder und Reime* (D. L. Ashliman, Trans., 2016). Munich, Germany: Verlag. Retrieved from http://www.pitt.edu/~dash/type0562.html#busch

The Gingerbread Boy. *St. Nicholas Magazine*, 2(7), 448–449. Retrieved from http://www.pitt.edu/~dash/type2025.html#gingerbread

Grimm, J., & Grimm, W. (1876). Elves and the shoemaker. In J. Grimm & W. Grimm (E. Taylor & M. Edwardes, Trans.), *Household tales*. London, England: Meek. Retrieved from https://www.worldoftales.com/fairy_tales/Brothers_Grimm/THE%20ELVES%20AND%20THE%20SHOEMAKER.html

Grimm, J., & Grimm, W. (1876). The frog prince. In J. Grimm & W. Grimm (E. Taylor & M. Edwardes, Trans.), *Household tales*. London, England: Meek. Retrieved from https://www.worldoftales.com/fairy_tales/Brothers_Grimm/THE%20FROG-PRINCE.html

Grimm, J., & Grimm, W. (1876). The golden goose. In J. Grimm & W. Grimm (E. Taylor & M. Edwardes, Trans.), *Household tales*. London, England: Meek. Retrieved from https://www.worldoftales.com/fairy_tales/Brothers_Grimm/THE%20GOLDEN%20GOOSE.html

Grimm, J., & Grimm, W. (1876). Hansel and Gretel. In J. Grimm & W. Grimm (E. Taylor & M. Edwardes, Trans.), *Household tales*. London, England: Meek. Retrieved from https://www.worldoftales.com/fairy_tales/Brothers_Grimm/Margaret_Hunt/Hansel_and_Grethel.html

Grimm, J., & Grimm, W. (1876). Little red-cap (Little Red Riding Hood). In J. Grimm & W. Grimm (E. Taylor & M. Edwardes, Trans.), *Household tales*. London, England: Meek. Retrieved from https://www.worldoftales.com/fairy_tales/Brothers_Grimm/Margaret_Hunt/Little_Red-Cap.html

Grimm, J., & Grimm, W. (1876). One-eye, two-eyes, three-eyes. In J. Grimm & W. Grimm (E. Taylor & M. Edwardes, Trans.), *Household tales*. London, England: Meek. Retrieved from https://www.worldoftales.com/fairy_tales/Brothers_Grimm/Margaret_Hunt/One-Eye,_Two-Eyes,_and_Three-Eyes.html

Grimm, J., & Grimm, W. (1876). Rumpelstiltskin. In J. Grimm & W. Grimm (E. Taylor & M. Edwardes, Trans.), *Household tales*. London, England: Meek. Retrieved from https://www.worldoftales.com/fairy_tales/Brothers_Grimm/RUMPELSTILTSKIN.html

Grimm, J., & Grimm, W. (1876). Tom Thumb. In J. Grimm & W. Grimm, *Household tales* (E. Taylor & M. Edwardes, Trans.). London, England: Meek. Retrieved from https://www.worldoftales.com/fairy_tales/Brothers_Grimm/TOM%20THUMB.html

Grimm, J., & W. Grimm. (1876). The twelve dancing princesses. In J. Grimm & W. Grimm (E. Taylor & M. Edwardes, Trans.), *Household tales*. London, England: Meek. Retrieved from https://www.worldoftales.com/fairy_tales/Brothers_Grimm/THE%20TWELVE%20DANCING%20PRINCESSES.html

Grimm, J., & Grimm, W. (1884). The Bremen town musicians. In J. Grimm & W. Grimm (M. Hunt, Trans.), *Household tales*. London, England: George Bell. Retrieved from https://www.worldoftales.com/fairy_tales/Brothers_Grimm/Margaret_Hunt/The_Bremen_Town-Musicians.html

Grimm, J., & Grimm, W. (1884). *The fisherman and his wife*. London, England: George Bell. Retrieved from https://www.worldoftales.com/fairy_tales/Brothers_Grimm/Margaret_Hunt/The_Fisherman_and_his_Wife.html

Grimm, J., & Grimm, W. (1884). Little Snow White. In J. Grimm & W. Grimm (M. Hunt, Trans.), *Household tales*. London, England: George Bell. Retrieved from https://www.worldoftales.com/fairy_tales/Brothers_Grimm/Margaret_Hunt/Little_Snow-white.html

Grimm, J., & Grimm, W. (1884). Rapunzel. In J. Grimm & W. Grimm (E. Taylor & M. Edwardes, Trans.), *Household tales*. London, England: Meek. Retrieved from https://www.worldoftales.com/fairy_tales/Brothers_Grimm/Margaret_Hunt/Rapunzel.html

Grimm, J., & Grimm, W. (1884). The wolf and the seven little kids. In J. Grimm & W. Grimm (E. Taylor & M. Edwardes, Trans.), *Household tales*. London, England: Bell. Retrieved from https://www.worldoftales.com/fairy_tales/Brothers_Grimm/Margaret_Hunt/The_Wolf_and_The_Seven_Little_Kids.html

Grimm, J., & Grimm, W. (1922). Snow White and Rose Red. In J. Grimm & W. Grimm, *Grimm's fairy stories*. New York, NY: Cupples and Leon. Retrieved from https://www.worldoftales.com/fairy_tales/Brothers_Grimm/Grimm_fairy_stories/Snow-White_And_Rose-Red.html

Jacobs, J. (Ed.). (1892). The three little pigs. J. Jacobs (Ed.), *English fairy tales*. New York, NY: Putnam. Retrieved from https://www.worldoftales.com/European_folktales/English_folktale_14.html

Leprince de Beaumont, J.-M. (1756). *Beauty and the beast*. Retrieved from http://pitt.edu/~dash/beauty.html

Perrault, C. (1697). Cinderella. In C. Perrault, *Histoires ou contes du tempes passe*. Retrieved from https://www.pitt.edu/~dash/perrault06.html

Perrault, C. (1697). The Sleeping Beauty in the woods (Briar Rose). In C. Perrault, *Histoires ou contes du temps passe*. Retrieved from https://www.worldoftales.com/Sleeping_Beauty.html

Perrault, C. (1901). Diamonds and toads. In C. Welsh (Trans.), *The tales of Mother Goose*. Boston, MA: Heath. Retrieved from https://www.worldoftales.com/fairy_tales/Charles_Perrault/THE_FAIRY.html (Original work published 1696)

Perrault, C. (1901). Puss in Boots (The Master Cat). In C. Perrault, *The tales of Mother Goose*. Boston, MA: Heath. Retrieved from https://www.worldoftales.com/fairy_tales/Charles_Perrault/THE_MASTER_CAT,_OR_PUSS_IN_BOOTS.html (Originally published 1696)

Steel, F. A. (1918). Henny Penny. In F. A. Steel, *English fairy tales*. London, England: Macmillan.

Steel, F. A. (1918). Jack and the beanstalk. In F. A. Steel, *English fairy tales*. London, England: Macmillan. Retrieved from https://www.worldoftales.com/European_folktales/English_folktale_13.html

Steel, F. A. (1918). The story of the three bears. In F. A. Steel, *English fairy tales*. London, England: Macmillan. Retrieved from https://www.worldoftales.com/European_folktales/English_folktale_89.html

Steel, F. A. (1918). The three sillies. In F. A. Steel, *English fairy tales*. London, England: Macmillan. Retrieved from https://www.worldoftales.com/European_folktales/English_folktale_96.html

Williams, F. W. (1918). The little red hen. (1918). In F. W. Williams, *The little red hen, and other stories*. Akron, OH: Saalfield.

Take a sneak peek at Gretchen Bernabei and Judi Reimer's best-selling writing book, plus two free lessons!

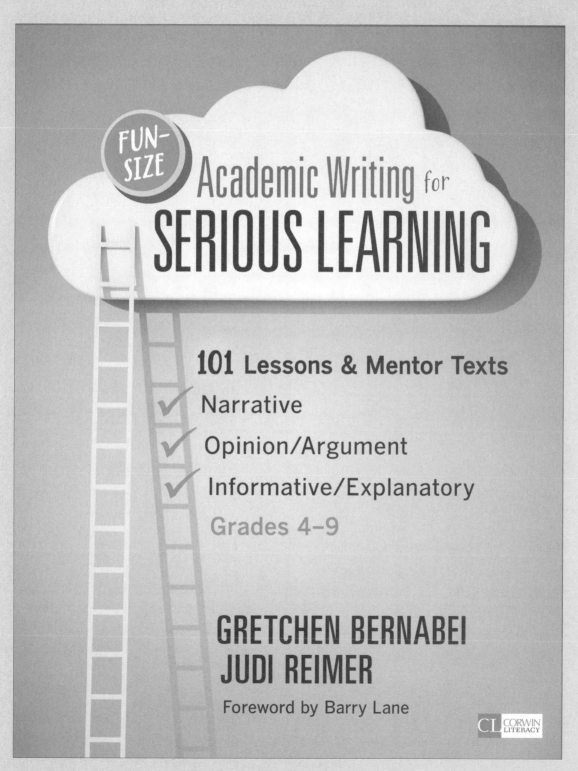

FUN-SIZE

Academic Writing for SERIOUS LEARNING

101 Lessons & Mentor Texts
✓ Narrative
✓ Opinion/Argument
✓ Informative/Explanatory
Grades 4–9

GRETCHEN BERNABEI
JUDI REIMER
Foreword by Barry Lane

CL CORWIN LITERACY

Contents

Part II. Informative/Explanatory 90

Part III. Opinion/Argument 152

Appendixes

Visit the companion website at **www.corwin.com/funsize**
for downloadable versions of all the student
essays and text structures.

Introduction

How This Book Began

One of the very first weird truths you learn about teaching is this: When kids hear something from other kids, they get it so much faster than when they hear the very same thing from us. It's inexplicable. But every teacher has seen it, no matter what the content.

You may be saying, "A concrete noun is something you can touch," and you see blinks.

One of them says, "Something you can touch?"

You say, "Yes, something you can touch." More blinks.

Then a kid pipes in. "Dude. You can touch it," and understanding dawns. Ohhh. You can *touch* it.

Maybe it doesn't matter how this happens, but just knowing that it does provides for us one of the very best tools in teaching. This book is built on two premises, and this is the first:

Students learn from each other faster and more deeply than they learn from us.

In *The Book of Learning and Forgetting*, Frank Smith (1998) opens our eyes about how the quickest, most powerful learning students do is by watching each other. We know this as parents, but we don't always remember it as teachers.

So one day, as we looked at student test essays that our state had released, we realized we'd discovered an instructional gold mine.

And the mining began.

We looked for and found high-scoring essays, obtained permissions from student writers and their parents, and began to explore ways to use these essays in our teaching, mostly as gallery walks.

But soon we realized how useful these essays could be for tightly focused, whole-group instruction in craft. Some demonstrated extraordinary word choice; some employed a sophisticated rhetorical device; some displayed an impressive range of sentence variety; some used powerful images. They were all enlightening in different ways. All provided opportunities to teach.

craft

In fact, we discovered the gold mine extended beyond test essays. We began gathering all kinds of writing, at all different grade levels, from all over the country. The pieces we collected range from informal journal entries to formal literary analysis, but they all have one thing in common: There's a craft nugget in each.

Each craft nugget became the center of a lesson in this book. Using the student essay as a mentor text, we worked backward, designing a lesson based on each one that would teach students how to *recognize* and *replicate* the craft move in their own writing.

The results have been astounding. Teachers all over the country have tried out these lessons in workshops. Here is a sampling of their responses:

"I can't wait to get back to class and try these out!"

"My students will be able to do this!"

"I finally feel like I have a tangible plan for teaching writing, and not just guessing. I also think the kids will *enjoy* it!"

"As teachers, we should aim at starting small and building, and this provides the tools and structure to do this. It is workable and doable with any student!"

We've received hundreds of emails from teachers, and have been encouraged, too, by their students' responses:

"We used these lessons and our 50% benchmark scores jumped to 88% passing on The Test..."

"My students actually asked to keep writing, and I *never* thought I'd see that happen."

Success is transformative for everyone.

The Deception of "Show, Don't Tell"

Ironic, isn't it? Those "show, don't tell" posters we put up in our classrooms? They tell. And they don't show *how*.

It took us twenty-five years to notice the irony. Asking students to "show, don't tell," is telling. Without showing *how*. Showing *how* is difficult without student models. Each one of the unique pieces of student work in this book *shows how to show*, not tell.

When your students experience these fun-size lessons, when they see how to show, you'll hear, "I can do that." When they hear the voices of other students, you'll see the understanding dawning. It's so palpable, you can touch it. Dude.

How the Lessons Work

We've divided up the book into the main kinds of writing taught, tested, and even outlined in the Common Core State Standards:

- narrative

- opinion/argument

- informative/explanatory

The sample pieces we have gathered fall into these main categories. Some states may use different language. For example, what Texas assesses as "expository" at Grades 4, 7, and 9 is known to the rest of the world as "argument." Persuasive writing, likewise, falls under the category of "argument" for the purposes of this book. Any teacher who is looking for a "how-to" or procedural paper will find it in the "informative/explanatory" section.

Each craft lesson is divided into sections:

- **What Writers Do:** describes a craft move that writers might make

- **What This Writer Does:** pinpoints that move in this specific piece

- **Activity for Your Class:** asks students to reread, identify something, and manipulate it in the student sample

- **Challenge for Students:** invites students to try out this move in their own writing

At the bottom of each craft lesson, we've also included the *text structure* of the piece. This isn't part of the craft lesson but an added feature. One way teachers ask their students to develop essays is to begin with a structure. We place one sentence in each box in the structure to create what we call a "kernel essay" that's modeled on the student mentor text used in that craft lesson. A "kernel essay" is like a kernel of corn, tiny but packed (Bernabei, Hover, & Candler, 2009). The structure, when imitated, provides students with a kernel of an essay.

Kernal essay — a short exemple essay

A collection of text structures like these can help students make organizational choices. You will find the collection of structures at the back of this book. (For more on this feature of the lessons, see How to Use Text Structures on page 6.)

Should the lessons be done in order? No. You should pick and choose on your own and will undoubtedly develop your own favorites.

Soon, you'll have student writing from your own class to demonstrate the craft lessons here, but these pieces of writing are a great starter set. We suggest that as your students write, you might keep some of their writing to use with the craft lessons, replacing the student pieces here. Your students will react more strongly when they recognize the names of the writers. But they will have no trouble identifying real student voices, even when the students come from another school.

You can use any lesson to jump-start and guide students as they begin a new piece of writing or to help them revise and enrich pieces they already have under way.

How to Find Quick Solutions to Writing Problems

What causes students to fail writing assignments or writing tests? Basically the same short list of problems:

- writing that wanders around without a plan

- vague writing

- not enough writing

- listy writing

- disconnected writing

- wordy writing

- boring writing

The lessons in this book focus on *solutions* to these problems. As you browse the table of contents, you will see that the craft lessons explicitly teach solutions, with those solutions modeled in the student pieces.

Learning to Read as Writers

At a recent NCTE conference, Kelly Gallagher talked about the importance of showing students mentor texts, texts written by professionals as well as student models. He said that he uses only excellent writing as mentor texts because "students see enough bad writing." We see his point.

But in *Teaching the Universe of Discourse*, James Moffett (1986) wondered at the wisdom of expecting students to imitate the prose of John Steinbeck. And Frank Smith's point that students learn most easily from watching the moves of other students is undeniable, too. To us, it is essential for students to see writing in all its various stages, the moves writers make along the way: in early forms, in developed forms, in polished forms.

How will they learn the habits of choice without seeing those choices in action? This leads to the second premise of our book:

Writers make choices.

Classrooms that show extraordinary student gains are classrooms with a safe writing climate. We create safe writing climates in our classrooms only by treating pieces of writing with respect. Most pieces of writing aren't finished, rubric-ready, evaluatable corpses. They are living, growing, organic, in-progress, complex groups of choices. The writer's question should not be, "*Is it done yet?*" or "*What grade did I get?*" but...

- "*What next?*"

- "*How does this work when you read it?*"

- "*What if we tinker with this or that... ?*"

This is how real writers work.

The pieces we share in class are conversations—breathing, ongoing, and revisable. Instead of "grading" a piece when they read it, it's much healthier and much more conducive to learning for students to read like a writer: to see, name, and learn from the moves the writer makes. Our goal is for students to

- accumulate choices

- enjoy the freedom to try out those choices

- get feedback from readers about how well their choices worked

This process is at the heart of learning to be an effective writer.

Or, to look at it another way, students might read a piece of writing—early, developed, polished, or Shakespearean—with this curiosity, through this lens:

- *What choices has this writer made?*

- *What structural moves?*

- *What detailing moves?*
- *What polishing moves?*
- *...and how do those moves work out?*

As students learn these moves from each other, they gain independence from us.

Naturally, we left some mistakes in. Some of these pieces were actually written in timed settings on "test day" of the state writing test. Some were written as classroom benchmark tests, some as regular classroom pieces. Some classroom pieces, of course, are more polished than others, having benefited from spell-check, conferencing with teachers or peers, proofreading steps, reference materials, and time. **It does some students a world of good to see mistakes in a high-quality piece**, potentially calming that demon-teacher-voice in their heads that shrieks at them, "If you can't write it perfectly, don't write it at all!"

If you wonder why we didn't clean them up, why we're modeling incorrectness, that's why. These are not corrected for perfection. There's not a paper written anywhere that couldn't stand a little more reworking or more editing. But each of these pieces does something magnificent, and we think it's good modeling to focus on *that*. We believe the most productive thing we can do is to notice strengths and build on them.

About the Grade Levels

At the top of each lesson, we included the grade level of the writer. We did this simply because it's interesting. But does that mean when I teach my fifth-grade class, I shouldn't use fourth-grade pieces? Or tenth? Of course not.

We learned long ago from Kenneth Koch's *Rose, Where Did You Get That Red?* (1973) that second graders can look at and imitate the masters. The opposite is also true. Older students can focus on and imitate moves made by younger writers as well. We remember well watching tenth graders absorb a lesson delivered via a fourth grader's writing. The tenth graders learned how to look for, find, and then plant different kinds of text in their writing, and the lesson stuck. Of course, the content of older writers' works will be different from the content used by younger students, but craft is for everyone. Anyone can use any lesson with any level. The teacher is the best judge of timing.

Again, classrooms that show extraordinary student gains are those that create a safe writing climate. We create safe writing climates in our classrooms one way: by treating pieces of writing with respect.

How to Use Text Structures

What are these boxes on the bottoms of the pages and what can you do with them?

As we mentioned above, those boxes are a graphic representation of the text structure used by the writer. Each structure provides us with dynamic additional activities for these lessons.

Guided by the structure, which is the "blueprint" of the piece, students can collaboratively deconstruct an essay and strip it down to its kernel essay form. A kernel essay consists of one sentence for each part of the structure.

Kernal essay definition

To collaboratively analyze the essay, take the following steps:

1. Give each student a copy of the student essay.

2. Read the piece of writing.

3. Show the text structure to the students.

4. Ask students to circle the parts of the essay that match each box in the text structure.

5. Ask students to write a one-sentence summary for each circled chunk of text.

6. Take turns reading the summary sentences aloud to hear the kernel essay of the piece.

To use the structure to generate new writing, continue with these steps:

1. Look again at the structure.

2. Invite students to write their own content for the structure, writing one sentence for each box of the text.

3. Flesh out the sentences with details to create a full essay.

Here is an illustration of the steps outlined above:

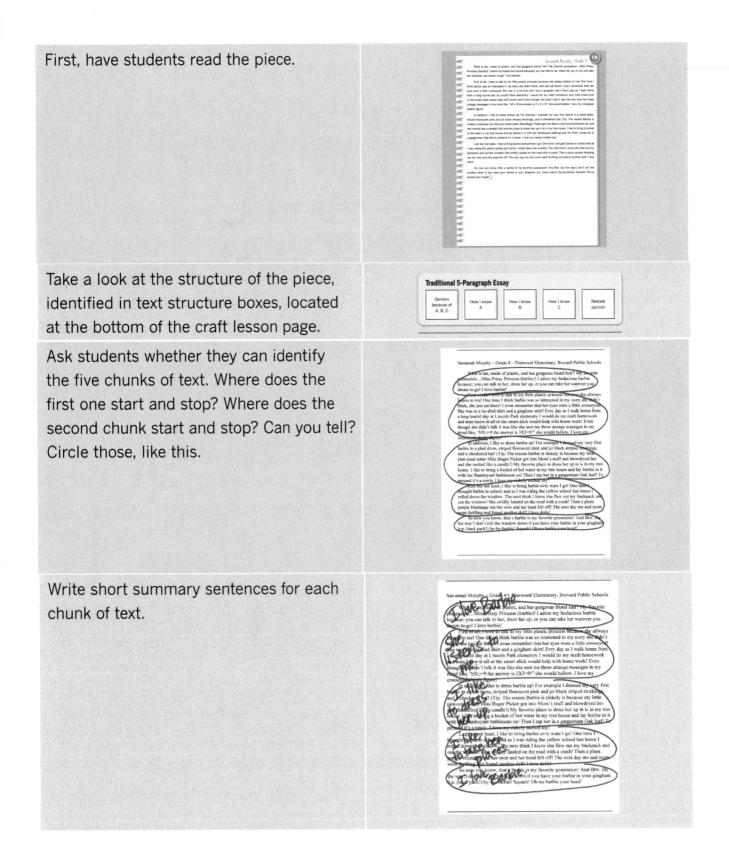

First, have students read the piece.

Take a look at the structure of the piece, identified in text structure boxes, located at the bottom of the craft lesson page.

Ask students whether they can identify the five chunks of text. Where does the first one start and stop? Where does the second chunk start and stop? Can you tell? Circle those, like this.

Write short summary sentences for each chunk of text.

Fun-Size Academic Writing for Serious Learning

Read the short sentences aloud to hear the kernel essay. (A kernel essay is one sentence for each part of the structure.)	*I love Barbie.* *She listens to me.* *I like to dress her up.* *I like to take her places.* *I love Barbie.*
Look again at the text structure.	**Traditional 5-Paragraph Essay** | Opinion because of A, B, C	How I know A	How I know B	How I know C	Restate opinion	
Have students use the structure as the basis for a new piece of writing by beginning with a kernel essay. Students use their own new content, one sentence per box.	*Horses are wonderful animals.* *It's fun just to be around them.* *You can get into great shape by riding them.* *They are as interesting as people.* *Horses are the best animals.*

Here is how the process would look on another piece, a narrative, with a different text structure.

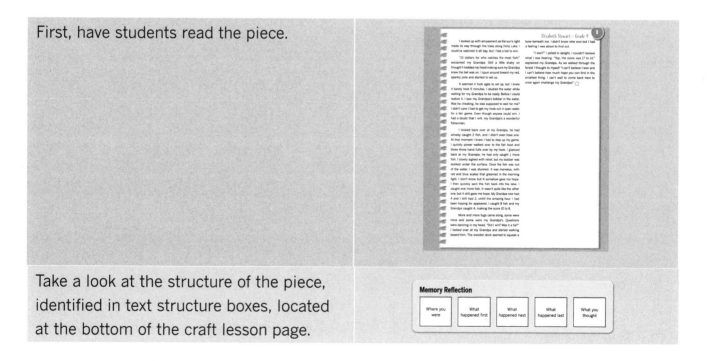

First, have students read the piece.	
Take a look at the structure of the piece, identified in text structure boxes, located at the bottom of the craft lesson page.	**Memory Reflection** | Where you were	What happened first	What happened next	What happened last	What you thought	

Ask students whether they can identify the five chunks of text. Where does the first one start and stop? Where does the second chunk start and stop? Can you tell? Circle those, like this.	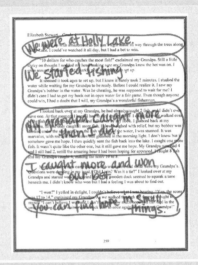
Write short summary sentences for each chunk of text.	
Read the short sentences aloud to hear the kernel essay. (A kernel essay is one sentence for each part of the structure.)	*We were at Holly Lake.* *We started fishing.* *My grandpa caught more than I did.* *I caught more and won our bet.* *You can find hope in small things.*
Look again at the text structure.	
Use the structure for a new piece by writing a kernel essay with new content, one sentence per box.	*Julian was in the living room.* *He bit down on his pizza slice and started to cry.* *His tooth almost came out.* *It finally came out after he went to bed.* *Nobody can be happy when their children are afraid.*

Fun-Size Academic Writing for Serious Learning

We included the text structure for every piece of writing to widen your instructional choices.

You may notice in the first example and in some other places in the book a text structure labeled "Traditional 5-Paragraph Essay." I am not a fan of teaching students this structure exclusively, as I hope the lessons throughout this book demonstrate! But I do think it's important that students learn to jump through any situational hoop that their academic life hands them. And some teachers in their futures will insist on this particular structure. Beyond that, though, for the function of this book, it's important to me that you see that this structure, *along with many others*, can work for a variety of purposes.

As a class, if you build a collection of text structures that you find useful, students may find themselves harvesting text structures from surprising sources and filling them with their own content—with surprising results.

Whether you begin with the text structures or the craft lessons that go with each piece of writing, we hope that you will enjoy the play of learning with the models and revel in the writing that your students produce.

Have a great time with these!

References

Bernabei, G. S., Hover, J., & Candler, C. (2009). *Crunchtime: Lessons to help students blow the roof off writing tests—and become better writers in the process*. Portsmouth, NH: Heinemann.

Koch, K. (1973). *Rose, where did you get that red?* New York: Random House.

Moffett, J. (1986). *Teaching the universe of discourse*. Boston: Houghton Mifflin.

Smith, F. (1998). *The book of learning and forgetting*. New York: Teachers College.

Color It Up

What Writers Do — Writers describe what they see, think, do, and say to tell a story. They describe what other characters do and say, too.

What This Writer Does — Elizabeth skillfully blends all four kinds of description in this piece, leaving readers with a perfectly clear picture of the whole memory.

Activity for your class:

1. Pass out copies and read the piece together with your class.

2. Have students highlight the following:
   - yellow—everything the narrator thought
   - blue—everything the narrator saw
   - pink—everything that anyone said
   - green—everything anyone did (not counting thinking or talking)

(This highlighting can be done by groups, partners, or individuals.)

3. Share and compare what you notice.

4. Create a class chart so that your class can remember the colors.

Challenge for students:

Highlight a story you've written, using the same color codes, just to see your own patterns. You may want to use the Memory Reflection text structure, below, to write a new personal narrative.

Memory Reflection

Where you were	What happened first	What happened next	What happened last	What you thought

I looked up with amazement as the sun's light made its way through the trees along Holly Lake. I could've watched it all day, but I had a bet to win.

"10 dollars for who catches the most fish!" exclaimed my Grandpa. Still a little shaky on thought I nodded my head making sure my Grandpa knew the bet was on. I spun around toward my red, sparkly pole and started to set up.

It seemed it took ages to set up, but I knew it barely took 5 minutes. I studied the water while waiting for my Grandpa to be ready. Before I could realize it, I saw my Grandpa's bobber in the water. Was he cheating, he was supposed to wait for me? I didn't care I had to get my hook out in open water for a fair game. Even though anyone could win, I had a doubt that I will, my Grandpa's a wonderful fisherman.

I looked back over at my Grandpa, he had already caught 2 fish, and I didn't even have one. At that moment I knew I had to step up my game. I quickly power walked over to the fish food and threw three hand fulls over by my hook. I glanced back at my Grandpa, he had only caught 1 more fish. I slowly sighed with relief, but my bobber was dunked under the surface. Once the fish was out of the water, I was stunned. It was marvalus, with red and blue scales that gleamed in the morning light. I don't know but it somehow gave me hope. I then quickly sent the fish back into the lake. I caught one more fish. It wasn't quite like the other one, but it still gave me hope. My Grandpa now had 4 and I still had 2, untill the amazing hour I had been hoping for appeared. I caught 8 fish and my Grandpa caught 4, making the score 10 to 8.

More and more tugs came along, some were mine and some were my Grandpa's. Questions were dancing in my head, "Did I win? Was it a tie?" I looked over at my Grandpa and started walking toward him. The wooden dock seemed to squeak a tune beneath me. I didn't know who won but I had a feeling I was about to find out.

"I won?" I yelled in delight, I couldn't believe what I was hearing. "Yep, the score was 17 to 14," explained my Grandpa. As we walked through the forest I thought to myself "I can't believe I won and I can't believe how much hope you can find in the smallest thing. I can't wait to come back here to once again challenge my Grandpa!" ☆

Sprinkling Writing With Humor

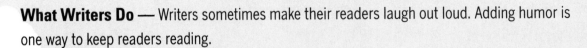

What Writers Do — Writers sometimes make their readers laugh out loud. Adding humor is one way to keep readers reading.

What This Writer Does — In her personal narrative about "a time you helped someone," Aine makes readers to laugh out loud and beg, "Again!"

Activity for your class:

1. Read the piece aloud or choose a student volunteer who will read with lots of animation.

2. After passing out copies, have students reread it, highlighting their three favorite lines.

3. Compare favorites and talk about why students chose the lines they did.

4. Notice how many readers chose lines because they were funny.

Challenge for students:

Write a composition about a memory, and see if you can sprinkle some humor into it. See if you can make your readers laugh. You can use the text structure below if you wish.

Memory Reflection

Where you were	What happened first	What happened next	What happened last	What you thought

Have you ever helped someone because he was your best friend? Well I have…and I never will again.

My friend Mark took me by the hand and dragged me to the school's wall. He popped his bright pink bubble gum bubble in my face. "Listen" he said. "I have a football game in Denver tomorrow, and I can't miss it."

"Okay" I said, "What about it?"

"Can you watch Rex?" he asked. Now I've watched his ant farm, his pet tarantula, and even his mouse. But Rex…NO WAY! I was not going to watch the dog who ripped my pants, ate my 50,000 dollar retainer, and bites me every week. "Come on," he said. "I'll take you to the Beatles concert."

"Okay" I said, being a little hesitant.

"Tomorrow morning at 8:00."

"Got it," I said.

When I got to his house the next morning, I saw Rex through the fence with his teeth oozing with spit.

"Hey," Mark yelled, "Come on in!" I ran inside and sat on a brown leather chair. "Here's his dog food," he said handing me a big blue bag. "He needs to be fed twice a day and you can let him out three times every day."

"Anything else?" I asked.

"Nope, just don't take him off his chain." Mark ran out the door, and drove off with his parents. I walked home and thought "this won't be so bad after all."

The next morning my mom drove me to Mark's house on her way to the grocery store. I got out of the car and ran inside the house. I picked up his food bowl and went to the back door. I opened it just a crack and peeked outside and there was Rex laying on the grass looking like he was going to cry. I walked over to him and put the food bowl on the ground. I unhooked the chain and…it was the worst mistake of my life. Rex darted toward me and ripped my pants, again! I was furious, but so was he. I ran to the fence and started to climb it. Jumped over it and my shoe fell off. I watched as he ripped the laces to shreds.

I ran home screaming like a girl. I bought Rex a shock collar and I am never going to feed him again. So now Mark asks Jimmy, a strong kid to feed him. I'll stick with my bunnies even though I love dogs. That day was truly the worst time I helped someone. ☆

Because...
ALL TEACHERS ARE LEADERS

GRETCHEN BERNABEI

This kid-friendly cache of 101 lessons and practice pages helps your students internalize the conventions of correctness once and for all.

GRETCHEN BERNABEI AND JENNIFER KOPPE

With 50 short texts written by famous individuals driven by "an itch" to say something, this book provides students with mentor texts to express their own thoughts.

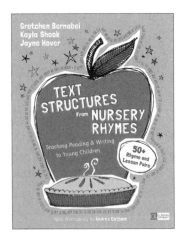

GRETCHEN BERNABEI, KAYLA SHOOK, AND JAYNE HOVER

In 53 lessons centered around classic nursery rhymes, this groundbreaking book offers a straightforward framework for guiding young children in their earliest writing efforts.

GRETCHEN BERNABEI AND JUDI REIMER

If ever there were a book to increase students' test scores, this is it. Its 101 student essays and one-page lessons deliver powerhouse instruction on writing well in any genre.

To order your copies, visit corwin.com/literacy

Do you have a minute? Of course not.

That's why at Corwin Literacy we have put together a collection of just-in-time, classroom-tested, practical resources from trusted experts that allow you to quickly find the information you need when you need it.

BERIT GORDON

Discover how to transform your classroom into a vibrant reading environment. This groundbreaking book combines the benefits of classic literature with the motivational power of choice reading.

M. COLLEEN CRUZ

By flipping the traditional "reading first, writing second" sequence, these innovative books let you make the most of the writing-to-reading connection via 50 carefully matched lesson pairs in each book.

NANCY AKHAVAN

With 75 tasks on beautiful full-color pages, this book offers a literacy instruction plan that ensures students benefit from independent effort and engagement.

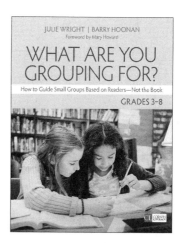

JULIE WRIGHT AND BARRY HOONAN

This book explains the five teacher moves that work together to support students' reading independence through small-group learning—kidwatching, pivoting, assessing, curating, and planning.

CORWIN

A SAGE Publishing Company

CORWIN HAS ONE MISSION: to enhance education through intentional professional learning.

We build long-term relationships with our authors, educators, clients, and associations who partner with us to develop and continuously improve the best evidence-based practices that establish and support lifelong learning.